# S-172

## LEE HARVEY OSWALD
### LINKS TO INTELLIGENCE AGENCIES

## GLENN B FLEMING

EMPIRE
PUBLICATIONS

First published in 2013

EMPIRE PUBLICATIONS
1 Newton Street, Manchester M1 1HW
© Glenn B Fleming 2013

ISBN: 978-1-909360-19-8

Printed and bound by CPI Group (UK) Ltd, Croydon, CR0 4YY.
Cover design, layout and illustration by Glenn B Fleming

# CONTENTS

For Helen

## ACKNOWLEDGEMENTS

Special thanks go to Ashley Shaw for his expertise on the manuscript and my publisher, John Ireland, for his continuing support. The publishers would like to thank Stuart Fish for his grammatical expertise.

## ABOUT THE AUTHOR

GLENN B FLEMING was born and raised in Manchester, England. He is an author, designer, photographer, film maker, illustrator, cartoonist and has written many articles and published several magazines on varying subjects.

His previous book on the JFK assassination – 'The Two Faces of Lee Harvey Oswald' published in 2003 – was unique; written as a novel, Fleming took us on a journey solely in the mind of President Kennedy's alleged assassin as he faced his demons that fateful weekend in November 1963.

'S-172: Lee Harvey Oswald - Links to Intelligence Agencies' looks at the story from the view that Oswald was an asset of the United States Intelligence community, a revelation dating from December 1963, only weeks after JFK was murdered. In 1976 it was revealed that the Central Intelligence Agency, after denying it for thirteen years, had, indeed, 'discussed the laying on of interviews' and shown 'intelligence interest' in Lee Oswald. In 1977, there were strong rumours of an Oswald '201 file'. According to many former CIA employees, if the CIA has a 201 file on Oswald that would prove that he must have had some kind of intelligence connections with the agency.

This statement became the basis of this work.

# FOREWORD

It is now half a century since President John F Kennedy was assassinated in Dallas, Texas. Many books, articles and documentaries have been devoted to what happened (and what did not happen) that sunny November day. Since then, many of the eye witnesses to the assassination have passed away, official (and unofficial) investigations have been opened and closed and opinions have changed and changed again. The official version of the assassination tells us that malcontent Lee Oswald fired three shots at Kennedy with a high powered rifle, left the scene of the crime, killed a policeman and then was himself shot down two days later by night club owner Jack Ruby whilst in the custody of the Dallas Police.

In 1991, Hollywood film maker Oliver Stone brought the assassination back to the attention of the world with his film 'JFK'. Based mainly on the best selling book 'Crossfire', written by the Dallas researcher Jim Marrs, Stone attempted to show the world what the JFK research community had suspected for many years: that former United States Marine Lee Harvey Oswald was innocent of the crime, that Oswald was employed by the United States Intelligence community and was working against the elements responsible for the president's murder. Oswald himself proclaimed that he was 'just a patsy'.

Following the public outcry generated by Stone's film, the United States Congress created the President John F Kennedy Assassination Records Collection Act (also known as the JFK Records Act) in an effort to release all relevant documents regarding the assassination. The Act became effective on 26 October 1992.

The Act directed the National Archives and Records Administration to establish a collection of records to be known as the President John F Kennedy Assassination Records Collection, stating the collection shall consist of copies of all US government records relating to the assassination of President John F Kennedy in 1963, and was to be transmitted to the National Archives. Assassination records also included those created or made available for use by, obtained by, or otherwise came into the possession of any state or local law enforcement office that provided support or assistance or performed work in connection with a federal inquiry into the assassination.

The Act requires that each assassination record be publicly disclosed in full, and be available in the collection no later than the date that is 25 years after the date of enactment of the Act (i.e., 26 October 2017), unless the President of the United States certifies that: (1) continued postponement is made necessary by an identifiable harm to the military defense, intelligence operations, law enforcement, or conduct of foreign relations; and (2) the identifiable harm is of such gravity that it outweighs the public interest in disclosure.

The Act established, as an independent agency, the Assassination Records Review Board (ARRB) to consider and render decisions when a US government office sought to postpone the disclosure of assassination records. The Board met for four years, from 1 October 1994 to 30 September 1998. When the Act was passed in 1992, 98 percent of all Warren Commission documents had been released to the public and by the time the Board disbanded all Warren Commission documents (except income tax returns) had been released to the public, with only minor redactions.

The ARRB began collecting evidence in 1992 and submitted its final report in 1998. The ARRB was not, however, enacted to determine why or by whom the murder was committed. Instead, it was to collect and preserve the evidence for public scrutiny. The Board collected a large amount of documents and took testimony of those who had relevant information of the events and, having completed its final report, the ARRB outlined the problems that government secrecy had created regarding the murder of President

Kennedy. During the 1990s it collected the assassination documents which have been slowly released for public scrutiny. Other information consists of a large number of documents from the Federal Bureau of Investigation (FBI) and the Central Intelligence Agency (CIA) that were required to cooperate with the turnover of relevant records held secret by these agencies.

As of 2013, there are still 50,000 pages of government documents relating to the assassination that have not been released.

'The very word 'secrecy' is repugnant in a free and open society; and we are as a people inherently and historically opposed to secret societies, to secret oaths and to secret proceedings. We decided long ago that the dangers of excessive and unwarranted concealment of pertinent facts far outweighed the dangers which are cited to justify it. Even today, there is little value in opposing the threat of a closed society by imitating its arbitrary restrictions. Even today, there is little value in insuring the survival of our nation if our traditions do not survive with it. And there is very grave danger that an announced need for increased security will be seized upon by those anxious to expand its meaning to the very limits of official censorship and concealment. That I do not intend to permit to the extent that it is in my control. And no official of my Administration, whether his rank is high or low, civilian or military, should interpret my words here tonight as an excuse to censor the news, to stifle dissent, to cover up our mistakes or to withhold from the press and the public the facts they deserve to know.'

QUOTE FROM A SPEECH GIVEN BY PRESIDENT JOHN F KENNEDY TO THE AMERICAN NEWSPAPER PUBLISHERS ASSOCIATION IN 1961.

# Lee Harvey Oswald
# Links to Intelligence Agencies

# MARINE, MOSCOW, MINSK AND MARINA

Since his defection to the Soviet Union in 1959, Lee Harvey Oswald has been thought to have had some kind of relationship with either the United States Government, the Soviet KGB, or both. We are led to believe that a sixteen-year-old Lee Oswald fed himself a hearty diet of Communist literature from his local library and wrote to the Socialist Party of America for information. He allegedly preached Socialism to his high-school friends and announced that he was looking for a Communist cell in his home town. Yet, another friend of Oswald's declared that there was no truth in these allegations.

Before his seventeenth birthday (and therefore prematurely), Oswald tried to enlist in the United States Marines Corps; at the time the most rabid bastion of anti-Communism in the Western world. He tried to cheat his way into the forces, asking his mother to help him falsify documents and, when discovered and his application turned down, began to read obsessively his brother's Marine Corps manual in readiness for the day he could successfully enlist. Oswald's mother would later say that Lee knew the manual 'by heart'. In some eyes, this would show an exceptional show of patriotism by Oswald, others may conclude something a little more sinister.

Oswald the boy finally joined the Marines barely a week past his seventeenth birthday, and, following his enlistment, Lee arrived at the Marine Corps Recruitment Depot in San Diego, California on 26 October, 1956.

Beginning his basic training, Oswald almost immediately bore the brunt of his fellow marines' taunts as his marksmanship was apparently so bad and less than his colleagues would accept. When Oswald couldn't even qualify as sharpshooter, the somewhat grand sounding name for the lowest score on the shooting range, his fellow marines nick-named him 'shit bird' because they felt Oswald was letting the platoon down. Sergeant, and later friend of Oswald, Nelson Delgado, has always publicly announced Oswald's proficiency with an M-1 rifle.

'We gave Oswald holy hell because he kept getting a good many Maggie's Drawers [Marine slang for complete misses of the target]. He was useless on the rifle range.'

Oswald, said Delgado, was always getting 'gigged' for having a dirty rifle. Oswald finally qualified as sharpshooter in December of that year, a full two months after joining the Marines. Three years later, firing for the record just before he left the service, he failed to qualify yet again.

Delgado, Puerto Rican by birth, taught Oswald rudimentary Spanish and found him to be very bright and likeable. Oswald, said Delgado, 'treated me like an equal' implying, of course, that others did not. Delgado and Oswald spoke at length about Marxism, Cuba and Castro. Oswald later asked Delgado how he could obtain some Marxist literature and possibly get in touch with some Cubans. Delgado told him to write to the Cuban embassy in Washington; Oswald did this and began to receive more mail than he had previously ever done.

According to another Marine colleague, Oswald was spotted by a young lieutenant reading this material. The lieutenant became quite excited and told all the men about his discovery. Apparently, and probably to the lieutenant's chagrin, the men laughed off this incident. Oswald himself didn't think that it was so funny. The lieutenant's warnings to his superiors seem to have fallen on deaf ears, because there is no evidence that Oswald was ever berated for his actions.

In January, 1957, Oswald was posted to Camp Pendleton, California, to complete advanced training.

The following spring, Oswald began learning radar and air traffic control at the Naval Air Technical Training Centre in Jacksonville,

Florida. Here, he showed particular interest and proficiency in Aircraft Maintenance and Repair. Such things are not unusual in military service, but these postings do require security clearances and security checks. Oswald, clearly of above average intelligence, passed his checks and was granted clearance at a 'confidential' level. At this time, he was promoted to Private First Class.

Around this time, Oswald was telling his Marine buddies that he used his weekend passes to go home to see his mother whom he said was living in his home town of New Orleans. Marguerite Oswald, however, was then living in Texas and Oswald's relatives in New Orleans could not remember him ever visiting them there during this period.

Oswald finished seventh in a class of 50 and qualified as a Military Occupational Speciality (MOS) of Aviation Electronics Operator. This grading led to a foreign posting to Atsugi, Japan, home of the First Marine Aircraft Wing. On 22 August, 1957, after a brief leave and assignment to El Toro Marine Corps Air station, Oswald boarded the USS Bexar for the trip to the Far East to begin his post with Marine Air Control Squadron One (MACS-1), approximately 25 miles south west of Tokyo. Also located in the remote Atsugi base were a number of buildings known as the 'Joint Technical Advisory Group', the CIA's main operational base, at that time, in the Far East.

Atsugi was also the home of the infamous U–2 aircraft. Oswald was clearly entering the world of military intelligence, albeit willingly or otherwise. The U–2 aircraft, known as The Black Lady of Espionage, was a high–flying spy plane that operated silently and successfully 90,000 feet above the USSR and China, gliding through the thermosphere, effortlessly photographing missile bases, seaports and other secret installations in remote areas of northern Asia. Few knew of a plane that could fly so high and to the obvious delight of American Military Intelligence, the Soviet Union, having long suspected that something was penetrating their air space, had no way of bringing the plane down as it flew high out of the range of any surface-to-air missiles.

The U-2 would later uncover Soviet missiles on mainland Cuba, initiating the October 1962 Cuban Missile Crisis that would almost escalate into world war.

Oswald's duties called for him to project the flight paths of all aircraft, friendly or otherwise, that came into the area he and his colleagues monitored. Lee and his fellows would also direct US aircraft to their targets via radar and radio. His unit would also track stray aircraft of any denomination. Occasionally, this routine boredom would be broken by an unlisted, unidentified utility plane with the code designation *Race Car.*

The pilot of *Race Car* would ask for weather and wind reports at 90,000 feet. At that time, the world altitude record was just over 65,000 feet and the radar height finding antenna only read up to 45,000 feet. Oswald must have come into contact with this phenomenal aircraft during the course of his duties and spoken with its various pilots and if he did so, he must have known the aircraft was friendly.

Oswald did well in his new profession. Captain Gajewski, one of the officers in charge of Oswald during this period, wrote that 'I would desire to have him work for me at any time. He minds his business and does his job well.'

Oswald and his buddies began to see more and more of the U-2 as it was wheeled out of its hangar and as it sped off on its spying missions. Pencil thin and painted black with little or no markings, the U-2 must have been an awesome sight.

Its hangars were jealously protected by guards armed with machine guns, and all personnel based at the Atsugi Base were under strict orders not to discuss what they had seen with anybody, including each other.

There is evidence, however, that Oswald walked freely around the Atsugi base with his camera in hand, unmolested and unperturbed. What was Oswald up to? Getting invaluable information for the Soviet Union, maybe? Had he already decided to defect to that country so early in his life and forsake his much loved and much sought after career in the Marines? Obviously, the secrets of the U-2 would have brought many riches to a young man willing to betray his country, but the young Oswald did not fit this scenario.

Of the many strange activities of the young Marine, one stands out from the rest. Oswald's former Marine buddy, David Bucknell, told of a conversation he had with Oswald after they both returned to the United States. Bucknell stated that, when the two were out in a bar drinking beer, they had been approached by two women and a conversation was struck up between the four of them. Later, Oswald told Bucknell that the incident reminded him of a similar one he had experienced in Japan. An 'attractive female' had approached him in a bar and asked him about his work at the Marine base. Oswald later informed his commanding officer of the conversation. The officer arranged a meeting with a man in civilian clothes. Oswald, it is said, took this man to be a representative of the intelligence community. The man told Oswald that he could do his country a great service by meeting the woman, a known KGB officer, and that he should pass on false information. Lee agreed and, by doing so, became an intelligence operative.

Bucknell also recalled, years later, that during 1959, before Oswald left the Marines, he and several others were ordered to report to the military Criminal Investigation Division (CID). There, a civilian tried to enlist as many of them as he could to take part in an intelligence operation against 'Communists' in Cuba. According to Bucknell, Oswald made several more trips to the CID and later told him that the man who had spoken to them at the CID meetings was the same man who had spoken to Oswald in Japan. Oswald confided to Bucknell that he was soon to leave the Marines and go to Russia on an intelligence mission that would make him a hero on his return.

Another of Oswald's acquaintances in Japan was Gerry Patrick Hemming. Hemming himself has told many investigators that he had been recruited by the Office of Naval Intelligence (ONI) whilst serving in Japan and when he returned to the United States, had been recruited into the CIA. He believes that Oswald had also been recruited by ONI, but states emphatically that Oswald never actually told him so.

As Oswald's tour of duty in the Far East came to an end, he was posted to Marine Air Control No. 9 (MACS-9) at El Toro, Santa Ana, California. Oswald was now being described as 'a good crew chief' and 'brighter than most people' by his superiors. He was part of a seven man radar unit.

At the El Toro Marine Base, Oswald began to study the Russian language. He applied to take a proficiency examination in written and oral Russian. He failed the test, but showed basic knowledge of the language. His buddies nicknamed him 'Comrade Oswaldskovitch', as much to their own amusement as Lee Oswald himself. To the young Marine, the nick-name was probably more palatable than the usual 'Ossie-rabbit', a character in a 1950s TV cartoon.

Oswald subscribed to Communist literature and studied it in the presence of his friends and superiors. Nothing was said to him about this anti-American stance. His skills steadily improved and he would answer his buddies with *da* or *nyet*, whilst addressing his companions as *Comrade*.

Several of Oswald's friends in the Marines made fun of him for his leftist leanings while it seems none of them took him seriously. One, Kerry Thornley, upset Oswald when he remarked to Oswald that Lee could change things when the revolution came. After this chance remark, Oswald appeared deeply hurt and never spoke to Thornley again. Another Marine buddy, James Botelho, said that he and the other Marines never believed that Oswald was a Communist or Marxist and, had they thought him to be, would probably have taken some form of violent action against him.

On 17 August 1959, two months before his twentieth birthday, Oswald applied for a hardship discharge from the Marine Corps.

His mother, Oswald stated for his case, had injured herself at her place of work and could no longer support herself. Around this time he applied for and received a passport, stating in his application form that he intended to visit various countries including Cuba and the Soviet Union. Two weeks later, on 11 September 1959, Oswald obtained his release and left the service. His passport was 'routinely' issued in time for his honourable discharge.

Oswald stayed with his mother for only two days. Her 'injury' had been caused by a chocolate box hitting her on the nose some months before. Oswald drew $203 from his only known bank account and bought a ticket for Le Havre, France aboard the freighter *Marion Lykes* for $220.75. He had told his mother he was to get work in New Orleans. Just before he sailed, Oswald sent a letter to his mother stating, 'I have booked passage on a ship to Europe. I would have had to go sooner or later and I think it's best I go now. Just remember above all else that my values are different from [my brother] Robert's or yours. It is difficult to tell you how I feel. Just remember, this is what I must do. I did not tell you about my plans because you could be hardly expected to understand'.

On 20 September 1959, still a teenager, Lee Harvey Oswald set sail across the Atlantic Ocean, bound for Europe. He would not see his homeland for another two and a half years.

Marine buddy Botelho's reaction when it was learned that Oswald had defected to the Soviet Union was not one of surprise. Oswald became the talk of the base. His colleagues realised that Lee, like them, had memorised all the radio codes concerning various aircraft missions. They also noted that those codes were not changed. This made Botelho suspicious of Oswald's intentions. He believed that Oswald was, indeed, a US intelligence officer and had gone to Russia as some kind of spy for the American Government. Botelho claims that the Oswald he knew was very anti-Communist.

Lee Oswald was the only US Marine to defect to a Communist country in peace time, a rather staggering event. Oswald's companions were asked several questions, but Botelho concluded that there was no real investigation because somebody from 'our side' had sent Oswald to the Soviet Union.

Years later, even his widow, Marina, came to believe that her husband was working for the United States Government in some capacity. Today, looking back at his character and observing that he had shown certain traits of professional training, Marina reminds us that Lee was taught Russian in the US Military to the extent that when she first met and spoke with him, she thought he was of Russian origin. He got in and out of the Soviet Union quite easily. She wonders if Oswald had rational reasons for actions that seemed inexplicable to her at the time; the night before the assassination of President John F Kennedy, he and Marina had argued over the telephone when she found out that he was living under the name 'O.H. Lee' in a boarding house in Oak Cliff, Dallas.

Oswald told her that he wasn't living under an assumed name and that his landlady remembered his name in the wrong order. Marina did not believe her husband then and to this day still wonders if Oswald had other reasons for lying to her about this use of an alias. She also stated that Oswald admired their young president and that Lee had said that Kennedy was 'good for the country'.

Oswald's widow also suspects that George de Mohrenschildt, the man who befriended them both when they moved to Dallas, was working for the American Government and may have been the influencing factor for her husband's six month sojourn to New Orleans in the summer of 1963. Since that dark day in Dallas half a century ago, much has been revealed about de Mohrenschildt, not least his liaisons with the United States Government in general and the Central Intelligence Agency in particular.

★

The Department of Defence destroyed its military files on Lee Oswald 'routinely' in 1973, whilst keeping files on Nazi war criminals from the 1930s and 40s. These files held information on Oswald prior to his arrest for the murder of John Kennedy on 22 November 1963.

Photographs appear to show that the Oswald who returned to the United States, was not the young Marine Oswald who entered the Soviet Union three years before. At the very least, the 'real' Oswald appears to have been the victim of imposture whilst in Russia, as he was later in Dallas and Mexico City. That Oswald was contacted by the Soviet Secret Police (NKVD) in Moscow is beyond question, if only as a matter of routine. Indeed, if the Soviets were aware of his proficiency at the Atsugi Base and his job there as a radar operator working with the U-2 spy plane, a fact that Oswald informed them of personally, he would have been a prime target for recruitment into Soviet Intelligence.

Oswald's military service and possible recruitment into Naval Intelligence is still shrouded in mystery even after 50 years. There are at least 17 intelligence agencies operating out of the United States, and many agents or officers dovetail and work as contract agents for any, some, or all. Speculation is that Oswald possibly defected to the Soviet Union under orders issued by the CIA.

A CIA memorandum released in the late 1970s revealed that an unidentified CIA officer hurriedly checked the Agency files in late November 1963 for information on Lee H Oswald following the assassination of John F Kennedy. His reason was that:

'We were extremely concerned at that time that Oswald, as an American returning from the USSR, might have been routinely debriefed by the Domestic Contacts Division (DCD)'. [The Domestic Contacts Division of the CIA monitors US Citizens leaving and returning to the United States from certain areas of the world]. The officer in question was apparently consoled by the fact he could find no trace of agency contact with Lee Harvey Oswald.

In February 1964, Soviet Intelligence officer Yuri Nosenko

conveniently defected to the West and readily answered a great many of the questions surrounding Lee Oswald's residence in the Soviet Union. Nosenko gave the American authorities the Moscow chronicle of the strange young man's life there. After Nosenko had acquired all the relevant papers on Oswald's stay in Moscow, the KGB told the American Government that they had no interest in Lee Oswald and that they were satisfied that the Soviet Union was not in any way connected to President Kennedy's assassination.

The CIA has always denied that the agency had something to hide regarding Lee Harvey Oswald. CIA Director John McCone, Warren Commission member, told the Commission under oath that 'my examination has resulted in the conclusion that Lee Harvey Oswald was not an agent, employee, or informant of the Central Intelligence Agency. The Agency never contacted him, interviewed him, talked with him, or received or solicited any reports or information from him, or communicated with him directly or in any other manner.'

In 1963, Richard Helms was serving in the CIA as Deputy Director for Plans. He later became director of the Agency. Helms had stated in 1964 that there was 'no material in the CIA, either in the records or in the minds of any individuals, that there was any contact had or even contemplated with him [Oswald].' Helms also stated that the entire CIA file on Lee Harvey Oswald had been presented to a member of the commission staff.

A document released in the late 1970s, however, revealed that the CIA had shown intelligence interest in Lee Harvey Oswald 'sometime in the summer of 1960.'

The bombshell document goes further, as the author of the document discussed 'the laying on of interviews through the Domestic Contacts Division or other suitable channels.' The writer also states that he didn't know what, if anything, happened beyond that discussion. It should be noted, of course, that in the summer of 1960, Lee Oswald was living in the Soviet Union.

Following the assassination of Kennedy, CIA Chief of Counter intelligence James Jesus Angleton contacted FBI Assistant Director William Sullivan and discussed what answers they should give, if they were asked to appear before the Warren Commission. Angleton foresaw many questions and recognised the need to pre-empt their interrogation. Among those questions could be Oswald's status with the CIA.

'Was Oswald ever an agent of the CIA?' To this question, Angleton told Sullivan, 'Our answer should be 'No.' '

The CIA apparently has 1,196 documents pertaining to Lee Harvey Oswald. Many of those documents are still classified and not available to the public until the year 2039, toward the end of September. The documents that are available are heavily censored. Oswald's '201' file, a file opened on any member of the public or otherwise that the CIA should take an interest in, was opened in December 1960, even though it holds documents dated as early as 1959 and the summer of 1960, when Oswald, of course, was already in the Soviet Union.

Senator Richard Schweiker of the Senate Intelligence Committee said in a 1978 interview with author Anthony Summers, 'Either we trained and sent him to Russia, and they went along and pretended they didn't know to fake us out, or in fact, they inculcated him and sent him back here and were trying to fake us out that way'.

★

Lee Oswald reached the Soviet Union on 16 October, 1959, two days before his twentieth birthday. His means of entry into that country is also mysterious. Normally, at that time, a tourist would have to wait up to two weeks before being allowed a visa. Oswald, presumably already screened by the Soviet Secret Police (NKVD), was issued with his Intourist visa within minutes of his application. Were the KGB or NKVD waiting for Oswald? Had he contacted them and told them of his desire to defect and pass on all he knew about his intelligence connections whilst serving in the Marine

Corps in Japan and his dealing with the U-2 spy plane? The Soviets must have been falling over themselves to get hold of this man.

John Donovan, a former lieutenant in the Marine Corps, testified to the Warren Commission that shortly before he left the Marines he and his fellows had: '…received word that he [Oswald] had shown up in Moscow. This necessitated a lot of change of aircraft call signs, codes, radio frequencies, radar frequencies. He had access to the location of all bases in the West Coast area, all radio frequencies for all squadrons, all tactical call signs and the relative strength of all those squadrons, number and type of aircraft in a squadron, who was the commanding officer, the authentication code of entering and exiting the ADIZ, which stands for Air Defence Identification Zone. He knew the range of our radar. He knew the range of our radio and he knew the range of the surrounding units' radio and radar.'

Two weeks after his entry into the Soviet Union, Lee Oswald walked into the United States embassy in Moscow and calmly told the consular officials that he wished to renounce his American citizenship. As they stared in disbelief at the young man, Oswald dramatically slammed his passport and a formal letter onto the desk and said, 'I affirm my allegiance is to the Union of Soviet Socialist Republics,' and that he had, 'voluntarily told Soviet officials that he would make known to them all information concerning the Marine Corps and his speciality therein, radar operation, as he possessed.' He also added that he might know 'something of special interest.' A reference, perhaps, to the top secret U-2?

United States Consular Official John McVicar was a little troubled by Oswald's outburst and felt that 'he was following a pattern of behaviour in which he seemed to have been tutored by a person or persons unknown.' McVicar went on to say that 'in short, it seemed to me there was a possibility that he had been in contact with others before or during his Marine Corps tour who had guided him and encouraged him in his actions.'

Of course, McVicar could have been wrong, but if he were

correct, then who might this person or persons be? To the casual eye, the evidence would seem to point to Soviet Intelligence. If one looks closer, other intelligence agencies would seem to be lurking in the background.

Yet another anomaly arises at this point. The man who dealt with Oswald at the US embassy, Richard E Snyder, was reputed to have had CIA links and had been working for the Agency since 1949. His file was later unobtainable 'as a matter of cover.' Snyder tried in vain to dissuade the young man from carrying out his threat. According to the Warren Commission, however, Oswald could not renounce his citizenship because his request fell on a Saturday, not a regular working day. Snyder told Oswald to think about what he was doing and return on the following Monday to further his request. Oswald did not return to the embassy but wrote a letter to embassy officials protesting the frustration of his act of renunciation and repeated his wish to dissolve his American citizenship. Because Oswald failed to appear in person at the embassy and failed to fill out the necessary documents, he never actually defected. Oswald even refused to see embassy staff personally when they contacted him later.

There is still uncertainty as to when Lee Harvey Oswald contacted the US embassy in Moscow. According to the Warren Report, Oswald appeared at the embassy on Saturday, 31 October 1959, two weeks after he entered the Soviet Union. A cablegram sent by the naval attaché in the embassy to the Navy Department in Washington, however, refers to a previous embassy dispatch dated 26 October 1959, dealing with Oswald's renunciation of US citizenship and his offer to furnish the Soviet authorities with information concerning his military expertise, namely radar systems and their operation.

Snyder sent a confidential letter dated 28 October 1959 to Gene Boster, Officer in Charge of USSR Affairs at the State Department. Snyder requested advice on how to handle an attempted renunciation of American citizenship. Snyder later testified that the letter was not directed at any particular individual. If Oswald did indeed make his contact with the embassy on 31 October, then the letter could not have been inspired by him. If Oswald on the other hand had contacted the embassy before that date, the letter takes on a totally different meaning.

Oswald, it will be remembered, had suddenly asked for and received, a 'hardship' discharge from the Marines to aid his ailing mother, who, Oswald cited, had injured herself whilst at work and had had to leave her place of employment. Mrs Oswald's injury, actually suffered months before, had been 'superficial'.

Lee Oswald, at home in Texas for only two days, told his brother Robert that he was returning to New Orleans in an effort to find work there. Oswald arrived in New Orleans and promptly boarded the ship Marion Lykes, bound for Le Havre, France. The ship, after crossing the Atlantic, was then to go onto Southampton, England. Oswald arrived in England on 9 October 1959. By midnight the following day, he was checking himself into the Torni Hotel in Helsinki, Finland.

Much speculation has arisen around this stage of his journey. Oswald's passport is stamped 'Embarked 10 Oct 1959.' Had Oswald left for Helsinki under a normal flight, he could not have reached Helsinki in time for his checking into the hotel. Many researchers believe Oswald may have been flown to Helsinki aboard a US military aircraft. This, of course, is only speculation.

Lee Oswald stayed in two of the most expensive hotels in Helsinki, abnormal behaviour for him, as he was always careful with his money. After visiting the Soviet Consulate, he obtained an entry visa within two days. An incredible feat. The Warren Commission itself reports that a normal application takes at least a week to be processed. Another discrepancy arises here. It was later revealed that Oswald did not in fact obtain his visa in Helsinki. A Swedish newspaper reports that Oswald appeared in Stockholm and applied and received his visa there.

Two days later, Lee Harvey Oswald, 'defector', ex-Marine and custodian of some of America's most guarded secrets, arrived in Moscow by train.

He was contacted by a Soviet Intourist representative and then checked into the Hotel Berlin, registering as a student. Later, speaking with his Intourist guide, Rima Shirokova, Oswald spoke of defection.

Having been interviewed many times over the following week, Oswald was informed, possibly to his dismay, that his visa had expired and he had two hours to leave the country or risk certain arrest and possible imprisonment. Oswald promptly slashed his wrists in an alleged suicide attempt. Reading Oswald's *Historic Diary*, supposedly written by Oswald at the time but now believed to be an elaborate fraud, Oswald describes his impending demise in these words, complete with the original spelling:

'I planned so much! 7.00pm. I decide to end it. Soak wrist in cold water to numb the pain. Than slash my left wrist. Than plaug wrist into bathtub of hot water. I think 'when Olga comes at 8 to find me dead it wil be a great shock. Some where, a violin plays, as I wacth my life whirl away. I think to myself. How easy to die and a sweet death, (to violins).'

Oswald's spelling obviously left a good deal to be desired, if, indeed, it was his. The *House Select Committee on Assassinations* concluded in 1979 that the Oswald 'diary' had, in fact, been written in one or two sittings and on the same paper.

Olga found Oswald unconscious and he was moved to hospital. Oswald was out of sight for the next eleven days and none of his actions are documented. After being interviewed by two American reporters, Aline Mosby and Priscilla Johnson [who later wrote the book Marina and Lee], Oswald disappeared for the rest of the year. Six weeks of Oswald's life (16 November to 29 December 1959) are totally unaccounted for and remain firmly wrapped in mystery and speculation. Priscilla Johnson was later the subject of speculation that she had spoken to Oswald in her alleged capacity of intelligence agent.

By early January 1960, Oswald had been moved to Minsk and worked in a radio and television factory. He had been issued with a Soviet Identification document designating him as a stateless person. Much later, Oswald himself proclaimed that he had, in fact, never pursued Soviet citizenship.

Arriving in Minsk with 5000 roubles, Oswald moved into a large apartment. With his continuing International Red Cross allowance and wages from the factory, Oswald was earning more than the factory director.

The city of Minsk, at that time, was the site of an espionage training school the CIA had been aware of since 1947.

An FBI document sent to the Warren Commission by Director J Edgar Hoover stated the director's fears. Hoover was concerned that Oswald may [later] have been sent back to the United States as a 'sleeper' agent, a man who would not be contacted for several years only to be used in some capacity later. Hoover's bureau also listed Oswald's fingerprints on their 'flash' notice in an effort to warn FBI agents that somebody may use Oswald's identity. On 3 June 1960, Hoover issued this declaration to the Office of Security, Department of State:

'Since there is a possibility that an impostor is using Oswald's birth certificate, any current information the Department of State may have concerning subject will be appreciated.'

At this time, on learning that Oswald was offering the Soviets military information and after failing to reach Oswald by certified letters, the Marine Corps officially changed Oswald's 'honourable discharge' to 'dishonourable.'

Six months after Oswald defected and spoke of telling all he knew to the Soviets, a U-2 spy plane crashed near the Russian city of Sverdlovsk. The 'shooting down' of this plane was, by coincidence, two weeks before the Summit meeting between President Eisenhower and the Russian Premier Khrushchev. The incident effectively ruined the talks. Eisenhower was further embarrassed by his opposite number in the Kremlin after he had indicated to the Soviet authorities that the U-2 had been a weather balloon lost over Soviet territory. Little did Eisenhower know that Gary Powers, the pilot of the U-2, had been captured along with his aircraft and the film he had exposed of Soviet military bases.

Powers, maintained that Oswald may have been responsible for his downfall. Years later, Powers would reveal that although he suspected that Oswald had indeed given the NKVD a great deal of information concerning the U-2, he believed that his plane had been sabotaged by person or persons unknown and not shot down by Soviet SAM missiles.

★

Meanwhile Oswald's mother Marguerite became increasingly concerned about her son's disappearance. On 28 January 1961 she caught a train to Washington, in an effort to seek out President Kennedy and ask him personally to locate Lee.

Mrs Oswald, not surprisingly, did not get to speak with Kennedy nor was she able to speak with her second choice, Secretary of State Dean Rusk. She did, however, speak with Eugene Boster, the White House Soviet Affairs Officer. Although neither Mrs Oswald, nor anyone else, had heard from her son for more than a year, Mrs Oswald quoted Boster as stating 'Oh, yes, I am familiar with the case.'

Marguerite Oswald became convinced that her son had defected to the Soviet Union in 1959 and was following orders from the US Government. Mrs Oswald first told her local newspaper of her opinion in January 1961, almost three years before Lee was accused of murdering JFK. Marguerite Oswald defended her view of this until her death in 1981. Mrs Oswald was convinced that the US Government knew exactly where her son was and what he was up to whilst in the Soviet Union. The record of Oswald's relationship with various offices of the US Government suggest she may have been correct.

Less than a week after her visit to Washington, a memo was

sent to the United States embassy in Moscow in an effort to locate Oswald. On 13 February 1961, the embassy received a letter from Lee stating: 'I desire to return to the United States, that is if we could come to some agreement concerning the dropping of any legal proceedings against me.'

In the letter, Oswald showed an astute awareness of his situation. He stated that he had never 'taken Russian citizenship' and if he could show the Soviet authorities his passport, he felt sure they would grant him an exit visa.

Oswald then sprang another bombshell on the embassy. In a letter following close behind the last, he stated:

'Since my last letter I have gotten married. My wife is Russian, born in Leningrad, she has no parents living and is quite willing to leave the Soviet Union with me and live in the United States. I would not leave here without my wife so arrangements would have to be made for her to leave at the same time I do.'

Oswald was obviously restless. Life in the USSR appeared not to be to his liking, despite his bravado of the previous years. He was ready to come home, but it would take almost another eighteen months to achieve that.

# Trucks, 'Oswalds' and a Mongoose

Following the assassination of President Kennedy, Oscar Deslatte, a Ford motor dealer in New Orleans, contacted the FBI. The name 'Oswald' had struck a chord with him in relation to the sale of several Ford trucks sometime prior to the assassination. Deslatte checked his files and discovered a docket in the name of 'Oswald' pertaining to the sale of the trucks in question. The problem soon became clear. The docket is dated 20 January 1960. Lee Harvey Oswald was living in the USSR at that time.

The FBI took charge of Mr Deslatte's docket and sent it to FBI headquarters in Washington, DC, for testing.

The 'Oswald' who visited Deslatte was accompanied by a swarthy Cuban. The pair had tried to buy 10 trucks from Deslatte during the build–up to the Bay of Pigs invasion, part of the CIA's *Operation Mongoose* war against Cuba's Premier Fidel Castro.

That these men were trying to buy these trucks at this time was not usual. American intelligence officers were quite open about their purchase of supplies and vehicles leading up to the invasion.

Deslatte recalled that the white male first identified himself as 'Joseph Moore' and asked for 'a good price' on the trucks because 'we're doing this for the good of the country'. 'Moore' also told Deslatte that he should write the name 'Oswald' on the docket because that was the name of the individual in charge of the money for his anti–Castro organisation and that 'Oswald' would be paying for the trucks if the deal were to go through. Oscar Deslatte could not identify photographs of Lee Harvey Oswald shown to him by the FBI as the man who had approached him in 1961. Also, Lee Oswald could not drive a car.

The docket, only released by the FBI in 1979 also reveals another tantalising clue. Marked clearly on it, is the name of the group wishing to purchase the trucks: *Friends of Democratic Cuba*. This organisation was run by none other than William Guy Banister – later linked to Lee Harvey Oswald after the latter's return to the United States. Banister, a former FBI agent, was at the time still engaged in undercover work for various intelligence agencies, worked out of 544 Camp Street, New Orleans. In the summer of 1963, Camp Street was a hot-bed of activity involving anti-Castro Cubans and operatives of the CIA. Lee Oswald was photographed passing out *Fair Play for Cuba* leaflets and was later arrested following a street scuffle. Banister, as will be shown later, was linked to this operation.

Another strange happening paralleled Oswald's visit to the USSR. Robert E Webster, a former US Navy serviceman, told officials he was defecting to the Soviet Union less than two weeks before Lee Oswald. Webster had been working in Moscow with a group of American plastics experts at an American trade exhibition and simply failed to return home with his co-workers. Webster had been employed with the Rand Development Corporation, one of the first US companies to sell technical products to the Soviet Union.

A link has been established between Rand Development and Rand Corporation, allegedly a CIA front organisation. The firms were once located across the street from each other in New York City; Rand Development held several CIA contracts and Henry Rand, president of the company and two top officials in that company, George Bookbinder and Christopher Bird were later connected with the Agency.

Webster, after declaring his allegiance to the USSR, took a Russian-born wife (although he had married in the United States). The couple had a child and suddenly, Webster decided he had had enough of the Soviet way of life and requested that he be repatriated at the earliest time possible. Webster and his Russian wife returned to the US at almost the same time as Lee Oswald, his Russian–born wife and baby daughter.

Webster told officials that he had never met or known Lee Harvey Oswald in Russia, but when Oswald was preparing to return to the United States, Oswald had casually asked embassy personnel about the fate of a young man named Webster who had come to the Soviet Union 'shortly before he did'.

Years later, Oswald's widow, Marina, told of meeting her husband after he had been working at an American Trade exhibition. Oswald, as far as has been reported, never worked at such an exhibition. Following the murder of John Kennedy, the United States authorities discovered an address in Marina's address book that matched that of Webster's Leningrad apartment.

Could Oswald and Webster have been part of a broader plan, executed by the US Government, running young, disenchanted defectors throughout the USSR?

There is some evidence that the Office of Naval Intelligence (ONI) ran a programme in the late 1950s of up to 40 young men who were made out to be poor, disenchanted Americans who turned onto the Communist way of life.

The US State Department had been monitoring these individuals, one of whom was Lee Harvey Oswald. Their task was to determine if any of the young men who returned had been 'turned round' by the Soviets and used against the US as spies. Five months before the assassination of JFK, this department still didn't know if Lee Oswald was, or had been, 'one of ours or one of theirs'.

Several researchers have become convinced that the Lee Oswald who left for the Soviet Union in 1959 was not the same man who returned to the United States and it has long been suspected that one or more people impersonated Lee Harvey Oswald in and around Dallas in the weeks before the assassination of President John F Kennedy. Could Oswald have actually been substituted by a KGB agent during his stay in the Soviet Union?

Several leading researchers into the JFK case have studied one of the more bizarre aspects of the whole 'Oswald' scenario: was the man arrested for shooting Dallas police officer Jefferson

Davies Tippit, then later charged with assassinating President John F Kennedy and then shot down by Jack Ruby, the real Lee Harvey Oswald?

Oswald had met Marina around 17 March 1961. Even Marina does not remember the exact date. They both attended a dance and Oswald had been introduced to Marina as 'Alik'. So good was Oswald's Russian at this point that Marina thought he was a native of the Baltic states. When he told her that he was an American from New Orleans, she was greatly surprised.

Six weeks after they met, after only two or three dates, Oswald proposed and Marina accepted. They married on 30 April 1961.

Marina had been born in the northern coastal town of Molotovsk on 17 July 1941. Marina never knew her father and before she was ten her mother died. Life with her stepfather was 'intolerable' and she moved into her uncle's house in Minsk. Her uncle just happened to be a top ranking official in the Soviet Ministry of the Interior (MVD). It is possible that Marina may have been issued with fresh documents, and therefore a fresh identity, to enable her to leave the Soviet Union with Oswald.

There are too many discrepancies regarding the true identity of Marina Prusakova. The CIA found her baffling. For example, one day after beginning her new career as a 'pharmacist' Marina suddenly quit the post and supposedly went on a long vacation which lasted several months. The CIA believed that she had possibly been whisked away to one of the many KGB training complexes. By coincidence, she 'disappeared' just before Lee Harvey Oswald reached Moscow. Maybe Marina had been groomed to meet Oswald? A CIA document released in 1976 reveals that Marina took yet another month long 'holiday' in which Marina herself admitted she stayed at a government 'rest home' in Leningrad in the autumn of 1960.

In Marina's address book, taken from her after her husband had been arrested for the murder of President Kennedy, the FBI found the name Lev Prizentse next to a Leningrad address. Marina stated that she had met this man at the 'rest home' in Leningrad. Following up this lead, the CIA discovered that the address was the same address where Robert E Webster, the previously mentioned American defector, had stayed. Webster, it will be remembered, had defected to the USSR shortly before Lee Oswald and had stayed in the same apartment as Oswald's future wife. Oswald had enquired about the welfare of Webster when he, Oswald, returned to the United States. Webster had met and married a Russian girl (believed by the CIA to be a KGB agent) and had a baby by her, before he, too, returned to the United States, supposedly disillusioned with life in the USSR.

The CIA must have been very concerned about the number of defectors returning with Russian wives and families.

There is no concrete evidence that Marina was an agent for Soviet intelligence or anybody else. She is, however, surrounded by almost as many coincidences as her late husband, Lee Oswald. Of course, Marina may have been steered toward the young American without her knowing she was being used.

After interviewing the Oswalds in the US embassy in Moscow, the embassy recommended that the State Department rule that Lee Oswald had not expatriated himself and that Marina's application for a visa to enter the United States should be approved. When Oswald returned to the US Embassy in July 1961 he convinced Snyder that he had learned his lesson and was indeed a loyal American. Oswald stated further that he had not carried out his threat to give the Soviet government any military secrets; that they had not asked him such questions and doubted that he would have complied if they had.

When asked, Marina told the embassy that she had never been a member of Komsomol (the Communist youth organisation), a statement which was later found to be false. The State Department took action to approve Marina's papers by putting pressure on the Immigration and Naturalisation Service (INS) to waive sanctions against her.

At the end of 1961 the Oswalds received their exit visas from the Soviet authorities. Oswald made futile attempts to raise cash from non-governmental sources in the United States. The International Rescue Committee, Inc.(IRC), describing itself as a 'strongly anti-Communist organisation', was one such source that Oswald contacted.

Oswald, turned down by everyone he approached for financial aid, turned to the State Department and asked the US embassy for financial assistance to cover travel costs to the US for himself, his wife and their new born baby daughter. The State Department authorised the embassy to make a loan of $435 to Oswald. Oswald signed a promissory note in June 1962 and also received his passport at that time. The passport was valid for only 30 days and listed 'good only for travel to the United States'. By January 1963, Oswald had paid off his debt to the State Department.

Almost two years later, the Warren Commission reviewed all transactions regarding Oswald and the US State Department from 1959 up to his death in November 1963 and concluded that Oswald had been treated properly, just as any other person would be, given his situation. If one reviews the relevant documents, however, there is a consistent pattern of unusual and favourable treatment of Oswald by the State Department. All obstacles seemed to have been removed for this self-declared enemy of his native country, confessor of top military secrets and his Russian-born wife.

Around this time, Marina noted a cooling in Oswald's demeanour toward her. This frostiness increased after they finally left the Soviet Union for the United States. She has stated that she felt as if Lee had acted out his love for her and was obeying some kind of orders to maintain their relationship.

The inconsistencies began to pile up. The Oswalds, if one believes the Warren Commission, crossed the Soviet border at Brest into Poland. Marina's passport is, however, stamped at Helmstedt, East Germany. Oswald's passport has no such stamp and he may have travelled a different route from Marina.

The Oswalds then moved on to Amsterdam and stayed in a private establishment recommended by someone in the US embassy in Moscow. Marina has described this place both as a 'private apartment' and as a 'boarding house'. The official record shows the Oswalds stayed at this establishment for only one night. After the assassination, Marina testified that they stayed for three nights. She also noted that the people spoke English and that the arrangements had been made previously. The Chief Counsel of the Warren Commission described this particular event as 'unexplained'. Little wonder many researchers believe that Oswald and Marina were debriefed by US Intelligence at this point.

Marina testified that she and her husband had arrived in 'New York by air then stayed in some hotel in New York City for one day and then went by train to Texas.' The Warren Commission, backed by documentation, stated that the Oswalds arrived in Hoboken, New Jersey via the ship SS Maasdam on 13 June 1962.

However they may have made the return trip to the United States, Lee Oswald and his family were back in the west. The enigmatic former Marine, still only 22 years old, was about to embark on the next phase of his mysterious, albeit short, life. People who manipulated Oswald's life as a teenager would influence his actions again and disappear into the background just as quickly.

Oswald was now falling into his own personal abyss but did he jump or was he pushed?

Anthony Summers, author of 'Conspiracy: Who Killed President Kennedy?' uncovered some tantalising information during the research of his book. By another coincidence, the CIA had borrowed 150 photographs taken by tourists who had returned from the Soviet Union in the early 1960s. They copied five from 150. To their amazement and no doubt everyone else's who has read anything about this case, in one of the photos is Lee Oswald, standing with his hands in his pockets talking to two American tourists as they travelled through Minsk in 1961.

Summers spoke with one of the tourists, Rita Naman. She and her friend Monica Kramer were travelling through the Soviet Union by car in the late summer of 1961. In Moscow in August of that year, Naman and Kramer were being taken by their Intourist guide to visit the Moscow Film Festival. Nothing unusual about that, but they were approached by a young man speaking English with an American accent. The man passed the time of day with the women and nothing more, but he did hold the women up by talking to them through the rolled down window of their car. Finally, the Intourist guide ordered them to move on.

Naman forgot about the man and might well have forgotten about the incident altogether if the same man had not turned up again ten days and 400 miles later in Minsk. This is where the photograph was taken.

Could Oswald have been in Minsk by coincidence? Oswald's own writings (albeit the suspect 'Historic diary') clearly show Oswald in Moscow that entire summer. Oswald and Marina had been summoned to the US embassy in the Soviet capital to discuss their future return to the United States. After a few days, Lee and Marina returned to Minsk, where by all accounts they stayed. Kramer and Naman met Oswald in Moscow three weeks after the Oswald's returned to Minsk.

The first reports talk of only two tourists. So who took the photograph? That question was answered later. Mrs Marie Hyde, another American tourist, had become separated from her guide and had asked Naman and Kramer if she could ride from Minsk through Poland and into the West. They agreed and Marie Hyde took the photograph of Oswald. The photo session was initiated by Mrs Hyde. Hyde took one photograph with Kramer's camera and then got Naman to take the second. Hyde confirms the essence of this story. When the trio reached the Polish border they were interrogated by the border police. Hyde was interrogated alone.

Naman and Kramer joked that their 'friend' was probably a spy. Was the CIA trying to contact Lee Oswald or using the women in an effort to locate and photograph him? Was the KGB using Oswald in an effort to determine what, if anything, Naman, Kramer and Hyde were up to in the Soviet Union? And that photograph is it a coincidence that out of all the photos taken by US citizens in the Soviet Union in that period, the CIA picked out the one that Oswald appeared in? The reason for the supposedly innocent encounter, if there was one, remains a mystery. Of course, it is possible that the entire Oswald defection story was just that – a series of coincidences only noticed by history because of the events that were to unfold 18 months later, following Lee Oswald's return to the United States.

After the assassination, the bewildered Marina Oswald was effectively placed under house arrest by the FBI and repeatedly warned that if she did not cooperate with the authorities she may be deported back to the Soviet Union. Squabbles aside, Marina loved Lee and felt she should stay in the United States for his sake and for the sake of their children.

After Oswald's death, her manner changed as she was continually browbeaten by the authorities. Oswald's mother, already estranged by language and accusation, was kept away from her daughter-in-law. After her son's funeral, filmed for posterity, Marguerite Oswald is seen passing Lee's five-week-old daughter to Marina, as they are led away by officials. Marguerite Oswald never set eyes on the remainder of her distant family again.

Marina was continually pressed for information regarding Oswald's alleged visit to Mexico in the September of 1963. In the first instance, Marina had no recollection whatsoever about such a trip and although she appeared several times before the Warren Commission in early 1964, Marina never mentioned any trip to Mexico by her late husband.

Toward the end of 1964, the United States authorities had been denying the press and Oswald's representative, lawyer Mark

Lane, access to Marina for the better part of a year fearing that she may have been influenced by their questions. In a sudden about face, the CIA and FBI declared that one Pricilla Johnson would be allowed to interview Marina. Johnson, described as a 'reporter', is to be found in an FBI report (Warren Commission document 49) stating that she was 'an employee of the State Department.' Johnson denied such a charge, but later retracted her statement of denial. The same Priscilla Johnson had interviewed Lee Harvey Oswald in Moscow after the latter's defection to the USSR in 1959. Following Johnson's appearance, Marina found the bus ticket stubs 'proving' that Oswald had, indeed, visited Mexico in September of 1963. Where did Marina find the tickets? Loose in the pages of a magazine, a year after the event.

In the years since that dreadful weekend, Marina is convinced Lee was some kind of agent of the United States Government. She points to the ease of Oswald's entry into and exit from the Soviet Union at the height of the Cold War together with his actions and moods at the time.

When she testified before the Warren Commission in 1964, she was, in her own words, 'just a blind kitten'. She admits to burying Lee, doing as she was told by the authorities to heap the blame on him.

For years after the event Marina refused to read, listen or watch anything related to the assassination. Now, although she dreads another investigation like the Warren Commission, she would like the truth to be revealed, once and for all.

# Nagell, Notebooks and New Orleans

Richard Case Nagell (born 5 August 1930) was a former United States military officer who claimed to have had foreknowledge of the assassination of President John F Kennedy. A decorated war hero in Korea, Nagell had resigned from the US Army in 1959, suffering severe disfigurement and permanent brain damage. Nagell's injuries had been sustained not only as a result of battle, but of a 1954 plane crash in which Nagell had been the only survivor. He suffered several concussions, one of which left a permanent depression on the side of his head, resulting in what his doctors called 'organic' brain damage. The doctors further stated that the damage gave Nagell the 'inability to distinguish between right and wrong'.

The military had been practically the only family Nagell had ever known and following his 1959 resignation from the military, Nagell found it difficult to re-adjust to civilian life; working briefly as a private investigator. Nagell also claimed to have had himself arrested in a bank shooting weeks before the assassination of JFK to avoid becoming a 'patsy'. In 1968, Nagell met with New Orleans District Attorney Jim Garrison, who at the time was investigating Clay Shaw's possible complicity in the assassination.

Did Nagell possess foreknowledge of the JFK assassination? Had he in fact been recruited by an agency of a foreign government to assassinate Lee Harvey Oswald in September 1963, and 'stop the clock' on the assassination? Did Nagell have personal knowledge of alleged conspirators such as David Ferrie, Guy Banister, Clay Shaw, Sergio Arcacha Smith, and 'Angel' and 'Leopoldo', two Cubans reportedly seen in the company of Lee Harvey Oswald by one Sylvia Odio?

Dick Russell's 1992 book 'The Man Who Knew Too Much'

reveals one side of the enigmatic Nagell. There is, however, another side to Richard Case Nagell.

Nagell had married a Japanese national by the name of Mitsuko Takahashi sometime in 1958; the union produced a daughter, Teresa, and a son, Robert. The children were barely old enough to walk before Mitsuko had taken them and walked out on Nagell. Following this setback, Nagell checked himself into a Veterans' Administration hospital, expressing depression and fear because of his inability to keep his marriage together and hold down a job. At one point, Nagell even described fantasies about murdering his wife.

On one occasion Nagell followed Mitsuko to her apartment and broke down the door. Nagell was arrested by local police on a 'drunk and disorderly' charge. Mitsuko consequently filed for divorce. A month later Nagell checked himself into a VA hospital again for a bullet wound to the chest; hinting that Mitsuko was responsible. After being examined, the doctor concluded, however, that the wound had been self-inflicted.

Since then, Nagell had become increasingly aware of how much his mental health was deteriorating; nervous and unstable, he had resigned from two jobs because of his inability to concentrate. He tried several times to obtain psychiatric treatment, but then would refuse to cooperate with doctors when his requests were granted. Nagell complained to the FBI that his wife had refused to comply with a court order granting him access to his children, but later admitted he there had been no such court order. Nagell appeared at the Outpatient Clinic of a VA hospital in Brentwood, California and was referred to the Neurological Clinic, appearing 'tearful, nervous and rigid'. Their report also stated that Nagell would only utter words 'Got to see my kids'.

On 20 September 1963, Richard Case Nagell appeared at the State National Bank in El Paso, Texas. He was armed with a fully loaded Colt .45 revolver. Three years after this incident he stated his whole purpose of entering the bank in El Paso that day was for the purpose of obtaining psychiatric help and treatment, and not for the purpose of actually robbing the bank. Nagell reportedly fired two shots into the plaster wall just below the ceiling; walked outside, sat on the steps leading to the bank and patiently waited for the police to arrive. As the State National Bank was federally insured, the FBI sent two agents to interview Nagell, by now waiting in police custody. The FBI report stated that 'When asked for his motive in attempting to hold up the bank, Nagell stated that he was unhappy with the American judicial system, because he had attempted, through judicial procedures, to get to see his two children, a girl and a boy, in custody of his divorced wife, and the California court had not executed an order in keeping with his request.'

Nagell was held without a trial for nine months in a county jail, where the FBI and Secret Service visited him on several occasions after the assassination; and, though there is no mention of Nagell in the Warren Commission's 26 volumes, FBI reports from December 1963 clearly state that he talked of having known Oswald in Texas and Mexico City.

Transcripts of assassination-related telephone conversations with President Lyndon Johnson show that LBJ's friend, federal judge and former Texas Congressman, Homer Thornberry, had been in touch with LBJ twice in the weeks following the assassination. Then, late in January 1964, Thornberry suddenly stepped in as the new judge in the Nagell case – where court transcripts indicated a concerted effort to suppress Nagell's efforts to describe his true motive for his alleged 'attempted bank robbery.' Following Nagell's conviction for attempted robbery, Judge Thornberry handed down the maximum sentence possible under the law to Nagell in June 1964: ten years incarceration.

As Nagell was waiting for his trial verdict and sentence, a declassified 20 March 1964 CIA file tells of the agency pursuing the significance of six names of CIA employees found in Nagell's notebook. The notebook had been taken by the FBI after Nagell's arrest. Dated 20 July 1963 and coming out of its Mexico City station, another CIA memorandum tells of an American using the name 'Eldon Hensen' who wanted to establish contact with the Cuban Embassy in Mexico City. Having picked up this information via a telephone tap, the CIA then dispatched someone posing as a Cuban Embassy officer to lure 'Hensen' to a hotel restaurant. The file describes Hensen's expressed willingness to 'help [the] Castro government in [the] US, [is] willing [to] travel, has many good contacts in [the] States, [and] can "move things from one place to another"'. Could 'Hensen' be on a similar mission to Nagell's own, masquerading as a 'double' agent?

Author John Newman, in his 1995 book "Oswald and the CIA", uses this incident to highlight the CIA's capability 'to enter surreptitiously into someone's life to control or manipulate it,' a scenario Newman cites as a precursor to the agency's shenanigans when Oswald paid visits to the Soviet and Cuban embassies in Mexico City two months later. Newman, however, doesn't mention the significance of the CIA files stating that Hensen 'agreed accept phone call with key word 'Laredo' as call from [deleted] contact.'

Dick Russell, author of "Oswald and the CIA" does mention this episode. Russell, who interviewed Nagell several times in 1978, discusses Nagell's own use of the same code name, 'Laredo.' Nagell, says Russell, used this code name when making contact with Soviet intelligence. Russell's last interview with Nagell was in April 1994. Russell gave Nagell Hensen's physical description. Nagell said, 'That fits somebody I'd run into at the time.'

Newman went further. He demonstrated how the CIA's 'paper trail' did add credence to the Nagell revelations. Here is the Newman's summary analysis of the three months preceding the assassination:

'The CIA was far more interested in Oswald than they have ever admitted to publicly. At some time before the Kennedy assassination, the Cuban Affairs offices at the CIA developed a keen operational interest in him. Oswald's visit to Mexico City may have had some connection to the FBI or CIA. It appears that the Mexico City station wrapped its own operation around Oswald's consular visits there. Whether or not Oswald understood what was going on is less clear than the probability that something operational was happening in conjugation with his visit.'

Newman concludes that 'We can finally say with some authority that the CIA was spinning a web of deception about Oswald weeks before the President's murder.' This is based upon an exhaustive survey of the now obtainable files previously denied to official investigations. Moreover, this information fits neatly with Nagell's earlier statements that the CIA's Cuban Task Force, then run by Desmond Fitzgerald, as well as the agency's Mexico City station, were deeply embroiled in the Oswald affair. It also backs up his claim that Lee Oswald did not know who was pulling his strings.

After some legal manoeuvring, Nagell was released after serving four years of his sentence. Although, by his own account, Nagell had 'betrayed the US many times', one thing was now certain. Regarding his mental health he could not survive without some form of governmental assistance.

Nagell is one of the many strange characters in the JFK assassination story. As with all strange characters, they become all the more interesting, when, on reflection, their story is not so far from the truth as first perceived.

In the fall of 1957, Nagell was reportedly working for the United States Army Counter Intelligence Corps (CIC), 441st Counter Intelligence Corps Group, at Field Operations Intelligence's Far East headquarters in Tokyo, Japan. According to Nagell, he was supervising a review of classified Military Intelligence files, but was also 'a non-paid, confidential informant' of the Central Intelligence Agency.

As Nagell told it, he became aware of Marine Lee Harvey Oswald during the former's military tour of Japan in November 1957, when Oswald and another American ostensibly visited the Soviet embassy in Tokyo. According to Nagell, Oswald was photographed by the Japanese as he entered the embassy. Nagell claimed that he and Oswald met soon after this, when each allegedly played a role in a CIA operation to convince Soviet Colonel Nikolai Eroshkin, a suspected member of the Soviet GRU, to defect to the United States. He also claimed that he and Oswald had together frequented the Queen Bee, a Tokyo nightclub rumoured to have been a hotbed of KGB activity at that time. Oswald had indeed been to the nightclub many times though no witnesses have come forward to say that Nagell was ever with him. Oswald contracted a venereal disease he described as 'acquired in the line of duty'. It should be noted that the Queen Bee was a pretty exclusive club thought to be way beyond the pay scale of Marine Oswald. Two years later, Lee Oswald defected to the Soviet Union.

Nagell claimed that in the fall of 1962, he began working undercover in Mexico City for one 'Robert Graham,' described by Dick Russell as to be a 'subordinate' CIA officer whose ultimate reporting reached all the way up to Desmond Fitzgerald in the CIA hierarchy. When an agency of the USSR purportedly offered Nagell an intelligence assignment related to the Cuban Missile Crisis, he allegedly consulted Graham for advice. According to Nagell, Graham instructed him to 'take the bait' signifying that Nagell would ostensibly be infiltrating the Soviet agency under Graham's supervision. At about this same time, Nagell was allegedly given an assignment concerning one Lee Harvey Oswald. By Nagell's account, 'Graham' subsequently gave him instructions to 'initiate certain action against Mr Oswald, who was the indispensable tool in the conspiracy' – to try to persuade Oswald 'that the deal [Oswald's involvement with the plan to assassinate JFK] was phony' and if that didn't persuade him, Nagell was to 'get rid of him [Oswald].'

'Graham' allegedly also assigned Nagell to infiltrate Alpha 66, a militant group of anti-Castro Cuban exiles, in order to verify whether there was any truth to the rumour that members of the group were planning an assassination attempt on Kennedy. Nagell claimed he had infiltrated the group and determined that it was planning an assassination attempt for the last week of September 1963, 'presumably' in Washington DC. Nagell claimed that two members of this group had posed as agents of Castro's G-2 intelligence service and had recruited Lee Harvey Oswald into the alleged plot, under the pretence that killing JFK would make Oswald a hero in the eyes of Castro and his followers.

As one time Nagell attorney, Bernard Fensterwald Jr, recalled, 'The USSR ordered Nagell to eliminate Lee Harvey Oswald because they thought it might be an extreme embarrassment to them if he was caught, not because he was one of them, but because of his history.' Oswald had, of course, defected to the Soviet Union in 1959 before returning to the United States in 1962.

Nagell said that he refused to go through with the 'removal' of Lee Harvey Oswald at which time 'Graham' allegedly revealed himself to be not simply an officer of the CIA, but actually a double agent in the employ of the Soviet government. 'Graham' purportedly threatened that if Nagell did not carry out his assignment to eliminate Lee Oswald, he would reveal to the FBI that Nagell had been performing services for the Soviet Union all along, and would thus face the full wrath of the US authorities. Later, Nagell would refuse to explain his reasons for turning down the Oswald assignment to assassination researchers; instead of committing murder, Nagell entered the State National Bank in El Paso and discharged his revolver.

Much later, Nagell would go on to name a number of individuals he described as Oswald's 'handlers' during the months preceding the assassination. One of them, he alleged, was none other than himself. The others, he stated, were men who would later became prime suspects in Jim Garrison's New Orleans based investigation into the JFK murder: New Orleans businessman Clay L Shaw, underworld pilot and Oswald's Civil Air Patrol officer David W Ferrie, Former FBI agent W Guy Banister, and anti-

Castro exile Sergio Arcacha Smith. Nagell also named the Cubans who ostensibly lured Oswald into the plot as 'Angel' and 'Leopoldo,' the same two men reportedly seen in Lee Oswald's company by eyewitnesses Sylvia and Annie Odio in late September 1963.

Nagell also alleged that on or about 17 September 1963, shortly before his arrest at the bank, he dispatched a registered letter to J Edgar Hoover of the FBI warning that one Lee Harvey Oswald and unnamed others were planning to assassinate John F Kennedy in Washington, at the end of September. The FBI subsequently denied ever receiving such a warning or letter from Nagell or anyone else.

Nagell assured assassination researchers that he did, indeed, possess other evidence that would support his story; claiming that sometime between August 23 and 27, 1963, he made 'a tape recording of four voices in conversation concerning the plot which ended in the assassination of President Kennedy.' No tape has ever been produced.

On or about 15 September 1963, Nagell said he met with Oswald for the last time, in New Orleans' Jackson Square. Nagell claimed to have arranged for a street vendor to snap a Polaroid photograph of the two men while they were talking, which he said he retained as evidence of their relationship. Again, this photograph has never been produced.

Central to Richard Case Nagell's story is the claim that he had a professional relationship with the Central Intelligence Agency, over a span of at least twelve years. Declassified CIA records demonstrate otherwise. While Nagell purported to have worked for the CIA as early as 1956, numerous documents show that he was unknown to the Agency until 1964, when the FBI forwarded information concerning his September 1963 arrest to them. It seems that at no time was Richard Case Nagell ever an employee or contract agent of the Central Intelligence Agency.

To counter such arguments, Nagell biographer Dick Russell cites page two of a four-page 1969 Military Intelligence report on Nagell, which reads, 'During the period from August 1962 to October 1963, Subject [Nagell] was intermittently employed as an informant and/or investigator for the Central Intelligence Agency (CIA).' However, the report explicitly cites an interview with Richard Case Nagell as the source of its information. Nagell also claimed to have worked for Soviet intelligence, the FBI, and Military Intelligence – after resigning his commission (his security clearances had already been revoked) – and he also hinted at involvement with the Defense Intelligence Agency (DIA).

Nagell's story first began to emerge in early 1967, following the announcement of New Orleans District Attorney Jim Garrison's inquiry into the John F Kennedy assassination. By his own admission, Nagell followed the press accounts of Garrison's investigation as avidly as he could and he informed the New Orleans District Attorney's office that he had inside knowledge of an assassination plot and that he had associated with Lee Harvey Oswald in New Orleans during the summer of 1963. Such a statement would obviously have piqued the interest of Jim Garrison, who was by now attracting a great deal of publicity to his investigation.

This contrasted somewhat with Nagell's only prior public statement on the matter, an FBI interview of 19 December 1963. 'For the record,' the report of this interview reads, '[Nagell] would like to say that his association with [Lee Harvey] Oswald was purely social and that he had met him in Mexico City and in Texas'. By the time Oswald visited Mexico City in late September 1963, however, Richard Case Nagell was in jail following the bank escapade, and there is no evidence whatsoever placing Nagell in New Orleans, with or without Oswald. Later, of course, Nagell would add not only New Orleans but also Japan to his list.

There are still problems with Nagell's account of his alleged 1957 acquaintance with Oswald, however. He specified November 1957 as the time that he and Oswald supposedly became involved in a CIA operation targeting Soviet Colonel Nikolai Eroshkin. Aside from questions about the dubious value of a teenage Marine private in sensitive intelligence matters, Lee Harvey Oswald was not on duty in November 1957; he was taken out of action on 27 October, 1957, when he accidentally shot himself in the forearm with a .22 Derringer. He was hospitalized for three weeks, and did not return to duty until 20 November 1957, just in time to ship out to the Philippines with his unit. He would not return to Japan until March 18 of the following year.

Nagell's claim about he and Oswald frequenting the Queen Bee together is equally problematic as Nagell hadn't mentioned the Queen Bee story prior to 31 May 1978. Edward Jay Epstein's Legend: The Secret World of Lee Harvey Oswald, published earlier that year, was the first time anyone in the general public had heard of Lee Oswald's 'visits' to the Queen Bee and it would seem a little more coincidental that Nagell now place himself there with Oswald. Moreover, it may be just as significant that Nagell also stated for the first time that George de Mohrenschildt had debriefed Oswald for the CIA, a claim advanced by de Mohrenschildt to Epstein during his interviews for that book.

Allegedly, Oswald's name next came to Nagell's attention in October 1962, in Mexico City. At this time, Nagell asserted, he was serving as an agent for the Soviet Union, and, while the claim cannot be verified one way or the other, Nagell related several accounts of his alleged involvement with the Soviets that, at best, are contradictory. Nagell claims he was approached in August or September 1962 whilst in Washington, DC by 'an individual whom he felt was either a Special Agent of the FBI or a Soviet Espionage Agent.' Nagell also claimed that at this person's instruction, he travelled to Miami, to meet with another contact. On another occasion he said it was a man he met in Mexico City who 'introduced him to individuals whom he believed may have been Soviet Agent[s].' On a third occasion, however, he suggested that his Washington contact might have actually been with the CIA.

Biographer Dick Russell writes, 'When Nagell signed his contract with the CIA [sic] in 1962, starting him on a 'double agent' mission vis-à-vis the Soviets, Nagell says it was a Fitzgerald subordinate who would serve as his CIA contact in Mexico City. According to Nagell, Desmond Fitzgerald definitely figures into the Oswald saga – to what degree we may never know, except perhaps through a no-holds-barred official inquiry.'

Again, it appears that Nagell's claim may have been untruthful as it seems Desmond Fitzgerald was not actually in Mexico City in the fall of 1962 and that he was not appointed to the Special Affairs Staff until late January 1963, prior to that he had been stationed in the Far East.

Nagell said his orders were to penetrate a group referred to in correspondence by the code name, 'Bravo Club.' In 1976 Nagell informed Dick Russell in writing that 'Bravo Club' was, in fact, another name for the notorious exile organization, Alpha 66. In a 1967 letter to friend Arthur Greenstein, Nagell had strongly implied that 'Bravo Club' was an Alpha 66 splinter group known as 'Commandos L'. However, in May 1967 Nagell 'made it expressly clear' to the New Orleans District Attorney's office investigator William R Martin 'that none of these [Cuban exile] organizations, acting as organizations, planned to assassinate, or in fact assassinated, President Kennedy. Rather, he stated that the Cubans who took an active part in the assassination acted as individuals and that they did not all belong to one organization or even to two organizations, even though they had all come together and become known to each other because of these organizations.'

Nagell claimed that during the first week of October 1962 (a week before public knowledge of the Cuban missile crisis), the Soviets heard a rumour that there had been a discussion within 'Bravo Club' speaking of assassinating President Kennedy. Nagell was allegedly then assigned to ascertain whether or not the rumour was true, and, that being the case, find out exactly who was involved, along with the motive and methods being discussed to initiate the plot. Nagell went on to say that he had barely begun his investigation when he was called to a particular location and informed by an unnamed person that the rumour was, in fact, true. Nagell then claimed to have been briefed regarding details about the alleged assassination plot, had managed to furnish a number of photographs of the alleged participants, and had then been instructed to return to the United States. Depending upon which version of Nagell's story one believes (if any), the location to which Nagell was summoned for this briefing was either the United States Embassy in Mexico City, the Soviet Embassy in Mexico City, or the Soviet Embassy in Washington, D.C..

Lee Harvey Oswald, according to Nagell, had been recruited into the plot as an assassin and patsy during the summer of 1963. As mentioned above, Nagell named a number of individuals as Oswald's 'handlers' during the months that followed, one of them being himself. The others, Nagell informed Jim Garrison in 1967, were the very men Garrison had targeted in his New Orleans-based investigation. It would appear that Nagell had never mentioned this information to anyone before he met up with Garrison and his team and it appears all of Nagell's statements about these men seem to have been lifted from media accounts of the day. For example, Nagell stated that during the summer of 1963 he had discovered that Oswald was 'undergoing hypnotherapy' from Garrison suspect David William Ferrie, an alleged CIA 'asset', in an effort to possibly groom Oswald into being a 'Manchurian Candidate' type of programmed assassin.

This was one of numerous stories presented in the New Orleans press and given the New Orleans District Attorney's office at that time, by former FBI man and avid anti-Communist Guy Bannister's associate and private investigator, Jack S Martin. Martin was a private investigator who worked out of Banister's office at 544 Camp Street/531 Lafayette Street, New Orleans, the same office address that was printed on Lee Oswald's *Fair Play for Cuba Committee* leaflets handed out by Oswald in the anti-Castro hot bed of downtown New Orleans in the summer of 1963. On the day Kennedy was assassinated, Banister and Martin were drinking together at a local bar. On their return to Banister's office, the two men, rather the worse for wear, got into a heated argument. According to Martin, Banister said something to which Martin replied, 'What are you going to do – kill me like you all did Kennedy?' An angry Banister then pistol-whipped Martin with his .357 magnum revolver, putting him in hospital. Banister, one of the principles surrounding Oswald's strange activities in New Orleans, was never questioned by the Warren Commission and died in June 1964, before he could testify.

Jack Martin told reporters in New Orleans and authorities that a man named David Ferrie, an associate of Mob leader Carlos Marcello, who in turn was a target for Attorney General Robert Kennedy, may have been involved in the assassination of JFK. Martin told police that Ferrie '...was supposed to have been the getaway pilot in the assassination.' He said that Ferrie had outlined plans to kill Kennedy and that Ferrie may have taught Oswald how to use a rifle with a telescopic sight. Martin claimed that Ferrie had known Lee Harvey Oswald from their days in the New Orleans Civil Air Patrol, and that he had seen a photograph, at Ferrie's home, of Oswald in a Civil Air Patrol group. Ferrie had always denied knowing Oswald, therefore denying he had ever met him. Then, after many years of denial, that photograph was subsequently confirmed to exist, and is now distributed widely.

Martin's accusations soon got back to Ferrie, who contacted several of his former Civil Air Patrol associates. Former cadet Roy McCoy told the FBI that 'Ferrie had come by looking for photographs of the cadets to see if Oswald was pictured in any photos of Ferrie's squadron.'

Jack Martin also told bail bondsman Hardy Davis that he had heard on television that Ferrie's New Orleans library card had been found in Oswald's possession when he was arrested in Dallas following the JFK murder. Davis reported this to Ferrie's employer, lawyer G Wray Gill. Ferrie subsequently visited both Oswald's former New Orleans landlady and a former neighbour about this report. Ferrie was, according to their report, able to produce his library card for FBI agents who interviewed him on 27 November 1963.

The question is: why would the FBI ask Ferrie if he had possession of his Library card if there was no link between it and Lee Oswald?

Martin also claimed that Ferrie had driven from New Orleans to Texas on the night of the assassination. (In fact, Ferrie and two friends drove 350 miles (560 km) to the Winterland Skating Rink in Houston, about 240 miles (390 km) south of Dallas, that evening.) Ferrie said that 'he had been considering for some time the feasibility and possibility of opening an ice skating rink in New Orleans' and wanted to gather information on the ice rink business. Ferrie stated that he had introduced himself to [rink manager] Chuck Rolland and spoke with him at length concerning the cost of installation and operation of the rink. However, Rolland said that he never spoke to Ferrie about running an ice rink. Rolland did confirm, however, that Ferrie had spent his time at the rink's pay phone, making and receiving calls.

On 25 November 1963, Martin was contacted by the Federal Bureau of Investigation. Martin told the FBI that Ferrie might have hypnotized Oswald into assassinating Kennedy. The FBI considered Martin's evidence unreliable. Nevertheless, FBI agents interviewed Ferrie twice about Martin's allegations; Ferrie claiming that in June 1963, he had been involved in an altercation with Martin, in which he had thrown Martin out of the office of lawyer G Wray Gill. The FBI also interviewed about twenty other people in connection with Martin's allegations, but said that it was unable to develop a substantial case against Ferrie. (An inquiry by the *House Select Committee on Assassinations* (HSCA), conducted a decade and a half later, concluded that the FBI's 'overall investigation of the 544 Camp Street issue at the time of the assassination was not thorough.').

Some of this information reached District Attorney of New

Orleans, Jim Garrison, who had become increasingly interested in the assassination after a chance meeting with Louisiana Senator Russell Long in late 1966. Garrison said that Long told him: 'Those fellows on the Warren Commission were dead wrong. There's no way in the world that one man could have shot up Jack Kennedy that way.' Intrigued by the enormity of a plot to murder Kennedy originating in his home town, Garrison quietly pursued the matter.

In December 1966, Garrison interviewed Jack Martin. Martin claimed that during the summer of 1963, David Ferrie, Guy Banister, Lee Harvey Oswald, and a group of anti-Castro Cuban exiles were involved in operations against Castro's Cuba that included gun running activities and burglarizing armouries. Garrison would later write that 'The Banister apparatus was part of a supply line that ran along the Dallas – New Orleans – Miami corridor. These supplies consisted of arms and explosives for use against Castro's Cuba.'

According to testimony by Banister's personal secretary, Delphine Roberts, Ferrie and Oswald were frequent visitors to Banister's office in 1963. She remembered Ferrie as 'one of the agents. Many times when he came into the office [Ferrie] used the private office behind Banister's, and I was told he was doing private work. I believed his work was somehow connected with the CIA rather than the FBI'. The *House Select Committee on Assassinations* (HSCA) investigated Roberts' claims and said that 'because of contradictions in Roberts' statements to the committee and lack of independent corroboration of many of her statements, the reliability of her statements could not be determined.'

As Garrison continued his investigation, he became convinced that a group of right-wing extremists, including Ferrie, Banister, and Clay Shaw, were involved in a conspiracy with elements of the CIA to murder John Kennedy. Garrison would later claim that the motive for the assassination was anger over Kennedy's attempts to obtain a peace settlement in both Cuba and Vietnam. Garrison also believed that Shaw, Banister, and Ferrie had conspired to set up

Oswald as a patsy in the assassination.

Nagell hinted at personal knowledge of Ferrie's involvement with an exile training camp during the summer of 1963 and such involvement with the camp, allegedly located off Louisiana's Lake Pontchartrain, had been asserted by Jim Garrison. There is no factual basis for the existence of such a camp at that time and place. Moreover, Ferrie's association with the exiles had ended in the fall of 1962, following his arrest on morals charges.

Another Oswald 'handler' named by Nagell was Garrison's chief suspect, Clay L Shaw. When Shaw was acquitted in 1969, Nagell seems to have dropped him from his tales. According to Nagell, yet another Oswald 'handler' was, indeed, Guy Banister, described by Nagell as 'a real asshole' and 'a guy who should have gone to jail.' Again, according to Nagell, Banister was a 'private detective who did a few jobs for the agency.' It was, however, none other than Jim Garrison who started the rumours of Guy Banister's alleged CIA connections. Likewise, Nagell's claim that Banister was 'partially responsible' for a 1963 FBI raid of an arms cache located off Lake Pontchartrain was simply another Garrison factoid with no basis in reality.

Nagell also supported Garrison's conviction that an Oswald impostor had been involved in framing the accused assassin well in advance of the assassination. According to Nagell, the impostor went by the name of 'Leon Oswald', a name that had shown up in the widely publicized statements of Garrison witness Perry Raymond Russo. It is, of course, also the given name of one of the men who turned up at Sylvia Odio's apartment in September 1963.

'I knew both of them,' Nagell told author Dick Russell referring to Lee [Oswald] and 'Leon'. 'I have been trained in observation, and there is no mistaking who was who. The other Oswald was working with anti-Castro Cubans. He was not pro-Castro. This 'Leon Oswald', the 'second' Oswald, allegedly registered at a hotel in Mexico City where I had once registered under a different name. I told [author Richard] Popkin he ought to check with the State Department, because somebody's got a picture of him.'

At times, Nagell seemed to support Richard Popkin's theory that Lee Harvey Oswald had been impersonated by such an individual in Dallas during November 1963. However, he also informed the New Orleans District Attorney's office that 'Leon Oswald' had been 'eliminated' in late September of that year. There is no evidence of Nagell being in New Orleans in 1963.

On 1 June 1964, Nagell wrote 'two Cubans were associating with Oswald in August and September 1963.' One of these men, he wrote, 'also fits the description of one of the two Cubans who allegedly visited Silvia [sic] Odio at Magellan Circle with Oswald in September 1963.' This Cuban, he wrote, 'was witnessed entering the On the Beach Bookstore on two separate occasions while he was under surveillance.'

On the Beach proprietor Vaughn Snipes told author Dick Russell, 'I just have no recollection of anybody I knew as a Cuban coming into the bookstore, or my having any contact with anyone who was a Cuban.'

Nagell seems to have brought all this information regarding these individuals after the fact only to boost his credibility; moreover, during the HSCA investigation of 1976–78 he spoke of underworld figures such as Sam Giancana, Johnny Roselli, Carlos Marcello, Oswald's friend George de Mohrenschildt and CIA officer David Atlee Phillips being involved in the assassination.

Nagell goes further and, seemingly, somewhat further over the top with his allegations. He claimed to have visited Cuba and to have personally warned Fidel Castro that Cuban exiles were plotting JFK's assassination, presumably because of the possible backlash this could pose to Castro considering the then current feeling between Castro and people intent of removing him from office. Nagell alleged Castro was a leading candidate for the position of the ultimate fall guy. The claim might have been a little more believable had Nagell not insisted that the meeting was with Fidel

Castro himself. 'To my knowledge I never talked to any of Castro's aides,' he stated later. Nagell then claimed to have contacted the New Orleans FBI about the alleged assassination plot, but, again, no documents support this. According to Nagell, he also sent warnings to Desmond Fitzgerald and another unnamed official of the CIA, as well as to his Soviet 'employers'.

The alleged warnings would seem to have provoked no action, despite Nagell's assurances that neither the Soviets nor the CIA wanted President Kennedy assassinated. Desmond Fitzgerald, a long-time friend of JFK (some even mistakenly believed the two to have been related), was as distraught about the assassination as anyone else could be that November weekend. Evan Thomas, a writer with *Newsweek* reported that Fitzgerald was at home watching television when Jack Ruby shot Oswald. Fitzgerald's wife Barbara was shocked to see her husband burst into tears. She had never seen him cry before. 'Now,' Fitzgerald had allegedly said at the time, 'we'll never know.'

In June 1966 Nagell underwent a psychiatric evaluation at Leavenworth. He initially refused to answer any questions, but after several days it was impressed upon him that his cooperation would be to his benefit. Nagell 'kept emphasizing throughout the various interviews that his whole purpose in entering the bank in El Paso, Texas when he is alleged to have attempted to rob the bank was for the sole purpose of getting psychiatric treatment.'

Nagell explained that, 'he had tried for admission to the VA Hospitals just prior to the alleged bank robbery. He stated that after getting married, his wife insisted that he resign [from the Army], which he did in 1959 and that his adjustment to civilian life was very difficult and made more difficult by his marital problems and finally resulted in his marriage breaking up.' The break up, which occurred in the spring of 1962, had a very traumatic effect on him; he alleged that his wife left him twice and after she left him for the second and last time, he noticed that he was starting to get nervous and emotionally unstable, and he had quit two jobs after that because he couldn't concentrate on his work. Nagell felt that he was slipping emotionally and finally tried for admission to a VA Hospital just prior to the bank shooting and was desperate for some type of psychiatric treatment for his psychiatric symptoms of nervousness, emotional instability and inability to concentrate.

The details in Nagell testimony seems doubtful at best. At one point he states that Oswald 'had CIA connections' and 'got paid by indirect means' but then goes onto to say 'If Lee Harvey Oswald worked for the CIA, he sure didn't know it.'

Nagell went onto make many statements which he would later deny or contradict. He was consistent in only one area: Nagell always insisted was that he had evidence to support his claims, evidence that would come out sooner or later. Unfortunately, nothing has ever been produced to substantiate anything he has said.

Nagell has claimed, as stated above, that sometime between 23 August and 27 August 1963, he made 'a tape recording of four voices in conversation concerning the plot which ended in the assassination of President Kennedy.' The conversation had been 'primarily in Spanish although on certain occasions certain of the participants lapsed into English.' When questioned as to the identity of the persons speaking on the tape, he would only state that one of them was 'Arcacha' and another individual whom he would only identify as 'Q'. Was Nagell referring to Garrison suspects Sergio Arcacha Smith and Carlos Quiroga, who had associated with one another in 1961–62? Arcacha is known to have left Louisiana by 1963. Nagell informed the New Orleans District Attorney office that the identities of the speakers on the tape were himself, Lee Harvey Oswald, 'Angel' (the Cuban exile reportedly seen with Oswald by Sylvia Odio), and an unidentified fourth party. In April 1967, Nagell told the New Orleans District Attorney's office that the tape was in the possession of a friend, one Frederick H John, who lived in California. Nagell promised the DA's Office that they would receive the tape as soon as possible. Garrison investigator

William Martin travelled to California to pick up the tape, but was told by John that it had been 'the subject of a burglary sometime in 1964.' On 8 July 1967, Nagell wrote his sister about the tape, saying, 'I can state with good foundation that if it was stolen, it was not stolen in 1964. In the same vein, I can also say that while the item involved may indeed no longer be available, it is not in the custody of the opposition either.'

However, another twist came in the late 1970s, Nagell assured Dick Russell that the tape was, after all, safe. In 1995 he told Noel Twyman that he himself had 'stashed' it away, along with other evidence; that it 'would be revealed in the event of his death. The truth will come out if I die,' he assured Dick Russell.

At the age of 65, Nagell died in November 1995 of arteriosclerotic heart disease in Los Angeles, California. The recording, along with all the other 'evidence', is still to surface.

Immediately following Nagell's death, the Assassination Records Review Board investigated the possibility that Nagell had left behind any information relevant to his claims. The board's Final Report notes, 'A member of the Review Board staff travelled twice to California to inspect the effects of Nagell in an attempt to find assassination records. During the first trip, the Review Board staff member, along with Nagell's son and niece, inspected Nagell's apartment in Los Angeles. During the second trip, the Review Board staff member inspected, again with the assistance of the son and niece, material contained in some footlockers found in storage in Phoenix, Arizona. The Review Board staff did not locate any of the items [Nagell had claimed to possess].'

But Nagell's story does not end there. No sooner had he disembarked at Kennedy International Airport in New York, following his release from federal prison, he was allegedly met by two individuals 'who identified themselves as representatives of the Central Intelligence Agency.'

'We pulled a lot of strings to get your freedom,' one of the men allegedly told him. Then he was reportedly handed the first of several cash payments of $500, and informed, 'More will come where this comes from. We appreciate your cooperation in prison.' Over the next three weeks Nagell allegedly received a total of $15,000 cash. It should be noted, however, that these alleged cash payments bear a close resemblance to the $505 monthly disability pension Nagell was receiving from the Army. Assuming he received these payments while still imprisoned, he would have had approximately $25,000 waiting for him upon his release.

In May 1968, Nagell allegedly had several meetings 'with a CIA official he knew only as Buehel.'

'Agent Buehel' supposedly told Nagell he was fully aware that his wife had divorced him while he was in Leavenworth. Nagell later told reporter Thomas C Lucey that the CIA had promised to reunite him with his family if he undertook an assignment for them. Are we to believe that not only has the CIA falsified its records to show no such relationship with Nagell, but that the Agency would offer contract employment to an individual who had been named in the January 1968 issue of Ramparts magazine as an agent of the CIA? Perhaps. Perhaps not.

Then, on 24 May 1968, Nagell received a new passport. Six days later he was on a plane to Zurich, Switzerland, claiming that his children 'were reported by a State Department official as living in Europe.'

Then, on 4 June 1968, Nagell was at the United States Embassy in Zurich, reportedly telling an 'incoherent story' about 'working for [a] US government secret agency on [a] mission to Geneva,' where he was to meet an unnamed Japanese individual or individuals. Nagell stated that Jim Garrison had warned him that his life could be in danger, so Nagell decided to inform the CIA that he was in Zurich. He returned the following day and asked to speak to a 'political officer.' Upon being introduced to the officer, Nagell then accused the officer of being 'an impostor'. A report of the ensuing encounter notes that Nagell appeared 'seriously incoherent, in fact, appears psychotic [and] possibly dangerous.'

On 10 June 1968, Nagell was ejected from a train in East Germany and ended up in police custody. He was detained for four months. Nagell later claimed that the entire incident had been planned by him and the mysterious 'Buehel'. The *Washington Post* reported that Nagell had been arrested for making derogatory remarks about East Germans.

On 23 October 1968, Nagell was released to American authorities at the Berlin border and received in West Berlin by attorney Wolfgang Vogel and Bruce Flatin, Chief of the Public Safety Division of the US Mission in Berlin. No sooner had Nagell crossed the border than he 'accused Flatin of wanting to kill him and ran back to East Berlin.' He was confined briefly to a military mental hospital. Nagell later told *Family* reporter Thomas C Lucey that Flatin was actually 'a longtime CIA member – and Flatin is not his real name.' Flatin would later respond to the allegation. 'Apparently [Nagell] has overlooked the fact that I am actually a career Foreign Service Officer of the Department of State, and that our family has been using the name Flatin since the Viking days in old Norge.'

According to Nagell, one of the men who negotiated for his release, attorney Ricey New, promised him 'legal assistance in obtaining a disability retirement from the Army if I stayed away from the West German news media.'

New denies this and allegedly told Nagell, 'That he had handled negotiations for the CIA and the Army in effecting the releases and exchanges of other American prisoners held by the East Germans.'

According to Nagell, New said, 'that I could consider him as a representative of the CIA.'

When Dick Russell spoke with Ricey New in 1978, New was operating a small law office ('basically just my wife and myself') in the United States. When asked if he was acting on behalf of the CIA in 1968, New replied, 'Certainly not, I never had any connection with them.' As far as New could recall, he thought, '[Nagell] had gotten off a train in East Germany and was wandering around the station there in an unauthorized area. They questioned him and kept him, on a violation of their laws.'

Ricey New suggested that Russell contact a former employee of the US Mission in Berlin, Andor Klay. Klay recalled Nagell somewhat enthusiastically.

'Nagell, yes! The Nagell case. Well, the question is not what he was doing over there, the question is what he was charged with. They can charge a man with anything. They probably thought at first he was some kind of spy – a military or CIA agent – and then later on perhaps they reached the conclusion that he was a nut.'

New insisted that was just his own speculation. 'you realize that at first he got himself involved in some shady activities so the East German police went after him and slapped him in jail, and then possibly it was during his trial there that his mental shape became questionable. There is, of course, intervention on our part for any and every American citizen. We went out of our way, either to try to get this man out or have some kind of exchange deal, or have the sentence reduced. It could well be the latter, some manipulations about reducing the sentence, or a realization on the part of the East Germans that the man was worthless. Or both.'

Russell then asked the question point blank: Was there no indication that Nagell was a spy?

'No, not on my side,' Klay replied. 'I mean, I can only tell you that from the files I had I am not competent to judge his mental condition, but assuming that he's okay mentally, then I would say there is probably a kind of morbid ambition to get on the front page of the papers or have himself accepted as a man who can perform great services for us.

'I think this was a somewhat confused man,' Klay added, noting Nagell's attempt to flee back to East Berlin. 'We struggled with him physically to put him in the car and took him out. But then he took his revenge in suggesting, giving all kinds of information – of course, most of it quite false – to this long overseas weekly newspaper [The Family] that was published. We could never really make head or tail of it.'

During a psychiatric examination at this time, Nagell himself claimed 'to have been tortured by East Germans,' and the psychiatrist noted that Nagell 'displayed [a] fixation' regarding his alleged relationship with alleged assassin Lee Harvey Oswald. However, Nagell denied 'any involvement in any [JFK] conspiracy and denied that he had any information of use to Garrison.' Further more, Nagell 'alleged that his fear that the CIA might try to 'eliminate' him was planted in his mind by Mr Garrison.' Nagell 'states he no longer believes it is realistic to think that the CIA was trying to kill him.' He admitted that his 'unstable personality and immature or impulsive behaviour [sic]' were the result of his 1954 plane crash.

Later Richard Nagell sought medical help at the US Consulate in Zurich after he claimed his American 'rescuers' had drugged him, thus preventing him speaking with anyone, especially members of the press. He then claimed he was referred to a civilian doctor who told him he'd been drugged with Seconal. The official record is somewhat different, however and the Consulate noted that Nagell 'claims to be ill from injections administered in East German prison'.

However, a psychiatrist at Berlin's US Army Hospital noted, 'Symptoms after such [a] long delay [are] extremely unlikely regardless of [the] nature of [the alleged] injections.'

Rather, it was observed that 'complaints [and] various efforts to delay and complicate matters' fit into the psychological pattern demonstrated previously by the patient.

Nagell finally returned to New York on 2 November 1968, reportedly travelling to Washington to another government agency. The State Department had, allegedly, offered to help Nagell find his children, though there are no records to support this statement. On or about 12 February 1969, Nagell was then allegedly attacked in New York with a 'practice Mark IV hand grenade thrown from a speeding automobile.' The alleged grenade attack failed to make the news. Nagell then reportedly flew to New Orleans and 'turned over what remained of the practice grenade to Mr Garrison in the presence of one of his investigators.' No one at the New Orleans District Attorney's office has ever come forward to confirm this; Jim Garrison does not mention the incident in his memoirs.

Nagell was soon back in Zurich. On 27 and 28 February 1969, he appeared at the US embassy and warned the interviewing Consul that 'unless promises made to him by US officials were honoured, he would reveal to the press [the] entire story of his alleged contacts with CIA and would expose individuals with whom he had dealt in the organization.' A 3 March 1969 CIA teletype states that Nagell 'has never had any CIA connections. No evidence [of] any current CIA relationships (ISR has no record). Past history indicates he [is a] fabricator and mentally disturbed individual.' It would seem the CIA were onto him and his past.

Then, barely a week later, Nagell again contacted the US General Consul in Zurich. On the 5 March, in more threatening fashion claimed he had radio [and] TV time [on the] evening [of] 6 March and that he would tell all about his alleged CIA contacts unless he receives assurance that promises made by US officials would be honoured. Two days later he returned to the embassy and 'stated that if he received no satisfaction by five o'clock that afternoon he would carry out his threats and expose US government on radio, television and in the press.' Nagell then, by all accounts, simply disappeared. A government teletype stated, that 'nothing further heard from him and no publicity given.'

Nagell would later claim he left Switzerland for Spain when a shooting attempt was made on his life, though, again no such attack was ever noted by anyone, never mind the press or police.

On 10 March 1969, the US Consulate in Zurich was 'advised by telephone from [the] US Consulate [in] Barcelona that Nagell had approached them and made similar threats.' Nagell now also claimed that he had been offered quite a sum to defect and would consider it if he had no hope of ever seeing his children again.

Nagell also claimed that he had left 'very compromising' classified documents with 'friends' in Switzerland who would forward them to the 'appropriate' newspaper representatives.'

The self-proclaimed 'spy' also raised the subject of his 1963 arrest. He claimed that 'the reason why he had been arrested in the first place was that he had worked with Lee Harvey Oswald in an assignment with a 'US intelligence agency.'

Nagell also stated that he had been held in the federal penitentiary for such a long period because he refused to reveal to the FBI any information about his intelligence activities. He also claimed he was visited by CIA agents while in prison who cautioned him to keep his mouth shut about his ties with Oswald.

In addition to stating his intention to 'defect to East Germany if he doesn't receive assistance from [the] US,' Nagell threatened to have himself arrested by Spanish police. Why Nagell would consider such an act a threat to the US government is unclear, but in light of his history, it seems a most revealing statement.

On March 12 Nagell appeared again at the Consulate and was shown a telegram demonstrating that the government was indeed trying to help him locate his children.

Nagell appeared happy with this action and left. He returned two days later, somewhat angry again but was advised to be patient. He said that 'although he had been offered a great sum and guarantee of a 'good life' if he defected, he basically did not believe that would be the case; he stressed that he had sacrificed much for his country and only asked that his right to see his children be recognized, saying that he needed something to hold on to – like his children – in order to restore some equanimity to his life.'

Nagell appeared yet again at the Consulate on 17 March, enquiring about any movement regarding his requests. Discussing the recent *Ramparts* article about the Kennedy assassination with the Consul, Nagell noted that 'the references to him in connection with the assassination' were 'completely erroneous.' He returned to the consulate the following day, ranting about doing something dramatic if he did not receive a positive answer from the Department of State regarding. The 'dramatic' action, he said during this particular altercation, would be to 'blow somebody's head off.'

On 7 April 1969, Nagell appeared at the US Embassy in Madrid, Spain where he 'proceeded to harangue [the] Consul for nearly two hours, accusing him of deliberately creating [a] situation to provoke Nagell into action harmful to him.'

The following day, Nagell left Spain for West Berlin. A Department of State telegram notes his return to Berlin and the fact that he has called at the US Mission on April 10 and 14. The Consular official was concerned about Nagell's 'irrational' behaviour, urging him to call on an Army psychiatrist in Berlin familiar with his case. On 15 April, the Psychiatrist's opinion was that '[Nagell is] mentally ill and should be hospitalized.'

On 14 April the Department of State in Washington informed the US Embassy in Madrid that the department had been unable to locate Nagell's family; they also said that, even if they had known where they were, they would have been unable to inform Nagell of their whereabouts unless his ex-wife gave her consent. The State Department also cautioned the Embassy to 'remember [that Nagell] is mentally unbalanced and may be dangerous.'

Nagell made an unsolicited appearance at Police Group West in Berlin on 15 April 1969. He said he wanted 'to talk to an official' because of information he had to offer 'concerning East bloc countries.' Nagell claimed that he had been involved in intelligence since the age of eighteen, 'with smaller tasks for the American Secret Service. He had been a member of the CIA during 1954 to 1956. During the following years he claimed [to have] worked for various secret services in the USA. During 1962/63 he had been again with CIA.' Nagell delivered a short statement about having been questioned about his passport the previous January. Nagell then left.

On 22 April 1969, Nagell suffered a head wound at a Berlin

bar and restaurant claiming he had been attacked by an unknown assailant, for reasons he did not know. The police report, however, gave a different account of the incident. The police report contained the testimony of an eye witness to the incident. The witness, one Werner Margret, stated that he had seen Nagell fall from his bar stool and strike his head. Margret also said that no other person was near Nagell at the time of his fall. The report concluded, not unreasonably, that the wound sustained by Nagell was most likely caused by this fall. The report also added that Nagell was in possession of a card identifying him as an employee of the CIA. The police thought Nagell to be 'mentally disturbed.' Nagell contacted a reporter, Thomas Lucey, about the incident and was by now stating that his 'unknown assailant' was, in fact, two strangers. One of these 'strangers', according to Nagell, had been following him for two days. Nagell left Berlin on 26 April but not before telling Lucey that he feared the next attacker would murder him.

On 5 May, Nagell was back in New York at the Regional Office of the Veterans Administration. Nagell wanted to be admitted to a VA hospital so injuries sustained in East Germany could be looked at. He was told he would have to wait for an appointment. Nagell then threatened to go to the local newspapers and to Washington, DC, in order to obtain satisfaction. The VA informed the Secret Service that Nagell 'is constantly appearing at their office and complaining of physical ills and requesting hospitalization. He is also constantly telling stories of his espionage activity and his importance to the United States Government.' They also told of Nagell's belligerence, which had been so bad at one point that GSA guards assisted in escorting him from the offices.

On 20 August 1969, a strange ad was placed in New York's East Village 'Other'. It read, 'Caught In The Act. Notice to the CIA and all SY shitheads who participated in Project Purple Shaft. After that fiasco in the GDR you worms did your best to screw, blue and tattoo me. You even tried to have my ass dusted in Berlin. Now it's my turn to do a little shafting. Cordially, R C Nagell.' Nagell, again full of bluster, did not carry out his threat.

On 14 April 1970, the well travelled Nagell was in Switzerland again reporting to the Zurich police that his raincoat had disappeared. He claimed that 'an important document intended for the American military authorities in Berlin was in the pocket. Document was entitled 'Fiscal Year 70 (USAREUR).' The police report noted that '[the] raincoat was found [a] short while later' in Nagell's hotel. There was no such document found in any of the pockets. The Hotel, not unsurprisingly, returned the raincoat to the Zurich police. Nagell subsequently picked it up from the police station. The police, unsure, or maybe uninterested simply concluded their report with the recommendation that someone advise the appropriate US Army authorities on the off chance they are missing copy of 'Fiscal Year 70 (USAREUR).'

Three days later the CIA noted Nagell's return to Zurich. A recommendation that Nagell be classified as 'a crank because he is mentally deranged. He was the sole survivor of an air crash and suffered brain damage. He has claimed CIA employment but was never connected with the Agency.' The CIA, by matter of course, would always deny he, or anyone else, had been in their employ.

In June of 1970, Richard Case Nagell was finally reunited with his two children in Los Angeles, there is no evidence of 'government assistance'. The reunion, however, was short lived. Barely a month later, he turned up at a VA hospital in Los Angeles where his behaviour was noted as 'very abusive'. A year later, unbelievably it would seem, Nagell finally obtained legal custody of his children.

Nagell then disappears from the radar again. Was he finally happy with his lot? Did he seek and obtain the treatment he needed for his health problems, managing to settle down to what most of us would call a 'real' life, with, at last, a family and hope?

In 1992, author Dick Russell succeeded in tracking down Nagell's son, 32-year-old Robert Lamont Nagell. Robert told of meeting his father for the first time in 1970 and of living with him for several years. Ultimately, Nagell snr decided that parenting just wasn't for him. Although they parted amicably, Robert never spoke to his father again.

San Diego researcher Noel Twyman was able to speak to Nagell twice over the telephone in the months before his death. Nagell expressed renewed fear for his life but said his private files were in safekeeping. He also added that there are individuals still alive who would be greatly 'embarrassed' in the event his materials should come to light.

Richard Case Nagell was found dead on 1 November, 1995. Nagell had not been seen for several days. At 9pm, Robert Lavelle, the landlord of the house where Nagell had been renting, unsuccessfully tried to open the lock in an effort to see if Nagell was still in the premises. Not being able to use a key, Lavelle then pried open a window and forced his way inside. Lavelle had discovered the already-decomposing body of Nagell in the bathroom. Upon his discovery, Lavelle alerted the police.

A spokesman for the Los Angeles Coroner's Office said Nagell had a history of heart disease, and that his body was discovered on the floor of the bathroom at his home in Rampart, Los Angeles. The two police officers who had entered Nagell's residence following the discovery of his body found no evidence of anything having been disturbed, though a number of weapons were found and inventoried. The house was then sealed off by the LA Coroner's office, pending the arrival of an executor named by Nagell to look after his estate and personal affairs. The LAPD were said to be watching the house to make sure that nobody attempted to break in. A curious message, however, went from the coroner's office to the LA Public Administrator, the public body charged with dealing with estates: 'When entering the house, beware of traps or pitfalls, due to deceased's CIA background connections'. Clearly, LA officials realized this was no ordinary case.

The Review Board had sent Nagell a letter, dated 31 October 1995, requesting that Nagell contact the Review Board's Executive Director to discuss any assassination records he might have in his possession. The request was sent too late as Nagell was already dead by that time. The Assassination Records Review Board did, however, make contact with Nagell's executor, but no report of this meeting is in the public domain.

A Review Board staff member travelled twice to California to inspect the effects of Nagell in an attempt to find assassination records. First, the Review Board staff member, along with Nagell's son and niece, inspected Nagell's apartment in Los Angeles. They found nothing out of place, or anything odd. The second trip saw the Review Board staff member, again with the assistance of the son and niece, inspecting material contained in footlockers that had been found in storage in Phoenix, Arizona and sent to Nagell's LA address.

Documentary material on Nagell from the US Secret Service and the US Army's Investigative Records Repository (IRR) was placed in the JFK Collection as a result of the JFK Act and the efforts of the Review Board staff. The CIA processed (as part of its sequestered collection) a 201 and Domestic Contacts Division file on Nagell. The Review Board staff also reviewed a CIA Office of Security file on Nagell. The entire file was designated an assassination record.

The strange story of Richard Case Nagell is one of the most intriguing, albeit frustrating, anecdotes in the entire Oswald affair. His family problems apart, given the latitude of Nagell's alleged 'relationship' with Oswald in those dark, cold war years so long ago, Nagell's obvious mental problems and his alleged ties with intelligence agencies, one thing stands out to this author: just where did he get the funds to fly around the United States and Europe as often as he did?

# Defectors, Informants and a Fly in the Ointment

The Federal Bureau of Investigation (FBI) were first interested in Lee Oswald following his defection to the Soviet Union in 1959. The Bureau interviewed Oswald's mother and brother Robert shortly after the disenchanted Marine had sailed across the Atlantic seeking the Communist way. Fort Worth FBI agent John W Fain reported that Robert Oswald, along with his family, were shocked that Lee had left the United States and embarked on such a trip. Lee, according to Robert, had never shown any tendencies toward Communism as far as he was concerned. Fain also questioned Marguerite Oswald with regard to a $25 money order she tried to send to Oswald. Fain later wrote another report on Lee Oswald before he arrived back in the United States. Much of the information in this report Fain gained from the Office of Naval Intelligence (ONI) in New Orleans.

When Oswald returned to Dallas with his family in June 1962, Fain and another FBI agent, Tom Carter, interviewed him at the local FBI office. Oswald furnished information to the FBI about his stay in the Soviet Union and the method of his return to the United States and that he had had to borrow over $400 from the State Department to pay for the trip home. Oswald flatly refused to answer questions on why he had gone to the Soviet Union in the first place. Fain and Carter reported that Oswald stated that he had not denounced his American citizenship and that he had not given his Soviet interrogators any military information. Fain and Carter's report speaks of Oswald's arrogant and impatient attitude towards them, although Oswald did tell them that if he were contacted by Soviet Intelligence under suspicious circumstances or otherwise, he would be in touch with the FBI immediately.

Fain and FBI agent Brown next spoke to Oswald two months later. Fain had decided that Oswald had been 'evasive' in his first interview and tried to glean more information from Oswald about his reasons for defecting. Oswald again stalled Fain and refused to answer his questions, but did repeat his statement about being contacted by any factions of Soviet Intelligence. At this point, Fain satisfied himself that Oswald was not a member of the American Communist Party and declared his Oswald file 'closed'.

Suspicion that Lee Oswald had been an informer for the FBI reared its head almost immediately after the assassination of John Kennedy. Texas Attorney General Waggoner Carr admitted such a belief early in the Dallas investigation of the alleged assassin and the matter was discussed at length by members of the Warren Commission in secret session held by those officers of state on 22 January 1964. The document relating to the meeting was withheld from the public for 12 years, being declassified on 4 March 1975.

Attorney General Carr held the view that Lee Oswald had been an undercover informer for the FBI and that his FBI code number was S-172 (or S-179) and that his pay had been $200 per month. It is alleged that upon his arrest on 22 November 1963, Oswald had a Government cash voucher in his possession. The fact that Oswald's tax return sheets for 1962 and 1963 are still being withheld by the authorities, could persuade anyone with an open mind looking into this revelation that something is not quite right.

Indeed, one only has to read the transcript of the meeting to see the concern of former CIA director Allen Dulles. Before we look at the transcript of that secret meeting, it must be said that Dulles had been sacked as head of the CIA in 1961 by John Kennedy, following the disastrous invasion of Cuba by anti-Castro Cubans and CIA operatives at the Bay of Pigs in April of that year. Dulles's covert mentality is stamped over the entire meeting, as he seeks to avoid the minutes being preserved:

*Mr Rankin*: When the Chief Justice (Earl Warren, head of the investigation) and I were just briefly reflecting on this (the Oswald–

FBI Informer rumour), we said if that was true and it ever came out, could be established, then you would have people think that there was conspiracy to accomplish this assassination that nothing the Commission did or anybody could dissipate.

*Rep. Boggs*: You are so right.

*Mr Dulles*: Oh, terrible.

*Rep. Boggs*: Its implications of this are fantastic, don't you think so?

*Chairman*: Terrific.

*Mr Rankin*: To have anybody to admit to it, why would it be particularly in their interest – I could see it would be in the interest to get rid of this man [Oswald] but why would it be in their interest to say he is clearly the guilty one? I mean, I don't see that argument that you raise particularly shows an interest. They [the FBI] would like to have us fold up and quit.

*Rep. Boggs*: This closes the case, you see. Don't you see?

*Mr Dulles*: Yes, I see that.

*Mr Rankin*: They found the man. There is nothing more to do. If he were not the killer, and they employed him, they are already it, you see. So your argument is correct if they are sure that this is going to close the case, they are worse off than ever by doing this.

*Rep. Boggs*: Yes, I would think so. And of course, we are all even gaining in the realm of speculation. I don't even like to see this being taken down.

*Mr Dulles*: Yes, I think this record ought to be destroyed. Do you think we need a record of this?

*Mr Rankin*: I don't, except that we said we would have records of meetings and so we called the reporter in the formal way. If you think what we have said here should not be upon the record, we can have it done that way. Of course it might . . .

*Mr Dulles*: I am just thinking of sending around copies and so forth. The only copies of this record should be kept right there.

*Rep. Boggs*: I would hope that none of these records are circulated to anybody.

Even at that early date, late January 1964, Warren Commission members were speaking of concealing evidence, in this case their very own words. The meeting lasted two hours. A rather long time to speculate that Oswald may have been involved with, or working for, the FBI. The complete transcript reveals the Commission members' reluctance to take on the powerful J. Edgar Hoover, then director of America's state police and founder member of the Federal Bureau of Investigation.

Another source of Oswald's relationship with the FBI came from the Secret Service, who in turn named Dallas deputy sheriff Allan Sweatt as their source. Obviously frustrated in their efforts to prove or disprove the rumour, realising that the FBI were telling them that Oswald had not worked for them in any capacity and that the FBI were unlikely to say anything else regarding the matter, the Warren Commission decided to drop the subject there and then.

Seven FBI agents are known to have been associated with Oswald from the period of his return to the United States in the summer of 1962 and his death some 18 months later. The first documented contact was a two hour interview on 22 June 1962. This FBI interview with a known defector was nothing out of the ordinary. Two months later, FBI Special agents Fain and Brown set up a stakeout from their car near Oswald's home. The agents testified later that they had interviewed Oswald in this way so as not to embarrass Oswald in front of his family. They did add that Oswald had said to them that it didn't matter either way to him and that in future they could, if they so wished, interview him in his home. They insisted that they stay in the car for the interview. Did these FBI agents recruit the vulnerable Lee Oswald as an informer at this meeting?

By 9 August 1963, Lee Oswald was following still another mysterious path after he had moved back to the place of his birth, New Orleans. Working solo on the streets of New Orleans, giving out Hands Off Cuba leaflets in the hotbed of anti-Castro activity, Oswald later hired a young man from the local employment office to help him.

One Adrian Alba had a strange story relating to Oswald. Alba worked in the Crescent City garage, situated next to the William Reilly Coffee Company. Oswald was working at the Coffee company at the time. Alba's garage had a contract to service a number of FBI and Secret Service cars in that area. Oswald, according to Alba, dropped into see him on many occasions and the two came to know each other pretty well. (Alba claims to have helped fix a sling to Oswald's Mannlicher-Carcano rifle, allegedly used by Oswald to murder JFK). Alba and Oswald spoke a great deal about weapons and Alba loaned Oswald several gun magazines.

A man described by Alba as an FBI agent visiting from Washington took command of a car from Alba's pool. The next day the car was parked by Oswald's place of work as Oswald approached it. Oswald bent down as if to look into the car and was handed a white envelope. Oswald pushed the envelope under his shirt and went back into the building. The car then drove off. Alba witnessed the same thing the very next day, but could not see what was handed to Oswald, but was sure that something had been. It must be stated that Alba did not tell the Warren Commission about any of this and, indeed, did not even recall the incidents until 1970. Oswald left the Reilly Company on 19 July 1963.

16 August saw Oswald on Canal Street where he soon found himself involved in a brawl with an anti-Castro Cuban named Carlos Bringuier. Bringuier was the New Orleans delegate for the *Cuban Student Directorate* (DRE), an anti-Castro group. (A Warren Commission Deposit (CD 205) indicates that Lee Oswald attended one such meeting of the DRE whilst he was living in Dallas).

The day before, Oswald had appeared in Bringuier's shop and

told the Cuban he wanted to help in the struggle to overthrow Castro and return the Caribbean island of Cuba to its people. Oswald told Bringuier that he was experienced in guerrilla warfare and would help to train any Cuban exiles Carlos wanted him to. Bringuier was, of course, suspicious of the ex–Marine and told him so. Oswald left a copy of the Marine Corps Training Manual containing details of commando and guerrilla warfare tactics to placate him. Oswald said he would return in a few days.

Three days later, Bringuier was told by a friend that the ex–Marine who had visited him previously was now passing out pro-Castro *Fair Play for Cuba* leaflets outside the International Trade Mart. Bringuier became incensed and left the shop to see for himself. Oswald, indeed, was there, along with a still unidentified young Latin man (photographed with Oswald), passing leaflets to pedestrians as they passed by.

As Bringuier approached Oswald, the ex–Marine turned to him and said, 'Go on, Carlos, if you want to hit me, hit me.'

A scuffle ensued and Bringuier kicked a pile of Oswald's leaflets into the road. As if pre–arranged, the local police turned up almost immediately and both men were arrested for disturbing the peace. Bringuier and his friends, the guilty party regarding the street brawl, were set free after being booked at the police station. Oswald pleaded guilty and was fined $10. Whilst under arrest at the local police station, Oswald strangely requested and received a private interview with an FBI Agent, in this case Special Agent John Quigley. Quigley interviewed Oswald for an hour and a half before later destroying his notes of the interrogation, stating that that was normal procedure after his notes had been returned to him, Quigley compiled a five page report on Lee Oswald. In the document is a close study of Oswald's background and activities on behalf of the *Fair Play for Cuba* (FPFC).

In 1964 Quigley told the Warren Commission that he had not heard of Oswald before he interviewed him in the New Orleans jail, but later admitted that he had reviewed a Navy file on Oswald at the request of the Dallas FBI office. The request from Dallas came in April 1961, while Oswald was in the Soviet Union and over a year before he returned to the United States.

When asked, Quigley could offer no reason as to why the ex–Marine and defector would want to speak with the FBI, but an FBI document released in 1977 tells of a New Orleans police intelligence officer informing Quigley that Oswald wanted to speak with someone in the FBI regarding information on his FPFC activities.

Police Lt. Francis Martello also interviewed Oswald and had the strong impression that Oswald had 'set them [Bringuier] up, so to speak, to create an incident'. Lee Oswald now had a police record in connection with his pro Castro/Communist activities.

Years later, two 'home movies' of the street incident surfaced. The FBI had apparently known about these movies shortly after the event, but had declined to view them. Neither film depicts exactly what happened, but this does not excuse the FBI's lack of interest. One of the movie makers informed his local bureau that he had filmed the event only days after the incident.

Would a real Castro supporter have asked for the presence of the FBI after such an arrest? Surely the miscreant would draw further attention to himself and risk possible future surveillance? Did Oswald perhaps explain to the FBI agent that he was working undercover for the FBI? We will probably never know, but there is still other evidence that Oswald was indeed a paid informant for the FBI.

A *WDSUTV* camera filmed one of Oswald's leafleting exercises. The film, though unclear, shows a white haired man walking toward Oswald as he passes out his leaflets. Many researchers believe this man to be Clay Shaw, the man later arrested by District Attorney Jim Garrison for complicity in the assassination of John Kennedy. In the film, the white haired man turns and enters the Trade Mart building by a side entrance. Oswald, preoccupied with leafleting up until he sees the white haired man, suddenly walks off in the direction of the man. Garrison later concluded that the white haired man in the film was, indeed, Clay Shaw. The man in the film appears to have Shaw's characteristic limp, though this is not conclusive.

On 23 August 1963, Oswald turned up on the local radio in New Orleans in a debate with Bringuier. WDSU's William Stuckey hosted a weekly radio show entitled 'Latin Listening Post'. Stuckey learned of Oswald's arrest and the apparent reasons behind it. After contacting Oswald, Stuckey invited Oswald to appear on his radio show, along with Carlos Bringuier and Edward S. Butler, the head of the staunchly anti–Communist Information Council of the Americas. Butler, it should be noted, also had an office in New Orleans Trade Mart building. Oswald was told he would be speaking about the Cuban issue, but when the debate began, Bringuier and Butler changed the course of the conversation to Oswald's defection to the USSR. In regard to how Stuckey and Butler learned of Oswald's past, Stuckey claims that both the FBI and Butler called before the debate and informed him that he had a defector on his hands. Butler, on the other hand, claims he had confirmed Oswald's credentials with the House Un–American Activities Committee offices. To confuse the issue more, if that were possible, FBI Special Agent John Quigley states in his report to FBI Headquarters that Stuckey advised him of Oswald's defection.

Oswald handled himself well in the face of the two rabidly anti-Castro supporters but made an amazing slip during the course of the debate. Dipping and diving amid the twin barrels of Butler and Bringuier, in answer to Stuckey's question pertaining to Oswald's means of survival in the USSR Lee Oswald made the following statement:

'I worked in Russia. I was under the protection of the – that is to say I was *not* under the protection of the American Government'

The Warren Commission would later edit that part of Oswald's radio broadcast when they published the 'entire' show in their volumes of exhibits (Stuckey Exhibit, volume 21, Hearings). They amended the mistake to read:

'I worked in Russia. I was not under the protection of the American Government.'

The tape is available from the National Archives in Washington.

## CUBANS, COUNCILS AND COMMUNISTS

Oswald is alleged to have had several meetings with Cubans and other government agents in a bar in New Orleans around the same time. Bar owner Orest Peña has stated that Oswald came many times into his bar. At this time Peña was also an FBI informant and was associated with the CIA – backed *Cuban Revolutionary Council*.

When Peña was called to testify before the Warren Commission in 1964, New Orleans FBI agent Warren de Brueys threatened Peña with violence if he referred to him at any time during the questioning. Peña need not have worried about de Brueys's manner. Commission council Wesley Liebeler would not let Peña speak freely about what he knew and so Peña decided to keep quiet anyway.

The day Quigley interviewed Oswald, New Orleans FBI office security clerk William S Walter claims that he saw an FBI 'informant' file on Lee Oswald in that office. Quigley denies this.

Dallas FBI Special Agent James P Hosty appears to be someone of high profile in Oswald's life. When Oswald was arrested for the murder of Dallas Police Officer J D Tippit on the afternoon of 22 November 1963, the arresting officers found a notebook in Oswald's trousers pocket. In the notebook, written in Oswald's hand, appeared Hosty's name, home address, telephone number and car licence number. J Edgar Hoover ordered this incriminating information be removed from Oswald's notebook and not be revealed to the members of the Warren Commission. Not until 11 February 1964 did the FBI finally correct the omission.

Agent Hosty had been assigned to investigate Oswald prior to the assassination of John Kennedy. Oswald had several altercations with Hosty and accused the FBI man of accosting and intimidating his wife in the months before the assassination.

On the afternoon of the assassination, Hosty had spoken to Dallas Police Lt Jack Revill.

'Jack,' said Hosty, 'a communist killed President Kennedy. Lee Harvey Oswald killed President Kennedy, we had information that he was capable of this.' Lt Revill reported this comment in a written statement dated 22 November 1963. That statement, however, was kept locked in a desk in the Dallas Police Department for five months. In October 1975, retired Police Chief Jesse Curry admitted that he had suppressed the Revill statement at the request of the FBI. Curry revealed the existence of the Revill statement in a registered letter to Commission Chairman Earl Warren on 24 May 1964. The letter told Warren that he, Curry, had instructed Revill to keep this information to himself after the Police Chief had been requested to do so by J Gordon Shanklin, then the Dallas FBI's agent-in-charge.

FBI Agent Hosty denied he said any such thing to anyone, at any time, about Oswald. Hosty told the Commission that his only reaction to Oswald being the suspect was one of, 'shock, complete surprise,' because he had no reason to believe that Oswald 'was capable or potentially an assassin of the President of the United States.' Hoover backed his agent and claimed the FBI did not have 'any indication that this man was a dangerous character'.

Three weeks before the assassination, Lee Harvey Oswald had ventured into the FBI office in downtown Dallas in search of agent Hosty. When the receptionist, Nancy Fenner, informed Oswald that agent Hosty was not available, Oswald left a note for him. Hosty brought the note to his superior Gordon Shanklin. Hosty was told not to mention the note during the investigation.

After Oswald was murdered by Jack Ruby, Shanklin again called Hosty to his office. Shanklin, according to Hosty, was visibly agitated and produced the note from his desk. Handing it to Hosty, Shanklin said, 'Oswald's dead now, there can be no trial. Here, get rid of this.'

Hosty tore the note up. As he did so, Shanklin said, 'No! Get it out of here. I don't even want it in my office. Get rid of it.' Hosty went to the men's room and flushed the note down the drain. The exact contents of the note have always been in doubt. Fenner maintains that the note said something like:

'Let this be a warning. I will blow up the FBI and the Dallas Police Department if you don't stop bothering my wife.' The note was signed by Lee Harvey Oswald.

Hosty, not surprisingly, denies this is what the note said. Hosty maintains that the note was folded and that Fenner could not have read it. Hosty remembers the note not being threatening and reading:

'If you have anything you want to learn about me, come talk to me directly. If you don't cease bothering my wife, I will take appropriate action and report this to the proper authorities.'

When Shanklin appeared before the House committee, he denied all knowledge of the Oswald note. Deputy FBI Director William Sullivan said Shanklin had discussed an 'internal problem' concerning a message from Oswald with him and that the existence of the note was common knowledge at the bureau headquarters.

Dallas FBI Special agent Kenneth Howe also remembered the note and testified that he discussed it with Shanklin the weekend of the assassination. Rumours of the existence of the note also spread through the Dallas police Department during the weekend of the assassination.

It is hard to imagine that if the Oswald note had said anything about destroying the Dallas FBI office, it would not have been destroyed after his death. More likely, it would have been produced as evidence of Oswald's violent nature the moment he was in custody, arrested for allegedly killing Dallas patrolman J D Tippit.

Some researchers maintain that the note was more than a menial communication with Hosty. As an FBI informer, Oswald may well have been warning Hosty about the coming assassination attempt on Kennedy, and others are convinced that it was Lee Oswald who sent the missing teletype (as described below) to the FBI.

Following this, however, Hoover was furious with Hosty. After Hosty had testified before the Warren Commission in 1964, Hoover took disciplinary action against Hosty, suspending him for 30 days and demoting him to an FBI office in Kansas City.

Years later, when the Oswald note was discussed before the *House Select Committee on Assassinations* (HSCA), the house reimbursed Hosty more than a $1000 in compensation.

★

Congressman Gerald R Ford, who served as a Warren Commission member in 1964 and was later chosen as Richard Nixon's successor as president in 1974, offers probably the most tantalising piece of evidence pertaining to Oswald's position within America's domestic intelligence community.

In an otherwise unremarkable book Ford co–wrote in 1965 entitled *Oswald: Portrait of the Assassin*, Ford reveals in the first chapter, 'The Commission gets its first shock':

> '*No sooner had the Commission investigating President Kennedy's assassination assembled its staff and tentatively outlined methods of operation than it was plunged into an astounding problem. On Wednesday, January 22 [1964], the members of the Commission were hurriedly called to an emergency session by the chairman [Earl Warren]. Mr J Lee Rankin, newly appointed general Council for the Commission, had received a telephone call from Texas. The caller was Mr Wagoner Carr, the Attorney General of Texas. The information was that the FBI had an 'undercover agent' and that that agent was none other than Lee Harvey Oswald, the alleged assassin of President Kennedy!*'

Several pages later Ford quotes Rankin telling the Commission:

> 'We do have a dirty rumour that is very bad for the Commission, the problem, and it is very damaging to the agencies that are involved in this and it must be wiped out

insofar as it is possible to do so by this Commission.'

★

Each time the FBI showed any interest in Oswald, he would lose whatever job he had at the time. In author Harold Weisberg's opinion, 'one of the obvious effects of this regular unemployment was to make [Oswald] dependent upon other sources of income that might be available to him. As an informant or other contact of a government agency he would have been compensated.'

While there can be no doubt that Oswald had connections with pro and anti-Castro factions in New Orleans in the summer of 1963, the true meaning of these connections remains hidden, buried deep within the framework of the United States intelligence community.

William Walter is the source of another potential bombshell. During the early hours of 17 November 1963, five days before the assassination of JFK, Walter claims that, while on night duty, he received a teletype message from FBI headquarters in Washington. The teletype was a warning of a possible assassination attempt on the president whilst in Dallas on November 22/23. Walter was alone when the message came in. The message was headed 'urgent' for all special agents and signed 'Director'. Walter called Special Agent in Charge (SAC) Maynard, who ran the New Orleans FBI office. Maynard in turn ordered Walter to immediately call the various Special Agents in the area. The response to the teletype demonstrated that the New Orleans office considered the message to be important.

After the assassination Hoover ordered all agents in New Orleans to review all their written reports dealing with the case to determine if there was anything in the reports that might 'embarrass' the Bureau.

Walter could not find the original teletype in the files of the New Orleans office and in 1979, the *House Select Committee on Assassinations* (HSCA) concluded that Walter's claims were 'unfounded' with this statement:

'[William] Walter admitted that he did not publicly allege the existence of this message until 1968. At that time, the FBI instituted an investigation that failed to find any corroboration for Walter's story. According to the Bureau, no record of a teletype or any other kind of communication reporting that there would be an attempt to assassinate President Kennedy in Texas could be found. Over 50 FBI employees of the New Orleans FBI office were interviewed by the Bureau, and none of them stated that they had any knowledge of any such teletype.

'Walter advised the committee that he did not know of anyone who could definitely substantiate his teletype allegation, although he suggested that his former wife, Sharon Covert, who also had worked for the FBI in New Orleans, might be able to do so. Sharon Covert, however, advised the committee that she could not support any of Walter's allegations against the FBI and that Walter had never mentioned his allegations to her during their marriage.

'More fundamentally, however, the committee was led to distrust Walter's account of the assassination teletype because of his claim that it had been addressed to the special agents in charge of every FBI field office. The committee found it difficult to believe that such a message could have been sent without someone 15 years later – a special agent in charge or an employee who might have seen the teletype – coming forward in support of Walter's claim. The committee declined to believe that that many employees of the FBI would have remained silent for such a long time. Instead, the committee was led to question Walter's credibility. The committee concluded that Walter's allegations were unfounded.'

Lee Harvey Oswald's interest in Cuba had begun in the late fifties, during his period of service in the United States Marine Corps. He and his sergeant, Nelson Delgado, had flirted with the idea of helping Castro in his fight against Fulgencio Batista, not unlike countless other US servicemen during the height of the Cold War. The swashbuckling ideology of Castro's and Che Guevara's revolution was not lost on many naive individuals.

Delgado remembers Oswald receiving mail from the Cuban consulate in Los Angles, California. Later, Oswald travelled to Los Angeles with Delgado and Oswald told Delgado that his purpose in visiting LA was to 'visit the Cuban consulate'. Reports of Oswald meeting with mysterious strangers whilst in LA abound, but Nelson Delgado believed the meetings were to do with 'the Cuban business'.

Former Marine Gerry Hemming, himself recruited by the Office of Naval Intelligence, recalls meeting Oswald in the Cuban consulate in Los Angeles. Hemming is sure that Lee Harvey Oswald was working for 'somebody' as an informer or such like. Indeed, Oswald approached Hemming and asked him several questions with a reference to Hemming's background. Hemming is of the opinion that Oswald was working for Naval Intelligence, but could not swear to it.

Oswald, barely a year back in the United States and under pressure from an allegedly failing marriage, told his wife Marina that he was returning to the place of his birth to find work there. Marina and their daughter, June Lee, would stay in the Dallas/Fort Worth area, staying with their friends, the Paines. Before he left for New Orleans, Oswald had written to the *Fair Play for Cuba Committee* (FPCC), a pro-Castro organisation operating out of New York City. The FPCC was under the most intense scrutiny before, during and possibly after its communications with one Lee Oswald, by the United States intelligence services, notably the FBI and Army intelligence. Oswald, in his letter, praised Castro and asked the FPCC for pamphlets, membership applications and advised them that he would willing to pass on any of his Marine training techniques should they so desire. Oswald mentions in his letter that he 'was thinking about renting a small office at my own expense.'

Vincent T Lee, the FPCC director in New York, advised

Oswald to do no such thing and warned him that any plans he (Oswald) may have could frighten away prospective supporters to the cause. Oswald would later totally ignore this advice.

Oswald boarded the overnight Greyhound Bus for New Orleans on 24 April 1963.

# PUBLIC ENEMIES, MISSILES AND THE CIA

The Eisenhower administration had marked Fidel Castro as a public enemy. Within the first year of his coming to power, Castro had denounced the United States as imperialists and vowed to spread the revolution to other South American countries. In his brother Raoul and to a greater extent the attractive and colourful Ernesto 'Che' Guevara, Castro appealed to the young factions of the Americas, including those of the United States.

In July 1960, the United States cut off all sugar importation from Cuba and the island faced economic ruin. Castro's eyes turned to the east. Although Castro's love affair with the Soviet Union was only a touch warmer than it was with America, Soviet Premier Nikita Khrushchev grasped a perfect opportunity that would eventually escalate into the Cuban Missile Crisis of 1962.

Eisenhower and his vice-president, Nixon, drew up plans for the return of Cuba to the predominantly right-wing exiles. The National Security Council (NSC) and the CIA recruited and trained an army of all too willing Cuban exiles, based in Guatemala, for the assault on that embittered island. Amongst the Cubans were American mercenaries and CIA operatives. One such CIA man was E Howard Hunt, known later for his part in the Watergate scandal that rocked America and sank Richard Nixon's presidency.

After his election, Kennedy vacillated and reduced United States input to a minimum, in an effort to sustain his 'deniability'. After coming to power, JFK and his staff had studied the plans drawn up by Richard Nixon *et al* before approving them. Kennedy's only reservation was that he be allowed to recall the invasion force during a period of 12 hours following the exiles leaving Puerto Cabezos, on the north east coast of Nicaragua.

JFK, vociferous in the 1960 presidential debates in his calls to aide the exiles to remove Castro, had upset the exiles' apple cart by refusing to send US aircraft to help soften up the beaches prior to those same exiles landing at the Bay of Pigs. Castro had possibly been tipped off and his troops lay in waiting. Although the exiles had attacked airfields with their B–26 bombers, not all Castro's aircraft had been destroyed. Castro launched his strike aircraft and they headed for the beaches.

General Charles Cabell, then acting Director of the CIA, sought approval from JFK for a final strike at Castro's Airforce and airstrips. Although Kennedy had never limited the number of airstrikes, Cabell decided to ask approval. Kennedy ordered that the airstrikes cease.

The expected uprising against Castro did not happen and the invasion force was either killed or captured.

Kennedy was extremely embarrassed by the whole episode while Castro showed the world newsreel of the captured men and equipment, condemning the United States and its administration for their participation and further embraced the Soviet Union. Kennedy showed deep remorse regarding the fate of the 1150 captured exiles languishing in Castro's jails and vowed to get them released. A month after the invasion, Castro offered to release the prisoners for the princely sum of 500 D–8 Super Caterpillar bulldozers. Kennedy offered farm tractors, realising that the bulldozers were more likely to be used in making airfields or missile bases than cultivating crops. Castro now wanted the dollar equivalent to the bulldozers, some $28 million. Meanwhile, the prisoners all received sentences of 30 years or, if Kennedy so desired, he could pay their 'fines' which now added up to $62 million. This bartering dragged slowly into late 1962 when a U–2 overflight discovered medium range missile bases being erected on the island.

President Kennedy pressed for the removal of Castro and factions of the CIA recruited members of organised crime to take care of the Cuban premier. This movement was codenamed *Operation Mongoose*.

Later, when Attorney General Robert Kennedy discovered the plans involving the Mafia, he ordered that they be stopped.

In 1963, New Orleans was the largest base for anti–Castro Cuban exiles in America operating outside Miami. In the two years since the abortive Bay of Pigs fiasco, New Orleans-based Cubans were smouldering in their hatred of Castro and Kennedy. *Operation Mongoose* grew swiftly. Task Force W, the CIA unit for Mongoose, soon boasted four hundred American employees in Washington and Miami, over fifty proprietary fronts, its own navy of fast boats, a small Airforce and 2,000 Cuban agents. The Miami headquarters became, for a while, the largest CIA station in the world, costing over $50 million per annum.

Cuba, the largest island in the Caribbean, was the focus of political unrest through out 1950s and 1960s; between 26 September and 3 October 1963, Lee Harvey Oswald allegedly visited the Soviet and Cuban embassies in Mexico City. The Central Intelligence Agency produced photographs of the individual they believed to be Lee Harvey Oswald leaving the Soviet embassy in Mexico City at the time in question.

These photos are clearly not of Lee Harvey Oswald.

# CUBAN EXILES, CASTRO AND THE BIG EASY

The problems with Oswald's trip to New Orleans began immediately. He apparently stayed with his aunt and uncle after arriving in New Orleans. Oswald's aunt Lillian remembers him calling their home by telephone from the bus station in New Orleans, on a Monday, whereas Oswald had left Dallas the previous Wednesday. Oswald would appear to have been missing for four days. As with other key times in his life, nobody could trace his movements or whereabouts. An interesting point should be remembered, though it may be a coincidence: Oswald's uncle Charles had been working in an underworld gambling syndicate known to have been connected with New Orleans Mafia kingpin Carlos Marcello.

Cuba appears to have been Oswald's main motive to be in New Orleans at that time, but his actions become blurred and contradictory upon close inspection. Over the years, many people thought that Lee Oswald had been recruited by Cuban intelligence to take action against Kennedy under orders from Castro. Castro, the same people argue, had discovered the CIA/Mafia plots against his own life and had sought revenge against the president. Oswald, an unbalanced maverick, trying to find his niche in history, had been persuaded by an individual or individuals unknown to strike at Kennedy. This would be quite possible were it not for the fact that Oswald was very definitely working for others in New Orleans at the time and simply could not have fired the shots that hit Kennedy and which still echo around Dealey Plaza to this day.

One theory has the right-wing exiles in New Orleans recruiting the left-wing Lee Oswald and using him in their plot to assassinate Kennedy, setting him up to take the blame for their actions.

This theory, on looking at the evidence and Oswald's actions and movements within the framework and backdrop of the emotionally charged New Orleans factions of that time, appears to be correct. There is, however, one reason that this particular scenario does not work.

Lee Oswald was very definitely affiliated with the most right-wing elements of New Orleans. If he were a left-wing/Cuban sympathiser, he could not have failed to see this. And, moreover, if he were genuinely sympathetic to Castro, these same elements could not have missed him either.

On the fringe of downtown New Orleans in 1963 was the Newman building (now demolished). The building was situated at 544 Camp Street, across the street from the government building which in 1963 housed the local CIA office. One block away south, is the William B Reilly Coffee Company Inc.

Oswald found himself a job at the Coffee Company, located at 640 Magazine Street. The company's owner, William Reilly, was a financial backer of the Crusade to Free Cuba Committee, one of many front groups raising money for the CIA backed *Cuban Revolutionary Council* (CRC). The CRC's address was 544 Camp Street.

544 Camp Street is the key to Oswald's allegiances that summer and the FBI, CIA and anti-Castro Cubans are all linked to Oswald during his six month stay there.

The dilapidated building was on the corner of Lafayette place and was a beehive of activity by anti-Castro groups. A side entrance at 531 Lafayette Place led to the same suite of offices on the second floor of the building, CRC headquarters and W Guy Banister & Associates.

Former FBI agent W Guy Banister worked out of that office. Banister, at best described as a racist, anti-Castroite and an alcoholic, wrapped tightly within a raging temper. He had been in charge of the FBI office in Chicago and was responsible for the capture and killing of America's 'public enemy number one' John Dillinger. He had been commended on his efforts by J. Edgar Hoover, before retiring in 1955 to become New Orleans deputy superintendent of police. Banister held this position for several years, before being 'retired' again for allegedly threatening a waiter with a pistol. He was regarded as one of the city's most vocal anti-Castroites and published the racist *Louisiana Intelligence Digest*, which depicted integration as a communist conspiracy. An un–named source close to the District Attorney's office in New Orleans revealed that Banister had been associated with the Office of Naval Intelligence through the recommendation of one Guy Johnson, an ONI reserve officer.

That someone like Oswald, if we believe that he was a pro–Castro sympathiser, to even get through the door of 544 Camp seems very unlikely. One member of CRC, Manuel Gil, was employed by the Information Council of the America's (INCA) and was responsible for tape recordings which were later broadcast in Latin American countries and in some Louisiana schools.

INCA was the owner and distributor of the broadcasts Oswald made whilst in New Orleans following his arrest when, as part of his 'cover', he engaged in allegedly pro-Castro debates. INCA was purely a CIA propaganda outfit.

Prior to the Bay of Pigs fiasco in 1961, the CIA was worried about the bitter disagreements between the major anti–Castro groups. In March 1961, in a safe house in Miami, the CIA ordered an amalgamation of the two main groups, the Frente Revolucionario Democratico and the Movimento Revolucionario del Pueblo.

Six days after this meeting the heads of the two movements signed a concord under which Jose Miro Cardona became the head of the CRC.

Also working from 544 Camp Street was the mysterious David William Ferrie. Ferrie, a brilliant pilot, had met Lee Oswald when the latter was just sixteen years old, when the young Lee had joined his Civil Air Patrol.

Ferrie worked for the CIA as a contract agent and also worked for mobster Carlos Marcello. He also allegedly flew an aircraft during the Bay of Pigs invasion. Ferrie, sacked by Eastern Airlines due to publicity concerning alleged homosexual activities, had also taught Oswald how to shoot a rifle with a telescopic sight. Now they were to meet again in the hotbed of New Orleans.

An FBI document in the National archives reveals that Ferrie had admitted being 'publicly and privately critical of Kennedy for withholding air cover at the Bay of Pigs' and that he had used expressions like 'he [JFK] ought to be shot'. The agents taking the interview were of the opinion that Ferrie did not mean the threat literally. (Ferrie, who always denied knowing Oswald, was arrested after the assassination of John Kennedy by New Orleans District Attorney Jim Garrison, who passed him over to the FBI for questioning. The FBI document of the interview is 40 pages long and is available to the public in 2039). When Oswald was arrested for the murder of Dallas police officer J.D. Tippit on 22 November 1963, he had in his possession a current library card belonging to one 'David Ferrie'.

On the day of the assassination David Ferrie was in a New Orleans courtroom with his boss Carlos Marcello. Only hours after the shooting, Marcello attorney C Wray Gill, visited Ferrie's home with the news of the library card discovery. An unknown source in Dallas had telephoned Gill saying that Lee Oswald's wallet contained a library card with Ferrie's name on it. Oswald's former landlady in New Orleans was paid a visit by a visibly agitated Ferrie who wondered if she knew anything about the card. Ferrie then rushed to an ex-neighbour of Oswald's and again asked for any information about the card that she might know, but was again frustrated from finding an answer. Immediately after searching for information about his library card and finding none, Ferrie made a phone call to Houston to reserve a room at the Alamotel, a Carlos Marcello owned motel. The reason for Ferrie's phone call is not known. After her husband's arrest that Friday afternoon, Oswald's wife Marina was taken into 'protective custody' and remained there for the next three months. During many hours of interviews, Marina was asked, amongst many other things, if she knew or had any knowledge of one 'David Ferrie'. Marina stated that she did not.

Guy Banister was also a member of the ultra right-wing John Birch Society, of Louisiana's 'Committee on Un-American Activities', a paramilitary group known as the 'Minutemen', head of the Anti-Communist Brigade of the Caribbean, and was an intermediary of the CIA and Caribbean insurgency movements. Before the Bay of Pigs invasion, Banister played the role of arms supplier, he and Ferrie being involved, according to Jim Garrison, in a raid on the Schlumberger Well Company munition dump near New Orleans. One witness saw 'fifty to one hundred' boxes marked 'Schlumberger' in Banister's office storeroom early in 1961. The boxes allegedly contained rifle grenades, land mines and 'little missiles'.

Jerry Milton Brooks, also a Minuteman from New Orleans, testified that he had known David Ferrie as a frequent visitor to Banister's office.

In the late 1940s and early 1950s he flew commercial light planes in Cleveland, Ohio. In the middle 1950s, Ferrie to all intents and purposes, disappeared. There is simply no trace of him. Then, as suddenly as he disappeared, Ferrie was back, this time flying for Eastern Airlines. Around this time, David Ferrie supposedly obtained an instrument rating at the Sunnyside Flying School in Tampa, Florida. This is unlikely, however, because there is no record of such a school existing.

No one who saw Ferrie could have possibly mistaken him for anybody else. Ferrie suffered from alopecia and had taken to wearing a deep red monkey hair toupee to cover his baldness. Ferrie also painted bright red eyebrows over his eyes. He supposedly suffered from cancer and kept scores of white mice in his apartment, running free, on which he experimented in search of a cure. Another side to Ferrie's continual hair loss comes from a former Eastern Airlines colleague. The unnamed colleague recalled that when he first met Ferrie, he was 'handsome and friendly' but soon became 'moody and paranoiac – afraid the Communists were out to get him.' Ferrie's personality changed at the same time as his hair began to fall out. After a bald spot had appeared on his head, Ferrie explained that it had been caused by acid from a plane battery dripping on his head. Then Ferrie's hair began to fall out in clumps. One unsubstantiated claim is that Ferrie was flying military aircraft, such as the U–2 spy plane, at high altitudes and had suffered a psychological reaction. Chinese Nationalist U–2 pilots reportedly have suffered the same hair loss phenomenon. In a speech before the Military Order of the World in New Orleans in 1961, Ferrie claimed that he had trained pilots in Guatemala for the Bay of Pigs invasion.

Ferrie worked on and off for Banister as an investigator and when Ferrie faced the hearing regarding his homosexual activities whilst working for Eastern Airlines, Banister showed up at the Miami hearing and delivered a plea on Ferrie's behalf. One of Ferrie's alleged covert tasks in New Orleans was to train small units of Cuban exiles in the swamp areas around Lake Pontchartrain, north of the City. Attorney General Robert Kennedy had the FBI shut down the camp. Large caches of arms and explosives were confiscated.

As with Lee Oswald, the CIA has always maintained that Ferrie was not an employee, in any capacity, of the agency. Former CIA executive Victor Marchetti revealed that DCIA Richard Helms and others within the agency had been worried when the Jim Garrison investigation had named Ferrie in its 1967 assassination probe. Marchetti asked a colleague what the problem with Ferrie was and was told that Ferrie had been a contract agent for the agency in the early 1960s and had been involved in some of the CIA's activities with regard to Cuba. Marchetti is convinced that Ferrie was a CIA contract officer, although his name doesn't appear in any agency files.

Sergio Arcacha Smith, New Orleans delegate to the Cuban Democratic Revolutionary Front, also worked from the office suite at 544 Camp Street. Smith had served in Batista's diplomatic Corps before the takeover by Castro's forces in 1959. Numerous witnesses attested that Smith was a confidant of Banister and Ferrie and that 544 Camp Street was a way station for the mixed bag of Cuban exiles and American 'adventurers' involved in the liberation movement.

Jim Garrison stated in 1967 that 'we have several witnesses who can testify that they observed Oswald [at 544 Camp Street] on a number of occasions.' One such witness, David L. Lewis, another one of Banisters 'investigators', said he was drinking coffee in the restaurant next to 544 Camp Street when in came Cuban exile Carlos Quiroga, who was close to Smith, with a young man he introduced as 'Leon Oswald'. A few days later, Lewis saw Quiroga, Oswald and Ferrie at 544 Camp Street. A few days after that encounter, Lewis interrupted a meeting in Banister's office and saw Oswald again with Ferrie and Quiroga. When Garrison interviewed Lewis later, he realised that Leon Oswald and Lee Harvey Oswald were probably the same man.

After Banister's death from heart failure some months after the JFK assassination, the FBI found several tantalising clues as to the workings of Guy Banister. Although his files had been raided by Ferrie and possibly others, curious files still remained. The titles of the files being: 'Central Intelligence Agency,' 'Ammunition and Arms', 'Anti–Soviet Underground,' 'Civil Rights Program of JFK,' 'B–70 manned Bomber Force,' 'US Bases, Italy,' *Fair Play for Cuba Committee* (FPCC). This was, of course, the faction set up by Lee Oswald in New Orleans, working out of 544 Camp Street. A police officer who saw the files stated that he had seen a file containing information on one 'Lee Harvey Oswald.' This file has unfortunately been destroyed.

Banister may have been keeping tabs on Oswald and the existence of a file does not necessarily mean that Oswald was working for Banister or anyone else, but it is known that Banister would hire young men to go to college campus's and seek out and infiltrate any Communist or Castro sympathisers. Two such recruits, Allen and Daniel Campbell, both former US Marines, were recruited by Guy Banister. Both had heard about the altercation outside the building when Oswald and an anti–Castro Cuban had tussled on the street. Later a young man with a 'Marine haircut' had come into the office and had asked if he could use the telephone. Daniel Campbell next saw this man on TV after President Kennedy had been shot. It was Lee Oswald.

Allen Campbell told the New Orleans authorities that he had heard that a pro–Castro sympathiser was handing out literature right outside Banister's office doorway. Banister, according to Campbell, laughed. Banister did become angry later when he noticed that the handbills Oswald was passing out on the street bore the legend: FPCC, 544 Camp Street, New Orleans, La.

Banister's secretary and lover, Delphine Roberts, asserts that Banister knew Lee Oswald personally and openly encouraged Oswald in his pursuits and had him mount his FPCC operation from an office at 544 Camp Street. Roberts was working for Banister at 544 Camp throughout the summer of 1963 and saw all of the strange characters passing through.

Author Anthony Summers interviewed Delphine Roberts in the late 1970s. She remembered Lee Oswald very well, even though she had avoided the New Orleans District Attorney's office and their investigation of businessman Clay Shaw. Banister had warned her not to speak with the FBI after JFK's death. Banister had kept her away from the office following Kennedy's death to protect her from the immediate uproar.

According to Roberts, Lee Oswald had walked into the office at 544 Camp and asked to fill out a form to enable him to become one of Banister's 'agents'. Roberts told Summers that she did not believe that was why Oswald was there and that she got the impression that Banister and Oswald had already met and were acquainted. After Oswald had filled out the form, Banister called him into his office. Roberts insists that Oswald's role in New

Orleans that summer was something to do with Cuba.

Oswald left the office after a lengthy conversation with Banister. During the weeks that followed she remembers Oswald coming and going from the office on lots of occasions. She was not surprised when she learnt that Oswald was working in the office above them. On several occasions, Banister took Roberts up to the next floor [where Oswald had been] and she saw various writings stuck on the walls pertaining to Cuba and lots of literature on the floor. She saw leaflets pertaining to the *Fair Play for Cuba Committee* and identified them as pro-Castro leaflets. Banister didn't comment about the literature.

The only time Banister lost his temper regarding the leaflets was when some of them found their way into her office. Banister raged that he didn't want any of them in his office.

Later, she saw Oswald giving out the leaflets in the street. She informed Banister. He said, 'Don't worry about him. He's a nervous fellow, he's confused. He's with us, he's associated with the office.' Delphine Roberts' daughter, also named Delphine, saw the young ex-Marine at the same time. She worked in another office and regularly saw Oswald coming and going. Although she never saw him speak with Banister, she knew that Oswald was using Banister's office. She told Summers: 'What I knew of Banister's work, I got the impression Oswald was doing something to make people believe he was something he wasn't. I am sure Banister knew what Oswald was doing.'

There are more witnesses who saw Oswald in the area. Some saw him giving out his leaflets and others saw him working from 544 Camp Street. At the same time Oswald was handing out his pro-Castro leaflets in New Orleans, David Ferrie was leading an anti-Castro demonstration only a few blocks away. Also denied by the authorities was Oswald's early relationship with David Ferrie, when the sixteen year-old Oswald was a member of Ferrie's Civil Air Patrol (CAP).

Ferrie's relentless pursuit of young boys had led him to be

dismissed from the CAP unit following allegations of drunken orgies involving several nude boys in his house. There is no evidence that Lee Oswald ever visited Ferrie's house at this time. Ferrie often encouraged his 'boys' to join the military when they reached seventeen. This behaviour fits the Oswald pattern as Oswald tried to enlist in the United States Marine Corps before he was seventeen. Turned away but not discouraged, Oswald studied his brother Robert's Marine Training Manual until, according to his mother, Lee 'knew it by heart.' Ferrie was vehemently anti-Communist and once spoke about bombing every 'damn Russian, Communist, Red or what-have-you to hell.' Considering his influence on the young minds in his CAP unit, one wonders if he indoctrinated them with anti-Communist propaganda. Remember, Oswald openly displayed pro-Communist tendencies while he was obviously quite the opposite.

In the summer of 1963, another bizarre episode in the life of Lee Oswald arises. Clinton, Louisiana is a small town approximately 80 miles north of New Orleans. Several witnesses claim to have seen a black Cadillac pull up to a line of Negroes registering to vote. After the assassination of Kennedy, several of these people recognised the thin white male in the car as Lee Oswald. Indeed, the thin white male had joined the line in an effort to be registered as a voter in the parish of Clinton. The man produced a Navy identity card in the name of 'Lee H Oswald'. The card had a New Orleans address. The registrar informed the young man that he had not been in the town long enough to qualify as a voter.

In the 1969 trial of Clay Shaw, witnesses from Clinton identified the two other men in the car as David Ferrie and Clay Shaw. Researchers now believe that the man identified as 'Shaw' was probably Guy Banister. Other witnesses in Clinton talk of Oswald getting a hair cut while in town and asking for advice on how to get a job as an electrician at the local hospital. Was Oswald involved in the FBI's Counter Intelligence Program (Cointelpro), a programme designed to infiltrate and destroy certain political groups and could he have been trying to infiltrate the local offices of the *Congress of Racial Equality* (CORE)?

In this writer's opinion, Oswald was clearly being used by elements of intelligence that he had no control over.

In 1961, David Ferrie flew mobster Carlos Marcello back to New Orleans against the direct orders of Attorney General Robert Kennedy. The Kennedys at this point were making more and more enemies in organised crime. Robert Kennedy was also up against Teamsters boss Jimmy Hoffa. The charges that led to Marcello's deportation were revised by Robert Kennedy's Justice Department. Amongst the people helping Marcello stay in the country were Guy Banister and David Ferrie.

Marcello, Florida crime boss Santo Trafficante, Chicago crime boss Sam Giancana and Hoffa were certainly no Kennedy lovers. They clearly recognised that, with the Kennedy Administration and the possibility of a Kennedy dynasty, the end of an era had come. The Kennedy brothers were no longer seeking the advice of their father Joe, who had once been connected to organised crime figures 'Lucky' Luciano and Meyer Lansky. Frank Costello, (who was also known as the 'prime minister of crime' during the prohibition era) was a partner of Kennedy patriarch Joseph).

Robert Kennedy, as head of the Justice Department and with his brother's full backing, was chasing after the mob and getting closer and closer. J Edgar Hoover's powerful FBI, so long ignoring the existence of organised crime and instead concentrating on 'the Red menace' and Martin Luther King's 'peace corps', was now being wielded by Robert Kennedy to crack down on the mobsters of America. Already losing an estimated 100 million tax free dollars from the lost casinos of Havana, the Mafia were desperate. Something needed to be done and quickly.

That something may have involved the enigmatic ex-Marine Lee Harvey Oswald.

## Mexico, Exiles and Revolutionaries

In late September 1963, when, according to the Warren Commission, Lee Harvey Oswald was staying at the Hotel del Comercio in Mexico City, three men appeared at the apartment of a Cuban woman named Sylvia Odio. Twenty-six year-old Odio had been born in Cuba in 1937 and her father had been involved in the struggle against Cuban President Fulgencio Batista, supporting the efforts of Fidel Castro to somehow remove the incumbent president. However, after Batista had been over thrown by Castro's revolutionary forces in early 1959, Odio's father had disagreed with Castro about certain issues and thus fallen from favour. In 1962 Mr Odio was arrested and sent to a detention centre on the Isle of Pines. Soon after her father's imprisonment, Sylvia Odio left Cuba and settled in Dallas, Texas. Sylvia Odio then became active in the anti-Castro movement and helped form an organization called Junta Revolucionaria.

Two of the men who turned up at Odio's apartment were introduced as Cubans and the other man was an American. The leader of the group introduced himself as 'Leopoldo' and he introduced the other Cuban as 'Angelo' and the American as 'Leon Oswald'.

Leopoldo said the men were on a trip and that they were working with the blessing of the *Cuban Revolutionary Council* and that they were members of the Junta Revolucionaria. Leopoldo said his group was trying to raise funds for anti-Castro operations and wanted her help.

Odio told them she was unwilling to take part in any actions that were criminal and therefore would not be helping their cause. The three men left.

The following day, 'Leopoldo' telephoned Ms Odio and asked her, 'What did you think of the American?' Odio said she had no opinion of the American. 'Leopoldo' then said, 'Well, you know, he's a former Marine and an expert marksman. He's kind of loco, kind of nuts. He could do anything – like getting underground in Cuba, like killing Castro. The American says we Cubans don't have any guts. He says we should have shot President Kennedy after the Bay of Pigs. He says we should do something like that.' The conversation ended and Sylvia Odio never heard from Leopoldo again.

It is believed that Bernardo De Torres, a Cuban, was 'Leopoldo' and Edwin Collins was 'Angelo'. Torres had been captured and detained following the failed 'Bay of Pigs invasion in 1961; he had been working for David Sanchez Morales as Chief of Intelligence for Brigade 2506. Torres was released and returned to the United States in December 1962. Collins, a former United States Marine, was born in Shreveport, Louisiana, held right wing political views and was suspected of working with the John Birch Society and the Ku Klux Klan in efforts to work against the Kennedy Administration. Collins was also a member of Interpen (Intercontinental Penetration Force) that was established in 1961 by Gerry Patrick Hemming. Other members of Interpen included Virgilio Gonzalez (later arrested as one of the Watergate burglars), Loran Hall, Roy Hargraves, William Seymour and Lawrence Howard to name but a few. Hemming served with Lee Oswald in the Marines in Atsugi, Japan. This group of experienced soldiers were involved in training members of the anti–Castro groups funded by the Central Intelligence Agency in the Florida Keys in the early 1960s. When the Kennedy Justice Department began to crack down on raids from Florida in 1962, Interpen set up a new training camp in New Orleans. The group carried out a series of raids on Cuba in an attempt to undermine the government of Fidel Castro. This involved a plan to create a war by simulating an attack on the US Naval Base at Guantanamo Bay. Edwin Anderson

Collins died in a boating accident in 1964.

Sylvia Odio, however, felt at the time of the visit by the three men that something wrong, something sinister and deliberate about the visit and the phone call; immediately suspecting there was some sort of scheme or plot afoot.

When Odio saw Lee Harvey Oswald's photograph on TV on 22 November 1963, she recognized Oswald as the American who had been with the two Cubans at her apartment. If this individual was Oswald, it proves a connection between Oswald and anti-Castro Cubans in the weeks before the assassination. If the individual was not Oswald, it would appear that someone may have been using his identity in the weeks leading to Dealey Plaza.

On the morning after the assassination, a Dallas police detective wrote a report on a lead he had received from an informant. It was that someone named 'Oswald' had attended meetings of an anti-Castro movement at an address believed to be on Harlandale Avenue in the Oak Cliff area of Dallas. At the time of this meeting, Lee Harvey Oswald was living in a rooming house on North Beckley Avenue, less than four miles away.

The informant reported that Cubans in the group had left that address in the past few days. The house in question was later found to be the local headquarters for Alpha 66, a militant Cuban exile group.

Although at the time of the JFK assassination, all US Government agencies denied any monitoring of Oswald's activities, it is now known that both the CIA and the FBI were keeping close tabs on the enigmatic marine defector. Oswald allegedly visited Mexico City between 26 September and 3 October 1963. The Warren Commission concluded that Oswald went to Mexico City directly after leaving New Orleans for the sole purpose of obtaining visas for Cuba and the Soviet Union. As with other key elements in this case, testimony is always conflicting and confusing.

Oswald, after six months in New Orleans and apparently having been deeply involved with many leading intelligence/underworld figures in that city, climbed aboard a Greyhound bus for the two day trip to Mexico City. Two Australian women later testified that they had had a conversation with Oswald and that he had told them of his tour in the Marines and his stay in the Soviet Union. The women found him open and honest.

A CIA teletype, written a month before President Kennedy undertook his fateful trip to Dallas, was received by the Departments of State, Navy, Immigration and the FBI concerning an individual who had been photographed entering and leaving the Soviet embassy in Mexico City. This was at the same time that the Warren Commission placed Oswald in that City. The cable reads:

'On October 1, 1963, a reliable and sensitive source in Mexico City reported that an American male, who identified himself as Lee Oswald, contacted the Soviet Embassy in Mexico City. The American was described as approximately 35 years old, with an athletic build, about six feet tall, with a receding hairline *it is believed that Oswald may be identical to Lee Harvey Oswald*, born 18 October 1939 in New Orleans, Louisiana.' (author's emphasis).

The description does not bare any comparison to Lee Harvey Oswald. Oswald was twenty three years old, five feet nine inches tall and of slim, if not wiry build, and weighed in at 150 pounds.

At 11.00 am on Friday 27 September 1963. Silvia Duran, a twenty-six year-old Mexican national working in the Cuban embassy in Mexico City, encountered a man who said his name was Lee Harvey Oswald and that he needed a Cuban transit visa. Oswald then informed Duran that he planned to leave Mexico in three days' time and planned to stay in Cuba for a couple of weeks before moving onto the Soviet Union. Oswald, in an effort to establish his identity, showed Duran his passport, some correspondence with the American Communist Party, his membership card for the *Fair Play for Cuba Committee*, a newspaper clipping about his activities in New Orleans and a photograph of himself in custody, accompanied by two police officers.

Duran was immediately suspicious of this Lee Harvey Oswald

as she could not understand why Oswald had not applied in advance by contacting the Communist Party in Cuba. Duran told him that he would need a passport photograph to apply for a visa for Cuba. He returned an hour later along with the photograph.

Duran then told Oswald she could not issue a transit visa without confirmation that he had clearance for travel to the Soviet Union and in any event it would be at least seven days before his transit visa could be issued. Oswald replied that he could only stay in Mexico for three days.

Duran then told him he would need to visit the Soviet embassy to get the necessary paperwork to apply for the visa. Oswald went to the Soviet embassy but was told by Vice Consul Oleg Nechiperenko that the visa application would be sent to the Soviet embassy in Washington and would take about four months to complete. Oswald then returned to the Cuban consulate at 4.00 and told Duran that he had been to the Soviet embassy and that they were willing to give him a visa straight away. Duran duly phoned the embassy to confirm this but was told that Oswald was lying and that the visa would not be issued for some time. After raised voices and a brief argument Oswald left the consulate. Six times Oswald needed to pass the newly installed CIA camera outside the building.

The CIA surveillance program worked and on Monday 30 September, Anne Goodpasture recorded details of Oswald's visits to the Cuban consulate. As Goodpasture noted, the two types of 'security' information that most interested the CIA station concerned 'US citizens initiating or maintaining contact with the Cuban and Soviet diplomatic installations' and 'travel to Cuba by US citizens or residents'.

The CIA tape of the Oswald call to the Soviet embassy was marked 'urgent' and was delivered to the station within 15 minutes of it taking place. Winston Scott read Goodpasture's report and next to the transcript of Duran's call to the Soviet embassy, he wrote: 'Is it possible to identify'.

Later, it emerged that the CIA station in Mexico was already monitoring Silvia Duran. According to David Atlee Phillips and Winston Scott, the CIA surveillance program had revealed that Duran was having an affair with Carlos Lechuga, the former Cuban ambassador in Mexico City, who was in 1963 serving as Castro's ambassador to the United Nations.

When Lee Harvey Oswald was arrested in Dallas shortly after the assassination, Duran immediately recognized him as the man who visited the Cuban consul's office on 27 September. This was reinforced by the discovery of Duran's name and phone number in Oswald's address book. However, Eusebio Azcue, another man who met Oswald in the same office as Duran, stated that the man he had encountered by the name of Oswald, had, in fact, dark blond hair and features quite different from those of the man arrested in Dallas.

Soon after the assassination, Scott contacted Luis Echeverria and asked his men to arrest Silvia Duran. He also informed Diaz Ordaz that Duran was to be held incommunicado until she gave all details of her contacts with Lee Harvey Oswald. Scott then reported his actions to CIA headquarters in Langley, Virginia. Soon afterwards, John M Whitten, the CIA head of the Mexican desk, called Scott with orders from Tom Karamessines that Duran was not to be arrested. Win told them it was too late but that the Mexican government would keep the whole thing secret. Karamessines replied with a telegram that began: 'Arrest of Silvia Duran is extremely serious matter which could prejudice US freedom of action on entire question of Cuban responsibility.'

Silvia Duran, her husband and five other people were arrested. Duran was 'interrogated forcefully' (Duran was badly bruised during the interview). Luis Echeverria reported to Winston Scott that Duran had been 'completely cooperative' and had made a detailed statement of the events. This statement matched the story of the surveillance transcripts, with one exception: the tapes indicated that Duran made another call to the Soviet embassy on

Saturday 28 September. Duran then put an American on the line who spoke incomprehensible Russian. This suggests that the man could not have been Oswald, as the real Lee Harvey Oswald spoke the Russian language well.

Thomas C Mann, the U.S. ambassador in Mexico, sent a message to Winston Scott that stated: 'Duran should be told that as the only living non-Cuban who knew the full story, she was in exactly the same position as Oswald prior to the assassination. Her only chance of survival is to come clean with the whole story and cooperate fully. I think she'll crack when confronted with the details.'

On 25 November, Gilberto Alvarado, a twenty-three year-old Nicaraguan man, contacted the US embassy in Mexico City and said he had some important information about Lee Harvey Oswald. The US ambassador, Thomas C Mann, passed the information onto Winston Scott and the following morning, Scott's deputy, Alan White and another CIA officer interviewed Alvarado. He claimed that during a visit to the Cuban Embassy he overheard a man he now recognised as Lee Harvey Oswald, talking to a red-haired Negro man. According to Alvarado, Oswald said something about being man enough to kill someone and he also claimed that he saw money changing hands. He reported the information at the time to the US Embassy but they replied: 'Quit wasting our time. We are working here, not playing.'

Winston Scott told David Atlee Phillips about what Gilberto Alvarado had said to Alan White. On 26 November, Phillips had a meeting with Alvarado in a safe house. Alvarado told Phillips that the red-haired black man had given Oswald $1,500 for expenses and $5,500 as an advance. Although he was not sure of the date, he thought it was about 18 September.

Thomas C Mann and David Atlee Phillips believed Alvarado, but Scott was not so sure. Scott argued that there was an 'outside possibility' that it might be a set-up by the right-wing government in Nicaragua who wanted the United States to invade Cuba.

However, as author Jefferson Morley pointed out in his book Our Man in Mexico: 'Speculation about Oswald's motives was to be cut off, not pursued.'

On 28 November 1963 , Scott contacted Luis Echeverria and told him that Washington wanted the Mexicans to interrogate Gilberto Alvarado. On 29 November, Scott received a message from John M Whitten saying: 'Please continue to keep us filled in on status of interrogations of Silvia Duran, Alvarado and others implicated as fast as you can get info.'

J Edgar Hoover sent one of his agents, Larry Keenan, to Mexico City. A meeting was arranged with Winston Scott, Thomas C Mann and David Atlee Phillips. Mann started the meeting by expressing the belief that Fidel Castro and the DGI were behind the assassination of John F Kennedy and that it was just a matter of time before the United States invaded Cuba. However, Keenan replied that Hoover, Lyndon B Johnson and Robert Kennedy all believed that Lee Harvey Oswald acted alone.

Thomas C Mann later told author Dick Russell: 'It surprised me so much. That was the only time it ever happened to me – We don't want to hear any more about the case – and tell the Mexican government not to do any more about it, not to do more investigating, we just want to hush it up. I don't think the US was very forthcoming about Oswald, it was the strangest experience of my life.'

Back in Washington though, J Edgar Hoover had not ruled out the possibility of a communist plot to kill President Kennedy. On 29 November 1963, Hoover told President Johnson on the telephone: 'This angle in Mexico is giving us a great deal of trouble because the story there is of this man Oswald getting $6,500 from the Cuban embassy and then coming back to this country with it. We're not able to prove that fact, but the information was that he was there on the 18th of September in Mexico City and we are able to prove conclusively he was in New Orleans that day. Now then they've changed the dates. The story came in changing the dates to the 28th of September and he was in Mexico City on the 28th. Now the Mexican police have again arrested this woman Duran, who is a member of the Cuban embassy, and we're going to confront her with the original informant, who saw the money pass, so he says, and we're also going to put the lie detector test on him.'

That evening Fernando Gutierrez Barrios told Winston Scott that Gilberto Alvarado had recanted and signed a statement admitting that his story of seeing Lee Harvey Oswald in the Cuban Embassy was completely false. He said his motive had been to try to get the United States to take action against Fidel Castro. A few days later Gilberto Alvarado reverted to his original story. He told his Nicaraguan handler that the only reason that he recanted was that his interrogators threatened 'to hang him by his testicles'. However, soon afterwards, he recanted again. David Atlee Phillips later claimed that Alvarado was 'dispatched to Mexico City by the Somoza brothers in what they considered a covert action to influence the American government to move against Cuba'. Jefferson Morley argues that Phillips is being disingenuous: 'Phillips knew all along about Alvarado's service as a CIA informant. Even the FBI knew all along he was under CIA control.'

Silvia Duran was subsequently questioned about her relationship with Lee Harvey Oswald. Despite being roughed up she denied having a sexual relationship with Oswald. She also claimed that Gilberto Alvarado was lying about money being passed to Oswald. Luis Echeverria believed her and she was released. However, Duran later admitted to a close friend that she had dated Oswald while he was in Mexico City.

Only a week after the JFK assassination, with Oswald now in Rose Hill Cemetery, Elena Garro reported that she had seen him at a party held by people from the Cuban consulate in September 1963. The following week, June Cobb, a CIA informant, confirmed Oswald's presence at the party. She also had been told that Oswald was sleeping with Duran. Winston Scott reported this information to CIA headquarters but never received a reply.

It emerged some time later that when Duran was interviewed by the Mexican authorities she described the man who visited the Cuban consul's office as being 'blond-haired' and with 'blue or green eyes'. Neither detail fits in with the authentic Oswald, who had dark hair and blue/grey eyes. However, these details had been removed from the statement by the time it reached the Warren Commission.

Duran was interviewed by the *House Select Committee on Assassinations* (HSCA) in 1978. This testimony remains classified. However, in 1979 Duran told the author Anthony Summers that she told the HSCA that the man who visited the office was about her size (5 feet 3.5 inches). This created problems as Oswald was 5 feet 9.5 inches. When Summers showed Duran a film of Oswald taken at the time of his arrest, Duran said: 'The man on the film is not like the man I saw here in Mexico City.'

The CIA stated that the Soviet and Cuban embassies were under 24 hour photographic surveillance during Oswald's alleged visit, but then told the Warren Commission that their cameras were turned off on Saturdays (the day 'Oswald' went to the Soviet embassy) and had failed on the day 'Oswald' went to the Cuban embassy. Despite this claim, the CIA sent photographs of the man they identified as Oswald to the FBI on the day of Kennedy's death, 22 November 1963. These photographs are clearly not of the 'real' Lee Oswald. CIA officials simply said there had been a 'mix-up' and left it at that. The CIA maintained that Oswald had made at least five trips to the two embassies and the HSCA were incredulous that he had not been photographed at least once. The CIA again passed over the issue by expressing the belief that the photos of the real Oswald had been 'lost or destroyed'. For whatever reason, the Warren Commission – no doubt holding its breath over the implication of Soviet or Cuban involvement with Oswald and the Kennedy assassination – based their published findings of Oswald's visit to Mexico solely on the CIA information. There is no day-to-day record of Oswald's activities in Mexico City.

Voice recordings of a person believed to be Lee Oswald speaking in Russian to the officials in the Soviet embassy were secretly taped by the CIA, but not passed on to the Warren Commission. When asked why, the CIA said they had been routinely destroyed before the murder of Kennedy. Fifteen years after the assassination a five page FBI document dated 23 November 1963, the day after the assassination, was released to the public. The document relates an intriguing story. While the FBI and Dallas Police were interrogating their prisoner, the CIA informed the FBI that their suspect had visited the Soviet embassy in Mexico City in September and October of that year.

The FBI agents claim to have listened to the tape recordings and state that, in their opinion, the voice on the tape was not Oswald. If this FBI document is authentic, who was speaking on the tape and when was the tape destroyed? The HSCA wrote a three hundred page report on Oswald's stay in Mexico, but declined to publish it in their final report, claiming they had withheld it to protect 'sensitive sources and methods' of the CIA. On the tape, 'Oswald' identifies himself and asks for an official by name, perhaps implying a relationship of some kind. 'Oswald' also asks: 'Are there any messages for me?' This further implies that 'Oswald' knew someone in the embassy.

'Oswald' is also believed to have met with certain officials of the Soviet embassy, one of them, Valeriy Vladirmirovich Kostikov, was alleged to be a high ranking KGB officer with connections to the Thirteenth Department whose responsibilities included assassination and sabotage. Several members of the Warren Commission, amongst them Congressman and later President Gerald R Ford, expressed the opinion that Oswald had gone to Mexico to meet with the KGB to plan Kennedy's assassination. They cited evidence revealing the fact that Oswald had an ongoing relationship with Soviet intelligence probably since being recruited in the Marines or when Oswald arrived in the Soviet Union. The reason Oswald visited the Cuban embassy, according to the

Commission members, was to plan his escape route after the murder. Other members of the Commission believed that Oswald went to Mexico in an effort to tie the Soviet Union and Cuba to the assassination, whether or not they actually were, and that Oswald was warning them of his actions.

President Lyndon Johnson, shortly before his death, stated in an interview that he 'never believed that Oswald acted alone'. Johnson was not, however, referring to any involvement with a foreign government. Indeed, the involvement of any foreign government with the assassination of Kennedy, had they been exposed, would surely have been suicidal.

It must be noted that the Warren Commission cited the CIA as their primary source of information on Oswald's activities in Mexico City. The CIA lied to the Warren Commission regarding the information they had. They knew Oswald had not been to either the Soviet embassy nor the Cuban.

Antonio Veciana, a Cuban exile with intelligence connections, was asked by his CIA case officer Morris Bishop to contact his (Veciana's) cousin, Guillamo Ruiez. Ruiez was an employee at the Cuban embassy in Mexico City in the autumn of 1963. According to Veciana, Bishop told him to contact Ruiez and his wife and offer them money to testify falsely that they had met with Lee Harvey Oswald in Mexico City sometime after 26 September 1963. If this incident is true, it would imply that someone was anxious to place Oswald outside of Dallas at that time and try to increase the suspicion of the Cuban government in a plot to assassinate Kennedy.

Edwin Juan Lopez, an HSCA research investigator has stated quite categorically that although Lee Oswald did not visit the Cuban or Soviet embassies in Mexico City he was, without doubt, in the city. Unfortunately, because of his HSCA 'Secrecy Oath', he cannot reveal the details of his investigation. Lopez and his colleagues meticulously sifted through the documents the CIA let them have pertaining to Oswald's visit to Mexico and this was their conclusion. Lopez goes on to say that not only was the man in the photos not Oswald, which is obvious, the man in question was an impostor, using Oswald's identity. There were no photographs of Oswald, even though the CIA had up to three surveillance cameras operating round the clock at the embassies at any one time. Lopez co-wrote a 280-page document that is now listed classified in the National Archives in Washington, DC. Lopez believes that Oswald was in Mexico at that specific time for a purpose and that Oswald was being set-up by the conspirators who went onto murder Kennedy.

That Oswald did not visit the embassies whilst in Mexico City was verified by the CIA officer David Atlee Phillips to author Mark Lane in the late 1980s. Phillips had been interviewed by Richard E Sprague, then general council to the HSCA. That interview remains classified. Other sources claim that 'Maurice Bishop' and Phillips are one and the same man. Veciana has testified that he met Lee Harvey Oswald in New Orleans whilst in the presence of Bishop.

Tape recordings were made by the CIA Mexico City station of conversations between the man who called himself 'Oswald' and Soviet embassy personnel. Transcripts of these conversations were also made. On the 9/28 transcript is the notation that the individual spoke in 'hardly recognizable Russian'. The real Lee Harvey Oswald spoke Russian quite well. Unfortunately these tapes have now vanished.

David Atlee Phillips, who was in charge of photo surveillance at Mexico City CIA Station, stated that the tapes were 'routinely destroyed' before the assassination. However, the HSCA concluded that based on cable traffic from Mexico City to Langley CIA headquarters 'after the assassination raised a possibility that at least one tape of Oswald's voice existed as late as 16 October 1963.'

Warren Commission staff lawyer W David Slawson has claimed to have listened to these very tapes and his belief that the tapes existed after the assassination is shared by the CIA Chief of

Branch responsible for Mexico City who testified that he 'believed the tapes did exist after the time of the assassination.' If Slawson listened to the tapes as part of his Warren Commission duties, they MUST have existed following the assassination. Someone is either mistaken or lying.

Moreover, David Belin, another Warren Commission staffer and long time defender of its conclusions, said in an interview with interviewer Ted Koppel on Nightline, 'The Warren Commission had access to the tape.' Again, if Belin is telling the truth (and he would have no reason to lie) why was the tape said to be destroyed before the assassination by the CIA?

The CIA forwarded photographs from surveillance cameras of the individual calling himself 'Oswald' to the Warren Commission. This man has been named as Johnny Mitchell Deveraux and bears no similarity to the historical Lee Harvey Oswald whatsoever. When it was discovered that the man in the pictures was not Oswald, the CIA claimed that it was a mistake and that they did not have a picture of the man at all.

David Phillips testified that the cameras were not in operation at the time Oswald visited the Cuban Consulate. However, based on CIA cables the HSCA was forced to conclude 'that it is probable that the pulse camera was in operation on the days that Lee Harvey Oswald visited the Cuban Consulate.' The Cuban government also lent doubt to the CIA's claims by supplying pictures taken by their spies showing the cameras in operation during the time in question. Again, David Phillips testified to something that was clearly not true. Had the real Oswald been photographed at that location, at that time, those photographs would have undoubtedly been used to incriminate him.

★

Oswald applied for a new passport in June 1963. Despite his past activities, including defecting to his country's most feared enemy and his possible recruitment to Soviet intelligence – not to mention his knowledge of the top secret U–2 spy plane – Oswald received his passport within 24 hours. A 'normal' tourist at that time would have had to wait at least three days, if not longer. On his application he acknowledged that he might be travelling back to the Soviet Union and other European countries. He also stated that his previous passport had been cancelled. Of course, the State Department surely had records of Oswald since they loaned him the money to return to the United States the previous year. Oswald visited the Mexican consulate in New Orleans and obtained tourist card number 24085. The card was valid for fifteen days only.

After the assassination of Kennedy, the FBI identified, with the exception of one person, each individual travelling on the Greyhound bus with Oswald. The FBI reported that they were unable to locate the holder of the card preceding Oswald, number 24084. Twelve years later, a document was inadvertently declassified and the holder of the card was revealed. His name was William George Gaudet, a CIA/OSS officer of more than twenty years standing. Gaudet told reporters that it was just a coincidence that his name appeared next to Oswald's. After the assassination, Gaudet, on receiving permission from his CIA superiors, was interviewed by the FBI. No record of that interview has ever been produced. Gaudet admitted 'knowing' Oswald in New Orleans, but had only seen him passing out his Hands off Cuba literature on various street corners. Gaudet said that Oswald was 'a strange man, an unusual man.' Gaudet told author Anthony Summers that he had seen Oswald in the presence of Guy Bannister in New Orleans in the summer of 1963 and that David Ferrie 'was with Oswald'. Gaudet has sided with the researchers who believe that anti–Castro factions were behind Kennedy's murder and that Oswald was just what he said he was: a patsy. Gaudet maintains that he flew to Mexico and did not ride the bus with Oswald.

The FBI later tracked down one Albert Osborne. He had accompanied Oswald on the bus. He had told the FBI that his name was, in fact, John Howard Bowen but later told the FBI that he was, indeed, Osborne. He denied having ever met Lee Harvey Oswald. Oswald used the name 'Osborne' when ordering his pamphlets and literature from the printer in New Orleans.

Who was using Oswald? Someone, it would appear, was trying to create a link between Oswald, the Soviet Union, Cuba and the assassination of John F Kennedy. The photographs of the individual shown above have allegedly been identified as a known 'hit-man' or hired killer. The possibility of such a person posing as Oswald in the weeks before the assassination of John Kennedy is an intriguing one. If this allegation were true and known at the time of the investigation, it should have been thoroughly explored by the members and staff of the Warren Commission. It was not, or if it were, then the findings are not available to the public.

The idea of a 'second' Oswald were laughed at by the Commission. Years later, declassified documents show that the idea was not far from the minds of certain FBI investigators. No less than FBI Director J Edgar Hoover considered the chance of someone impersonating Oswald three years before the assassination a possibility and issued a memorandum to that effect. Oswald was known to be in the Soviet Union following his defection at the time of Hoover's concern.

'Since there is a possibility that an impostor is using Oswald's birth certificate, any current information the Department of State may have concerning the subject (Oswald) will be appreciated.'

Hoover's warning was issued to the Departments various offices. This memo was not declassified until 1975. The memo was also withheld from the Warren Commission and its staff.

'Oswald' turned up in various places whilst riding the exhaustive route to Mexico City on his Greyhound bus.

A young man described as loud, rude and arrogant walked into the Selective Service Office in the Texas capital, Austin. The man in question asked Mrs Lee Dannely if she could help him overturn his dishonourable discharge from the Marines. (Oswald had left the Marines in 1959 on an honourable discharge. This was changed to dishonourable after his defection to the Soviet Union.) The man said he was registered in Florida but lived in Fort Worth, Texas and complained that he was having trouble maintaining employment because of his undesirable discharge. Later that same day, 'Oswald' was seen by other people in and around Austin.

A telephone call from someone claiming to be Lee Oswald was placed to the home of Horace Elroy Twiford in Houston. Twiford was a member of the Socialist Labor Party. He had received Oswald's name from the party's headquarters in New York.

Mrs Twiford answered the phone and spoke with 'Oswald'. 'Oswald' told her that he was a member of the *Fair Play for Cuba Committee* and that he hoped to see her husband for a few hours before he flew to Mexico. Mrs Twiford informed 'Oswald' that her husband was not available to speak with him at that moment but would speak to him another time. 'Oswald' declined and again spoke of his impending trip to Mexico.

The direct result of the United States Congress passing the 1992 'JFK Records Act' was fulfilled six years after its inception. Approximately six million pages of documents had been made available to the public including documents that indicate just what the CIA had been hiding in its files regarding the murder of John Kennedy for almost half a century – that the CIA had, indeed, been involved in a cover-up relating to Lee Oswald's mysterious visit to Mexico City in the fall of 1963.

The Warren Commission report stated that Lee Harvey Oswald travelled to and was in Mexico City in late September and early October of 1963. During his one-week stay, Oswald supposedly endeavoured to obtain visas from both the Cuban Consulate and Soviet Embassy in that city. However, intelligence documents released in 1999 establish that, after he failed to procure the visas, CIA intercepts showed that someone impersonated Oswald in phone calls made to the Soviet Embassy and the Cuban Consulate and linked Oswald to a known KGB assassin – Valery Kostikov – whom the CIA and FBI had had under surveillance for over a year before Oswald allegedly visited the city.

The news of this impersonation and the link to Kostikov, learned within hours of President Kennedy's assassination, so alarmed government and intelligence officials that the subject dominated their discussions in the immediate weeks following the assassination. It also became, during the next 40 years, one of the CIA's most closely guarded secrets on the Oswald case.

## VISAS, CABLES AND TAPES

Shortly after Oswald's 27 September 1963 visit to the Cuban consulate in an effort to obtain a visa for that country, the CIA station in Mexico informed its headquarters about Lee Oswald's alleged activities and requested more information on the individual. However, headquarters lied to its own station, saying that no information on Oswald had been received by headquarters since his return to the United States eighteen months earlier. Documents show, however, that most of the half–dozen agency employees who participated in the drafting and dissemination of this false story had signed for and read various FBI reports received on Oswald during those months, especially during the two weeks before this deception was created.

Following President Kennedy's assassination, documents show that the Agency created two more false stories in connection with Oswald's Mexico City visit. The first cover story was that the CIA's tapes of the phone calls had been erased before the assassination; the second cover story was that the CIA did not realize Oswald had visited the Cuban consulate until they looked into the matter after the assassination.

The cover–up was apparently put in motion the day after the assassination (Saturday, 23 November 1963, when Oswald was still in police custody) by Anne Goodpasture (unless, of course, someone else altered the cables she sent after the fact) in the CIA station in Mexico City. At least two Oswald impersonated calls were intercepted: One on Saturday, 28 September 1963, allegedly from the Cuban Consulate to the Soviet Embassy (Soviet officials have always maintained they never received such a call). The second call occurred Tuesday 1 October 1963 from somewhere in Mexico City, again to the Soviet Embassy. In both calls the impersonator made statements that were inconsistent with the experiences Oswald had had in both the Embassy and the Consulate.

Files released in the mid-1990s show Goodpasture sent a cable at noon (1pm EST) on 23 Nov 1963 stating that a voice comparison (between two intercepted phone calls on 28 September 1963) had not been made at the time of Oswald's visit because one tape had been erased before another had been received. It was unlikely this would have happened, however, as tapes were kept for at least two weeks before erasure; it was necessary to deny that a voice comparison with the Cuban Consulate tape (recorded on 1 October 1963) had taken place, in order to facilitate the cover story that the station had been unaware that Lee Oswald had visited the Cuban Consulate in Mexico City.

Goodpasture's cable only ruled out a voice comparison at the time, leaving the issue of what tapes had survived unresolved. So, at 2:37 EST the following day (Sunday, 24 November 1963) Goodpasture sent another cable confirming all the tapes had been erased.

Whether these cables were inserted or altered after the fact is no longer an issue here; they only constitute the extant record and are not true Goodpasture's *Washington Post* article a year later clearly indicate a voice comparison had been made by Finglass (alias for Mrs Tarasoff, a CIA translator who transcribed the tapes) after headquarters had responded to their first cable. Her changing story at least raises the possibility that her cables were altered after the fact by someone other than her. A 30 September 1963 tape existed because of the recollection of the CIA translator who transcribed it, the afore mentioned Mrs Tarasoff. Tarasoff remembers not only transcribing it, but also the fact that the Oswald voice was the same as the 28 September 1963 voice; in other words the same Oswald impostor. Mrs Tarasoff remembers that 'Oswald' asked the Soviets for money to help him defect, once again, to the Soviet Union. In addition, the CIA officer at the Mexico City in charge of Cuban operations, David Atlee Phillips, in sworn testimony to the *House*

*Select Committee on Assassinations* (HSCA), backed up Mrs Tarasoff's claim about the tape and the request for money to assist in another defection to the Soviet Union. But the Phillips story has a twist; the day before his sworn testimony, Phillips told a different, more provocative version to Ron Kessler of the *Washington Post*. He told Kessler that on this tape Oswald asked for money in exchange for information. Why was this crucial transcript destroyed? What could have motivated Phillips to tell two different stories in less than 24 hours?

Ms Goodpasture's erasure cables are contradicted by her own 1995 deposition to the Assassination Records Review Board in which she stated she thought a tape dub had been hand-carried to the Texas border the night of the assassination and that a copy of the tape was made at the CIA telephone tap center. Goodpasture added that she was sure a copy of the tape would have been sent up to Washington as soon as it had been made.

Newly released internal CIA documents from the weeks following the assassination reveal that another copy of the 1 October intercept was found at that time and that 'the actual tapes' were reviewed. Moreover, the Assassination Records Review Board also verified that in 1964 two Warren Commission attorneys, William T Coleman and W David Slawson, had travelled to the Mexico City station and listened to the tapes. There is no mention of this in either the Warren Commission's 26 volumes or its final report, which were published in September 1964.

Meanwhile, the FBI had to cooperate with the Agency for the CIA's erasure story to work. FBI headquarters in Washington was still asking on the Monday after the assassination (the day after Lee Oswald was murdered by Jack Ruby) for the CIA tapes that had been sent from Mexico City to Dallas early Saturday. The FBI office in Mexico City provided the cover on the Monday afternoon after the assassination, sending a cable to headquarters saying that the tapes had been destroyed. FBI Director Hoover, after learning of this deception, stated that he was not amused. Eighteen days after the assassination, he censured, demoted or transferred everyone in the FBI that had been touched by the 'Oswald in Mexico City' story. Hoover was still angry about it in January 1964, when his subordinates sent him a memo on illegal CIA operations in the US which stated that the CIA had promised to keep the Bureau informed. Hoover pulled out his pen and, in his characteristic large, thick handwriting scrawled, 'OK, but I hope you are not being taken in. I can't forget CIA withholding the French espionage activities in USA nor the false story re Oswald's trip in Mexico City only to mention two of their instances of double dealing.'

The CIA, however, were suppressing more than just the Mexico City tapes; someone made the decision soon after the assassination to deny that anyone within the CIA – including the Mexico station – knew of Oswald's visits to the Cuban consulate until after JFK's murder. The Mexico City station's chief, the head of Cuban operations, and the others involved with Cuban operations all maintain that they knew about the visits and informed headquarters at the time. They also maintain that there was an additional Oswald phone call not accounted for in the extant records. Later, memos confirm what the station personnel said: One is a memo concerning Deputy Director Richard Helms' discussion with the Warren Commission in 1964; the other, a memo by Counterintelligence Chief George Kalaris to the House Select Committee on Intelligence Activities in 1975. Both affirm the station knew and reported to headquarters Oswald's Cuban contacts.

If the recollections of all these people are correct, the record has clearly been altered. Helms, after being shown the documents in 1994, agreed it was obvious the CIA had known at the time, and, in his opinion, the reason for the cover-up was to protect the Agency's sources and methods. Yet, this can only be part of the answer. Recall that in its 10 October 1963 response to the Mexico City station, CIA headquarters had feigned ignorance of Oswald's Cuban connections in Dallas and New Orleans. This was therefore only an internal matter before Dallas and the assassination, still some six weeks away.

Supporting the theory is the CIA memo sent to the FBI on 16 September 1963 – the day before Oswald obtained his permit to go to Mexico. The Agency said it was considering countering the pro-Cuba *Fair Play for Cuba Committee* (FPCC) activities in foreign countries by planting deceptive information to embarrass the FPCC in areas where it had support. Given Oswald's activities on behalf of FPCC in New Orleans that summer, activities closely documented in the local newspapers, on radio and on television, did the US authorities have advance knowledge that Oswald would be paying a visit to the Cuban Consulate in Mexico City that fall? It certainly makes sense that Oswald would have been closely monitored by the FBI following his very public stance in New Orleans.

HSCA investigators including its first chief, Richard Sprague, felt there was reason to believe some cables concerning Oswald's alleged Cuban Consulate visit were either destroyed or altered.

Shortly before Oswald arrived in Mexico City, the incoming FBI reports to the CIA about his activities in Dallas and New Orleans were not put in his 201 file (where all previous FBI and State Department reports on Oswald had been filed), but were diverted into a different folder, filed as FPCC (100-300-11). Agency components in possession of these files during Oswald's trip, and at the time of the exchange of information, included the Operations section of the Counterintelligence Staff (CI/OPS) and the Counterintelligence section of the SAS (SAS/CI). It was these components whose reputations were on the line when Oswald was later publicly accused of being JFK's assassin.

Whatever SAS/CI and CI/OPS had been up to was swept away by the story that no one knew of Oswald's contacts with the Cuban consulate; Mexico station chief Win Scott was indignant about this lie. In his memoir, Scott mocked this cover story and said that his station had immediately cabled headquarters with 'every piece of information' about Oswald's visits to the Cuban consulate in Mexico City.

As proven by the documents, the intelligence cover-up on Oswald and Mexico City was real. The question is: why?

The impersonated phone call linking Oswald to Kostikov and the visit to the Cuban consulate certainly raised the possibility that Oswald not only had not acted alone, but was in the employ of Castro and/or the Soviets. And, if this were the case, then the CIA and FBI, by failing to act for six weeks upon the possible Oswald/ Kostikov link, clearly failed President Kennedy.

Was the cover-up merely protecting sensitive sources to hide incompetence, or were the possible implications running far deeper? If the Kremlin had ordered JFK's murder, either using their agents or Cubans, the nightmare scenario of nuclear exchange would have presented itself to the White House within hours of the president's murder and this author believes such an 'executive action' would have been utter suicide.

Although it is unclear when President Johnson was first informed of Oswald's visit to Mexico City, at 10.00 am on Saturday, 23 November 1963, Johnson asked FBI Director Hoover if there was any new information pertaining to Lee Oswald's visit to Mexico. At this point – barely 24 hours after the assassination – Hoover told Johnson about the Kostikov link and that it was not Oswald's voice on the tape.

Over at the Justice Department, with Attorney General Robert Kennedy absent and in mourning that weekend, Deputy Attorney General Nicholas Katzenbach handled the case. Katzenbach met with Hoover on Sunday, 24 November 1963, just a short while after Jack Ruby had murdered Oswald. Katzenbach then prepared a memo for Johnson's top aide, Bill Moyers, stating that the public had to be 'satisfied' that Oswald had acted alone and that the 'evidence' would have convicted him at a trial. Katzenbach warned that speculation about Oswald's motive had to be 'cut off' and that the thought that the assassination was a communist conspiracy

# Dramatis personæ

Lee Harvey Oswald

Jack Ruby

David Ferrie

Clay L Shaw

J D Tippit

Richard Case Nagell

W Guy Banister

George de Mohrenshildt

Albert Osbourne

Carlos Bringuier

Edward Lansdale

Roscoe White

'Maurice Bishop'

David Atlee Phillips

Edwin Walker

Gerry Patrick Hemming

# *Dramatis personæ*

Loren Eugene Hall

Jack Martin

Marina Oswald

Ruth Paine

E Howard Hunt

Antonio Veciana

W Wray Gill

Sylvia Odio

Frank Sturgis

Waggoner Carr

Gerald Ford

James P Hosty

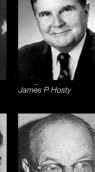
Tracy Barnes

Lawrence Howard

Dr Mary Sherman

Oscar Deslatte

*Civil Air Patrol Cookout, 1955*

*David Ferrie (second from left, wearing helmet)*

*Lee Oswald (far right)*

# Dramatis personæ

J Edgar Hoover

Jim Garrison

Carlos Marcello

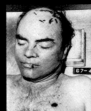

Eladio Del Valle

*(Above): CIA surveillance photograph from the Soviet Embassy in Mexico: this individual was identified as Lee Harvey Oswald*

*(Above): Clay Shaw always denied he knew or had met David Ferrie. This photograph (circa 1949) shows David Ferrie (second from left) and Clay Shaw (standing, centre) at a social gathering.*

or a 'right-wing conspiracy to blame it on the communists' had to be rebutted. After the Sunday meeting Hoover observed, 'The thing I am concerned about, and so is Mr Katzenbach, is having something issued so we can convince the public that Oswald is the real assassin.'

To head off any congressional investigations, President Johnson decided to create a blue-ribbon commission, headed by Chief Justice Earl Warren and composed of men like Senator Richard Russell amongst others. Russell refused the assignment, stating not only he didn't like Warren but couldn't work with him either. Johnson pulled rank on the Senator telling him that he had no choice in the matter; it already had been announced, that he could work with anyone for the good of America, and that Oswald's apparent connection to Castro and Khrushchev had to be prevented 'from kicking us into a war that can kill forty million Americans in an hour.' Warren had initially refused to take the job even after both Attorney General Robert Kennedy and Solicitor General Archibald Cox had requested him to do so. Lyndon Johnson told Russell he had 'ordered' Warren to come to the White House and in that meeting Warren had twice refused the president's request.

Johnson told Earl Warren that 'a little incident in Mexico' would make it look like Khrushchev and Castro had ordered Kennedy's murder. LBJ said to Warren that it was therefore his 'patriotic duty' to head the investigation. Warren had wept, finally agreeing to take the assignment. Almost a decade later Earl Warren himself told the same story – except for the tears. He said that Johnson felt the argument that Khrushchev and Castro had killed Kennedy might result in nuclear war between the two countries, thus starting World War Three; Warren stated he responded, 'Well, Mr President, if in your opinion it is that bad, surely my personal views don't count.'

So as the FBI record indicates, President Lyndon Johnson, Deputy Attorney General Katzenbach, and FBI Director J Edgar Hoover declared and accepted that they would be in line with a lone-assassin scenario. This decision was made no later than Sunday, two days after the assassination; Lee Oswald never had a chance and would now take his place in history along side those other Presidential assassins John Wilkes Booth, Charles J Guiteau and Leon Czolgosz.

Two days later, in a 26 November 1963 phone call, Katzenbach informed the FBI that, 'there might have to be some so-called editorial interpretation' for any subsequent FBI report that would be released to the public.

It is clear that, for the lone-assassin scenario to stand up to the obvious up coming scrutiny, the Mexico City evidence (the tapes of the impersonation and various cables) had to be destroyed, suppressed or at least altered. The problem, however, was that news of the impersonation was already spreading.

Memos were already circulating at the highest levels of the US government concerning Lee Harvey Oswald and his possible connection to Valery Kostikov and the latter's role in KGB assassination operations in Central America. Over at the FBI building in Washington DC, the documentary record within the first 24 hours was already considerable; there were those lower down in the FBI who had listened to the tapes, and memoranda were circulating among the top four men in the FBI and veteran Secret Service Chief James J Rowley. The situation over at Langley was similar; personnel at the CIA Mexico City station and memoranda about the voice comparisons began circulating among senior officials by Sunday, 24 November 1963, two days after the assassination.

The staff of the Mexico CIA station and others at headquarters such as Richard Helms (head of the CIA's 'Operation Mongoose', involved in plots to remove Castro and based in Miami in November 1963) and George Kalaris would have little reason to contradict the record unless the record is untrue. Lies were told in the days after the assassination, that much is evident, lies that could only uphold the lone-assassin theory – even if created for the purpose of preventing war and saving millions of lives.

Of course, this also enabled the JFK conspirators to avoid the scrutiny of a serious, unbiased investigation into the President's murder and, yet, even with the release of these documents, there are still glaring omissions: Oswald's Marine Corps G-2 files and some of the FBI files pertaining to him from 1959–60 (when Oswald was in the Soviet Union) remain classified.

What information could those files possibly hold?

# ALPHA 66, BISHOP AND CHECKMATE

A long suppressed secret government document lends credence to the contention that Lee Harvey Oswald was seen in Dallas with a US intelligence agent about two months before the President's murder, along with unproven reports that a violent Cuban exile group – perhaps with the help of an American intelligence agency – was involved in the assassination. In 1978, the *House Select Committee on Assassinations* (HSCA) investigated the reports but said it was unable to substantiate the claims of either theory. The clues, however, tend to tell a different story.

Those reports centre on a shadowy figure by the name of 'Maurice Bishop', who was said to have been an intelligence agent during the early 1960s.

Cuban exile Antonio Veciana, founder of the Alpha 66 Cuban exile group that launched repeated guerrilla raids against Fidel Castro's regime, testified before the House committee that he considered 'Bishop' his US intelligence contact; that he met with Bishop more than 100 times from 1950 to 1963 and that Bishop had directed him to 'organize' Alpha 66. Veciana also stated that not only had Bishop paid him to carry out these tasks, but he had met briefly with Bishop and a person he identified as Lee Harvey Oswald in Dallas sometime around September 1963, some two months before Kennedy's assassination.

G Robert Blakey, chief counsel to the House committee, decided not to credit Veciana's claim because, among other things, there was no actual proof that a 'Maurice Bishop' existed. (The reader should not be confused with Maurice Rupert Bishop, the late Grenadian politician and revolutionary).

However, a document released by the US Assassination Records Review Board in 1993 supports the contention that Bishop actually *did* exist, thus verifying Veciana's story. Sources stated that a US Army intelligence report dated 17 October 1962 describes a man who fits the profile of 'Maurice Bishop'. Moreover, the official stated that Bishop used a different name but fitted 'Bishop's' profile very closely.

The document is a report from one Colonel Jeff W Boucher, an Army intelligence officer, to Brigadier General Edward Lansdale, assistant to Secretary of Defense Robert McNamara. L Fletcher Prouty, a former United States Air Force Colonel who served under President John F Kennedy as Chief of Special Operations for the Joint Chiefs of Staff, identified Landsdale in a series of photographs as the man walking past the so called 'tramps' who were arrested in Dealey Plaza minutes after the JFK assassination.

An intelligence operative described as fitting Bishop's profile 'has contact with the Alpha 66 group' and that Alpha 66 'was going to conduct raids against Cuba'.

Alpha 66 leaders, the document stated, had told the operative they 'desired support of the US Army in the action phase' including funds, equipment and arms. 'In return the group would provide intelligence information, would furnish captured equipment, and could land agents in Cuba. The group estimated it would require $100,000 to complete the balance of its program, consisting of four more raids on Cuba.'

The document also stated that a unit of Army intelligence had approved debriefing Alpha 66 frogmen who had conducted underwater operations against Castro; exploring the possibility of buying captured Soviet equipment from Alpha 66 and briefing Lansdale on the Alpha 66 proposal to furnish intelligence information and material for financial support.

If Veciana was indeed present in 'Bishop's' office with Lee Oswald that day, a whole can of worms is opened; what, indeed, would a lonely, malcontent nobody like Oswald be doing talking with Cuban exiles and American Intelligence?

It is widely believed that 'Maurice Bishop' was none other than

David Atlee Phillips, a Central Intelligence Agency officer for 25 years and only one of a handful of people to receive the Career Intelligence Medal. Phillips ultimately became the CIA's chief of all operations in the Western hemisphere. In 1975 he founded the Association of Former Intelligence Officers (AFIO), an alumni association comprising intelligence officers from all services.

Phillips was born in Fort Worth, Texas in October 1922 and established his ties to the intelligence community during military service with the US Army Airforce in the Second World War. Serving as nose gunner, Phillips' aircraft had been shot down and the crew captured. Phillips went to organise an escape committee and ultimately enabled himself and several of his colleagues to escape captivity.

Phillips joined the CIA as a part-time agent in 1950 in Chile, where he owned and edited 'The South Pacific Mail', an English-language newspaper that circulated throughout South America and several islands in the Pacific. He became a full-time operative in 1954, and operated a major psychological warfare campaign in Guatemala during the US coup and its aftermath. Phillips served primarily in Latin America, including Cuba, Mexico, and the Dominican Republic. Phillips died in 1988 from cancer.

Winston Scott, CIA Station Chief in Mexico City, asked Phillips to assume the post of Chief of Covert Action which, according to Phillips, was 'a job E Howard Hunt had held in the early fifties and in which Hunt had handled, among others, an American contract agent named William F Buckley'. According to *House Select Committee on Assassinations* (HSCA) investigator Gaeton Fonzi, Phillips became Mexico City's Chief of Cuban Operations in September 1963, just before Lee Oswald visited the city. Gaeton Fonzi believed Phillips was Bishop. In the HSCA's 1979 report, it stated:

'The committee suspected that Veciana was lying when he denied that the retired CIA officer was Bishop. The committee recognized that Veciana had an interest in renewing his anti-Castro operations that might have led him to protect the officer from exposure as Bishop so they could work together again. For his part, the retired officer aroused the committee's suspicion when he told the committee he did not recognize Veciana as the founder of Alpha 66, especially since the officer had once been deeply involved in Agency anti–Castro operations. Further, a former CIA case officer who was assigned from September 1960 to November 1962 to the JM/WAVE station in Miami told the committee that the retired officer had in fact used the alias, Maurice Bishop. The committee also interviewed a former assistant of the retired officer but he could not recall his former superior ever having used the name or having been referred to as Bishop.'

The report went on to dismiss Veciana's testimony about the meeting:

'In the absence of corroboration or independent substantiation, the committee could not, therefore, credit Veciana's story of having met with Lee Harvey Oswald.'

So, Fonzi believed that 'Maurice Bishop' was none other than David Atlee Phillips, the spymaster responsible for the 'Oswald in Mexico City' deception. Clearly from this document, however, we can see that Oswald was exactly the intelligence operative, either working for the United States Office of Naval Intelligence or a CIA contract agent, many believe he was.

It should be noted that three months after the HSCA report was released in 1979 (along with Veciana's testimony) there was an attempt on Veciana's life when persons unknown fired four bullets into his truck while Veciana was driving; the shots only grazed Veciana though he was hospitalized for two days.

— A foot note to Alpha 66, the group 'Bishop' financed, was found to be responsible for the blowing up of Cubana Airlines Flight 455, off the south coast of Barbados, on 6 October 1976. This act of terror resulted in the loss of 73 lives.

★

In 2003, Robert Blakey, staff director and chief counsel for the Committee, issued a statement on the Central Intelligence Agency:

'I no longer believe that we were able to conduct an appropriate investigation of the [Central Intelligence] Agency and its relationship to Oswald. We now know that the Agency withheld from the Warren Commission the CIA-Mafia plots to kill Castro. Had the commission known of the plots, it would have followed a different path in its investigation.'

'The Agency unilaterally deprived the commission of a chance to obtain the full truth, which will now never be known. Significantly, the Warren Commission's conclusion that the agencies of the government co-operated with it is, in retrospect, not the truth. We also now know that the Agency set up a process that could only have been designed to frustrate the ability of the committee in 1976-79 to obtain any information that might adversely affect the Agency. Many have told me that the culture of the Agency is one of prevarication and dissimulation and that you cannot trust it or its people. Period. End of story. I am now in that camp.'

## The Search For Bishop

The following is from Volume 10 of the HOUSE SELECT COMMITTEE ON ASSASSINATIONS:

(168) One of the factors utilized in the committee's efforts to locate Maurice Bishop was the description of him provided by Veciana. When he first met him in 1960, Veciana said, Bishop was about 45 years old, about 6 feet, 2 inches tall, weighed over 200 pounds, and was athletically built. He had gray-blue eyes, light brown hair, and a light complexion. (151) Veciana said, however, that Bishop appeared to spend much time outdoors or in sunny climate because he was

usually well tanned and there was some skin discoloration, like sun spots, under his eyes.(152) He appeared to be meticulous about his dress and usually concerned about his weight and diet.(153) In the latter years that Veciana knew him, Bishop began using glasses for reading.(154)

(169) Shortly after he revealed his Bishop relationship to Senator Schweiker's investigator, Veciana aided a professional artist in developing a composite sketch of Bishop. Schweiker's office provided the committee with a copy of the sketch. Veciana told the committee that he considered the artist's composite sketch of Bishop a 'pretty good' resemblance.(155)

(170) Prior to the committee's efforts, Senator Schweiker's office, as well as the Senate subcommittee he headed, looked into certain aspects of Veciana's allegations. Schweiker, for instance, requested the Belgian Embassy to conduct a record check for information about a passport issued under the name of 'Frigault'. The Belgian Embassy said that, without additional identifying information, it could not help.(156) In addition, Schweiker's investigator showed Veciana numerous photographs of individuals who may have used the name of Bishop, among them Oswald's friend, George de Mohrenschildt, who was then a teacher at Bishop College in Dallas. The results were negative.(157)

(171) It was Senator Schweiker who focused the committee's attention to David Atlee Phillips, former chief of the Western Hemisphere Division of the CIA Deputy Directorate of Operations, as perhaps having knowledge of Maurice Bishop. Immediately after receiving the Bishop sketch, Schweiker concluded that Phillips, who had earlier testified before the Senate Select Committee on Intelligence Activities, bore a strong resemblance to the sketch.

(172) When Veciana was shown a photograph of David Phillips by Schweiker's investigator, he did not provide an absolutely conclusive response. (158) For that reason, it was decided that Veciana be given the opportunity to observe Phillips in person.(159) Schweiker

arranged for Veciana to be present at a luncheon meeting of the Association of Retired Intelligence Officers in Reston, Va., on September 17, 1976.(160) Phillips was one of the founders of the association. Veciana was introduced to Phillips prior to the luncheon.(161) He was introduced by name but not by affiliation with Alpha 66 or involvement with anti-Castro activity.(162) According to Schweiker's investigator, there was no indication of recognition on Phillips' part.(163) Following the luncheon, Veciana had the opportunity to speak with Phillips in Spanish. (164) Veciana asked Phillips if he was in Havana in 1960 and if he knew Julio Lobo.(165) Phillips answered both questions affirmatively and then asked Veciana to repeat his name.(166) Veciana did and then asked, 'Do you know my name?' Phillips said he did not. (167) Phillips was asked if Veciana was on Schweiker's staff.(168) He was told that he was not, but that Veciana was helping Schweiker in his investigation of the Kennedy assassination.(169) Phillips declined to be interviewed by Senator Schweiker's investigator, but said he would be happy to speak with any Congressman or congressional representative 'in Congress'. (170) Following the encounter of Veciana and Phillips, Schweiker's investigator asked Veciana if David Phillips was Maurice Bishop.(171) Veciana said he was not.(172)

(173) Schweiker's investigator expressed some doubt about Veciana's credibility on the point, however, because of Veciana's renewed interest in continuing his anti-Castro operations and his expressed desire to re-contact Bishop to help him.(173) In addition, Schweiker's investigator expressed doubt that David Phillips, who was once in charge of Cuban operations for the CIA and whose career was deeply entwined in anti-Castro operations, could not recognize the name of Veciana as being the founder and vociferous public spokesman for one of the largest and most active anti-Castro Cuban groups, Alpha 66.(174)

(174) The committee considered other factors in examining Phillips, including his principal area of expertise and operations

until 1963. (175) In 1960, when Veciana said he first met Bishop in Havana, Phillips was serving as a covert operative in Havana. (176) From 1961 to 1963, Phillips was Chief of Covert Action in another relevant country. When Oswald visited the Cuban Consulate in Mexico City in 1963, Phillips was also in charge of Cuban operations for the CIA in the same country. Phillips had earlier lived in and had numerous associations in another relevant country. (177) He had also served as chief of station in several other places of general relevance.(178)

(175) The committee developed other information that further gave support to an interest in Phillips in relation to Bishop. In Miami, its investigators interviewed a former career agent for the CIA, who for present purposes will be called Ron Cross. From September 1960 until November 1962, Cross was a case officer at the CIA's JM/WAVE station, the operational base which coordinated the Agency's activities with the anti–Castro exiles. (179) He handled one of the largest and most active anti–Castro groups.(180) At the time that Cross was at the Miami JM/WAVE station, David Phillips was responsible for certain aspects of the CIA's anti–Castro operations. Cross coordinated these operations with Phillips, who would occasionally visit the JM/WAVE station from Washington. (181) Generally, however, Cross worked with Phillips' direct assistant at the station, who used the cover name of Doug Gupton.

(176) In his book about his role in the Bay of Pigs operation, former CIA officer E. Howard Hunt used a pseudonym when referring to the chief of the operation.(182) The chief of propaganda was David Phillips, Hunt called him 'Knight.'(183)

(177) When asked by the committee if he was familiar with anyone using the cover name of Bishop at the JM/WAVE station, Cross said he was 'almost positive' that David Phillips had used the cover name of Maurice Bishop.(184) He said he was 'fairly sure' that Hunt himself had used the cover name of Knight.(185) Cross said,

however, that the reason he was certain that Phillips used the name of Bishop was because he recalled sometimes discussing field and agent problems with Phillips' assistant, Doug Gupton, and Gupton often saying, 'Well, I guess Mr Bishop will have to talk with him.' Cross said: 'And, of course, I knew he was referring to his boss, David Phillips.' (186)

(178) The committee ascertained that the cover name of Doug Gupton was used at the JM/WAVE station by a former CIA employee.

(179) The committee staff interviewed Doug Gupton on August 22, 1978, at CIA headquarters.(187) Gupton said he worked for the CIA from December 1951 until his retirement.(188) Gupton confirmed that he was in charge of a special operations staff at the Miami JM/WAVE station and that his immediate superior was David Phillips. (189) Gupton acknowledged that Ron Cross (cover name) was a case officer who worked for him and that he saw Cross on a daily basis.(190) Gupton said he did not recall whether E Howard Hunt or David Phillips ever used the name of 'Knight.' (191) He said he does not recall Phillips ever using the name of Maurice Bishop.(192) When told about Cross' recollection of him referring to Phillips as 'Mr Bishop,' Gupton said: 'Well, maybe I did. I don' remember.'(193) He also said, however, that he never heard the name of Bishop while he was stationed in Miami.(194) When shown the sketch of Bishop, he said it did not look like anyone he knew.(195)

(180) Explaining his working relationship with David Phillips, Gupton said he was in contact with him regularly in Washington by telephone and cable, and that Phillips visited Miami 'quite often.' (196) Gupton said, however, that there were two sets of operations. His set of operations was run out of Miami and he kept Phillips informed of them. Phillips ran another set of operations personally out of Washington and, Gupton said, Phillips did not keep him briefed about them.(197) Gupton also said he knew that

Phillips used many of his old contacts from Havana in his personal operations.(198)

(181) David Atlee Phillips testified before the committee in executive session on April 25, 1978. He said he never used the name Maurice Bishop.(199) He said he did not know of anyone in the CIA who used the name Maurice Bishop.(200) He said he had seen Antonio Veciana only twice in his life, the second time the morning of his hearing before the committee when Veciana, who had testified earlier, emerged from the hearing room while he, Phillips, was in the hallway.(201) Phillips said the first time he met Veciana was at a meeting of the Association of Former Intelligence Officers in Reston.(202) He said that Veciana was brought to that meeting by an investigator from Senator Schweiker's office but, said Phillips, Veciana was not introduced to him by name but only as 'the driver'. (203) He said Veciana asked him some questions in Spanish, but at the time he did not know who Veciana was or why Senator Schweiker's office had sent him to the meeting.(204)

(182) Phillips also testified that he had never used the name Frigault and had never used a Belgian passport. (205)

(183) Phillips was shown the sketch of Maurice Bishop but could not identify it as anyone he knew. He said, however, 'It looks like me'. (206)

(184) In sworn testimony before the committee in executive session on April 26, 1978, Antonio Veciana said that David Atlee Phillips is not the person he knew as Maurice Bishop.(207) He said, however, that there was 'physical similarity'.(208)

(185) On March 2, 1978, the committee requested the CIA to check all its files and index references pertaining to Maurice Bishop. (209) On March 31, 1978, the CIA informed the committee that its Office of the Inspector General, its Office of the General Counsel, its Office of Personnel, and the Deputy Directorate of Operations had no record of a Maurice Bishop.(210)

(186) On August 10, 1978, B H, a former covert operative of the CIA, was interviewed by the committee in a special closed session. (211) B H was a CIA agent from 1952 to 1970.(212) Between 1960 and 1964 he was assigned to Cuban operations.(213) As such, he testified, he was involved in 'day-to-day' operations with David Atlee Phillips. He characterised Phillips as 'an excellent intelligence officer' and 'a personal friend.'(214)

(187) When asked if he knew an individual named Maurice Bishop, B H said:

'Again, Mr Bishop was in the organization but I had no personal day-to-day open relationship with him. Phillips, yes; Bishop, no. I knew them both.'(215)

(188) Although he couldn't describe Bishop's physical characteristics, BH said he had seen him 'two or three times'(216) in the 'hallways or cafeteria'(217), at CIA headquarters in Langley. B H said he thought Bishop worked in the Western Hemisphere Division (218) and that he had position 'higher than me.'(219) He could not be more specific. The two or three times he saw Bishop, he said, was between 1960 and 1964 when he himself was in Cuban operations, although, he said, he did not know if Bishop worked in that area also.(220)

(189) Asked how, if he did not personally know Bishop, he knew the person he saw at CIA headquarters was Maurice Bishop, BH said: 'Someone might have said, 'That is Maurice Bishop,' and it was different from Dave Phillips or Joseph Langosch, guys that I know.'(221)

(190) When shown the sketch of Maurice Bishop, however, BH could not identify it as anyone he recognized.

(191) On August 17, 1978, the committee deposed John A. McCone, the Director of the Central Intelligence Agency from October 1961 until 30 April 30 1965.(222)

(192)  During the course of the deposition, the following questions and answers were recorded:

Q. Do you know or did you know Maurice Bishop?

A. Yes.

Q. Was he an agency employee?

A. I believe so.

Q. Do you know what his duties were in 1963?

A. No.

Q. For instance, do you know whether Maurice Bishop worked in the Western Hemisphere Division or whether he worked in some other division of the CIA?

A. I do not know. I do not recall. I knew at that time but I do not recall.

Q. Do you know whether Maurice Bishop used any pseudonyms?

A. No; I do not know that.(223)

(193) In view of the information developed in the interviews with B H and former Director McCone, the committee asked the CIA to renew its file search for any files or index references pertaining to Bishop.(224). It also asked for a written statement from the CIA indicating whether an individual using either the true name or pseudonym of Maurice Bishop has ever been associated in any capacity with the CIA. (225)

(194) A reply was received on 8 September 1978, from the CIA's Office of Legislative Counsel indicating that all true name files, alias files and pseudonym files were again checked and, again, proved negative. 'No person with such a name has a connection with CIA,' said the reply. (226) Added the Agency: 'Quite frankly, it is our belief from our earlier check, reinforced by this one – that such a man did not exist, so far as CIA connections are concerned.'

(227)

*On October 19, 1978, the committee's chief counsel received a letter from the principal coordinator in the CIA's Office of Legislative Counsel The letter said, in part:* 'This is to advise you that I have interviewed Mr McCone and a retired employee concerning their recollections about an alleged CIA employee reportedly using the name of Maurice Bishop.

'We assembled photographs of the persons with the surname of Bishop who had employment relationships of some type with CIA during the 1960's, to see if either Mr McCone or the employee would recognize one of them.

'Mr McCone did not feel it necessary to review those photographs, stating that I should inform you that he had been in error.

'The employee continues to recall a person of whom he knew who was known as Maurice Bishop. He cannot state the organizational connection or responsibilities of the individual, not knowing him personally, and feels that the person in question was pointed out to him by someone, perhaps a secretary. He is unable, however, to recognize any of the photographs mentioned above.

'In summary, Mr McCone withdraws his statements on this point. The employee continues to recall such a name, but the nature of his recollection is not very clear or precise. We still believe that there is no evidence of the existence of such a person so far as there being a CIA connection.'

(195) Additional efforts to locate Maurice Bishop were made by the committee in file requests to the Federal Bureau of Investigation. (228) and to the Department of Defense. (229) Both proved negative. (230)

(196) Although file reviews of Maurice Bishop proved negative, the committee learned that Army intelligence had an operational interest in Antonio Veciana during one period. (197) Veciana was registered in the Army Information Source Registry from

November 1962 until July 1966.(231)

(198) The nature of the Army's contact with Veciana appeared to be limited to attempting to use him as a source of intelligence information about Alpha 66 activities, with Veciana, in turn, seeking to obtain weapons and funds. (232) Veciana acknowledged and detailed to the committee these contacts with Army intelligence and said that, aside from keeping Bishop informed of them, they had no relationship with his activities wit Bishop.(233)

(199) Given the Army's acknowledgement of an interest in Veciana and Alpha 66, the committee made the assumption that the CIA may also have had a interest in Veciana and his Alpha 66 activities as part of its pervasive role in anti–Castro operations during the 1960's.

(200) In a review of its own files on March 15, 1978, the CIA noted that Veciana had contacted the Agency three times – in December 1960; July 1962 and April 1966 – for assistance in plots against Castro. (234) According to the CIA: 'Officers listened to Veciana, expressed no interest, offered no encouragement and never re–contacted him on this matter. There has been no Agency relationship with Veciana.'(235)

(201) The committee's own review of the Agency's files basically confirmed the stated conclusions about the meetings with Veciana in 1960 and 1966. Review of the files pertaining to 1962, however, revealed that on July 7, 1962, Veciana received $500 from a wealthy Puerto Rican financier and industrialist with whom the CIA had a longstanding operational relationship.(236) Although the files do not explicitly state whether the money originated with the CIA or the industrialist, and even though during this same period the Agency was using the Puerto Rican, it appears that in Veciana's case the money was provided by the industrialist, and not by the Agency.

(202) Finally, to locate or identify Maurice Bishop, the committee

issued a press release on July 30, 1978 and made available to the media the composite sketch of Bishop. The sketch was part of a release of several other items, including two sketches and three photographs. The committee warned that it should not be assumed that the release indicated the committee believes the person in the sketch was involved in the Kennedy assassination, only that information resulting from possible citizen recognition of the sketch might 'shed additional light on the assassination'. The committee asked that anyone who had information contact the committee by mail, not by telephone.(237)

(203) By November 1, 1978, the committee received from the general public a total of four written responses relating to the Bishop sketch. The three photographs were identified, the two sketches were not. (238)

(204) No definitive conclusion could be reached about the credibility of Antonio Veciana's allegations regarding his relationship with a Maurice Bishop. Additionally, no definitive conclusions could be drawn as to the identity or affiliations of Bishop, if such an individual existed. While no evidence was found to discredit Veciana's testimony, there was some evidence to support it, although none of it was conclusive. The available documentary record was sufficient to indicate that the US Government's intelligence community had a keen interest in Antonio Veciana during the early 1960s and that he was willing to receive the financial support he needed for the military operations of his anti-Castro groups from those sources. From the files of these agencies, it thus appears reasonable that an association similar to the alleged Maurice Bishop story actually existed. But whether Veciana's contact was really named Maurice Bishop, or if he was, whether he did all of the things Veciana claims, and if so, with which US intelligence agency he was associated, could not be determined. No corroboration was found for Veciana's alleged meeting with Lee Harvey Oswald.

Submitted by: GAETON J. FONZI, Investigator.

★

In August 1975, twelve years after the deaths of John Kennedy and Lee Oswald, Texan researcher Penn Jones received a typewritten letter* in Spanish from Mexico City. The letter was signed with the initials 'PS' Jones had the letter translated:

*Dear Sir,*

*At the end of last year I gave Mr [Clarence] Kelly, the director of the FBI, a letter from Lee Oswald. To my understanding it could have brought out the circumstances to the assassination of President Kennedy.*

*Since Mr Kelly hasn't responded to that letter, I've got the right to believe something bad might happen to me, and that is why I see myself obligated to keep myself away for a short time.*

*Convinced of the importance of that letter mentioned and knowing that you have been doing some investigation independently of the assassination, I'm sending you a copy of the same letter.*

*Enclosed with the above typewritten letter was a photocopy of the 'Oswald' note. It read:*

*Dear Mr Hunt,*

*I would like information concerning [sic] my position.*

*I am asking only for information. I am suggesting that we discuss the matter fully before any steps are taken by me or anyone else.*

*Thank you,*

*/s/ Lee Harvey Oswald*

Jones also sent this letter to the FBI and he too received no reply. Handwriting experts in Dallas compared the note to known handwriting of Oswald and found it to be authentic. The experts did not know the identity of the person in question before their work was done. Questions and rumours arose and some sources suggested that the 'Mr Hunt' could have been Texan oil millionaire HL Hunt. Eight years after Jones received the note, it was learned that the FBI had thought that the 'Mr Hunt' may have been HL Hunt's son, Nelson Bunker Hunt. The FBI record of the investigation has never been made public.

Jones, however, believes the 'Mr Hunt' to be none other than Watergate plumber and former CIA man E Howard Hunt. Jones explains that the note originated from Mexico and that Hunt was allegedly stationed in that City at the time of Oswald's visit there in 1963. Howard Hunt was also in charge of Anti-Castro Cubans at that time also. Jones told Jim Marrs, author of 'Crossfire', 'Knowing Hunt's background with the Cuban Revolutionary Committee and the CIA, it makes more sense that the note is addressed to E Howard Hunt.'

The FBI and *House Select Committee on Assassinations* (HSCA), however, both appear to have forgotten the letter. The matter rests there as with many other areas concerning the mysterious life of Lee Oswald. The existence and wording of the note implies to some researchers the genesis of the assassination, Oswald's role and the identity of other key players.

* The matter of the 'letter', however, did not rest there; another twist, if not deception, would surface an incredible thirty six years after the assassination. In 1999, former KGB archivist Vasili Mitrokhin indicated that E Howard Hunt had been targeted as part of a (fabricated) conspiracy theory disseminated by a Soviet 'active measures' program. The 'theory' was designed to discredit the CIA in particular and the United States in general. By Mitrokhin's account, the KGB had created a forged letter from Oswald to Hunt implying that the two (Oswald and Hunt) were linked as conspirators in some kind of operation. Copies of the 'letter' were then forwarded to 'three of the most active conspiracy buffs' in 1975, one of them being Penn Jones. Mitrokhin claimed that the photocopies were accompanied by a fake cover letter from an anonymous source alleging that the original had been given to then FBI Director Clarence Kelley and was apparently being suppressed by that agency. While this author cannot find any evidence to support this theory, if true, it would bring Soviet Intelligence into play.

# Rifles, Senators and Loyalists

In 1963, Senator Thomas Dodd of Connecticut, acting as head of the Senate's Juvenile Delinquency Subcommittee, was experimenting with ordering arms from mail order houses in an attempt to gather information allowing Congress to stem unregulated traffic. Senator Dodd instituted the program on behalf of Colt and other small firearms producers in Connecticut who complained of foreign imports. It is thought Oswald might have participated in this program; Dodd, a former FBI agent and long-time J Edgar Hoover loyalist, was also a leading member of the Cuba Lobby (which grew out of the right-wing, red-hunting, China Lobby) through which he was in touch with some of the same Cuban-exile mercenaries that Lee Oswald mingled with down in the Big Easy. Dodd was also investigating the *Fair Play for Cuba Committee* (FPCC), a pro Castro organisation; Oswald was photographed in New Orleans giving out 'Hands Off Cuba' leaflets only a day after proclaiming his 'anti' Castro stance. Was Oswald trying to infiltrate the anti Castro group or the pro Castro group. Or both?

According to a standard textbook by criminologist Charles O'Hara, it is clear how Lee Oswald, working in a legitimate undercover capacity for Dodd, could have easily been manipulated into simultaneous conspiracies involving a Mannlicher-Carcano, the alleged JFK murder weapon: 'In the investigation of subversive activities and systematic thefts undercover operations are almost indispensable. Undercover work is most successfully used when there is knowledge that certain persons are engaged in criminal activity, but proof which may be used as evidence is lacking. The effective undercover agent is, perhaps, the only means of obtaining detailed information concerning a subversive group or organization.'

Two of the gun mail-order houses Dodd's subcommittee was investigating were the ones from which Oswald allegedly ordered his Smith and Wesson .38 revolver (Seaport Traders of Los Angeles) and his Mannlicher-Carcano carbine (Klein's of Chicago). Oswald, we are told, ordered his pistol two days before Dodd's subcommittee began hearings on the matter on 29 January 1963. The subcommittee's sample statistics later showed a purchase in Texas made from Seaport Traders. One of the groups being investigated for firearm purchases was one whose members Oswald had in his address book, the American Nazi Party. One of the investigators looking into interstate firearms sales at this time was Manuel Peña, the Los Angeles police lieutenant who was later one of the pivotal officers investigating Robert Kennedy's assassination, barely five years in the future. It was Peña who traced Oswald's telescopic sight to a California gun shop. And one of the primary culprits, robbing domestic manufacturers of profits, was the cheap, almost unreliable, Italian made Mannlicher-Carcano.

According to author George Michael Evica, he has 'beyond speculation learned that according to two unimpeachable sources, Senator Thomas Dodd indeed caused at least one Mannlicher-Carcano to be ordered in the name of Lee Harvey Oswald (or in the name of 'Alek Hidell') sometime in 1963.' Evica has yet to produce this evidence, tantalising as it is.

After the assassination, Dodd, using CIA sources, helped the Senate Internal Security Subcommittee publish a story that Oswald had been trained at a KGB assassination school in Minsk. At the time, Dodd was on the payroll of the American Security Council, 'the leading public group campaigning to use US military force to oust Castro from Cuba, and to escalate the war in Vietnam.'

★

After his return from New Orleans and Mexico City in October 1963, Lee Harvey Oswald rejoined his estranged wife, Marina, in Dallas and moved back with her into the home of Ruth Paine.

The Oswald's had actually reunited in New Orleans when Ruth had driven Marina to see Lee that summer. Because Marina was pregnant with their second child, it was decided between the trio that Marina should return to Dallas with Ruth and that Oswald would join them later.

Ruth Paine's house was located in Irving, a suburb of Dallas. Ruth and Michael Paine had also separated and the move was convenient to all parties. Ruth Paine has testified that she and Oswald did not exactly see eye-to-eye on most things. Despite the obvious prickliness between them, Ruth and Lee maintained a peaceful relationship for the sake of all parties.

One of the most interesting possessions found amongst Lee Oswald's personal effects, located in an old Marine seabag, following his arrest on 22 November 1963, was a small Minox camera. This three-inch camera, known as a 'spy' camera and used by Germans and the allies alike during the Second World War, was not freely available to the public in 1963. This, in itself. does not mean that Oswald was a spy, but when the find was listed as a camera by the Dallas Police Detectives Rose and Stovall, the FBI pressed their law-enforcement colleagues to change their story. Rose refused to change his inventory list, made out later on 26 November, insisting that the object he and Stovall found was, indeed, a camera. Dallas District Attorney Bill Alexander also upholds Rose's contention that the object was a camera, having seen it himself shortly after it was discovered. Alexander adds that he personally operated the shutter on the camera after being shown the item.

The camera, according to Rose and Stovall's report, was even loaded with film. The inventory list was witnessed by FBI agent Warren De Brueys, the FBI agent who had monitored Oswald in New Orleans in the summer of 1963. Although Detective Rose had refused to change his list, the camera became a 'Minox light meter' in the FBI inventory. Following his retirement from the FBI, Warren De Brueys, however, could not remember what the object in question had been.

Could the FBI's insistence that the object first identified by Dallas police officials as a camera, then by themselves as a light meter, be connected with the Bureau's paranoia that Oswald may have had some official link with that agency? Any student of the Kennedy assassination can clearly see that probably every US Government agency was compromised in some way the instant the bullet blasted JFK's head apart on Elm Street.

The *Dallas Morning News* found out later from the Minox Corporation that the serial number on the camera did not tally with any serial number on any Minox camera distributed commercially in the United States. The News also found that the Minox Corporation did not sell one light meter in the United States in 1963.

In 1979, the FBI released 25 photographs under the Freedom of Information Act (FIA) claiming they were taken by Oswald with a Minox Camera. The photographs depict scenes believed to be in Europe and several military scenes in Asia or Latin America. Oswald is not known to have travelled to Asia or Latin America whilst serving in the US Marines or otherwise and, considering his short but extensively documented life, it would appear that he did not. The photographs pose another unanswered question: if Oswald did not, in fact, take the photographs himself, what were they doing in his possession? With the Minox camera, the Dallas Police also found three other cameras, a 15–power telescope, a compass and two pairs of field glasses. The cost of this sophisticated equipment must have been in excess of hundreds of dollars and must have been outside Oswald's documented expenses. He lived on the breadline for the better part of his life.

In 1976 it was revealed that the CIA, after denying it for thirteen years, had, indeed, 'discussed the laying on of interviews' and shown 'intelligence interest' in Oswald. In 1977, there were strong rumours of an Oswald '201 file'. According to many former CIA employees, if the CIA has a 201 file on Oswald that would prove that Lee Oswald must have had some kind of intelligence connections with the agency.

The CIA, however, told the HSCA in the late seventies that there was nothing unusual about a member of the public having a 201 file and that Oswald may have had 'potential intelligence or counter intelligence significance', an obvious reference to his stay in the Soviet Union.

The HSCA immediately ran into problems when they uncovered that the CIA had opened a 201 file on Oswald in October 1959, around the time of his defection. They had previously said they had opened the file in December 1960, when Oswald was already living in the Soviet Union. The CIA had kept hidden for almost fifteen years the fact that they had any file on Oswald and had now lied about the original inception of the file. Why?

The file was kept under the name Lee Henry Oswald and the HSCA began to consider the possibility that the agency were keeping dual files. Recently obtained documents reveal that Oswald's file, whoever's name it was filed under, was enough to fill 'two four draw safes.' After enquiring about the Oswald file, the HSCA were presented with an almost empty folder. Up to thirty seven documents pertaining to a possible Oswald/CIA relationship were missing.

The FBI stated after examining Oswald's possessions following the assassination that 'nothing was noted which would indicate that these specimens would be particularly useful in the field of espionage' and that the items had been searched for microdots. The word microdot appears in Oswald's address book, next to the address of Jaggers-Chiles-Stovall, a Dallas graphic arts company used by the US Army map service. A good deal of the work done by Jaggers-Chiles-Stovall involved material obtained by U-2 aircraft similar to the ones that Oswald himself had seen whilst serving in the Marines in Atsugi, Japan.

Microdots contain millions of words reduced to the size of a punctuation mark that can be put into a book or document. After being collected, the microdot is enlarged and the information revealed. Obviously, this mode of passing on information has little value outside the world of espionage.

As we have discussed above, Oswald lived in New Orleans in the summer of 1963 and visited the local library many times. Following Oswald's arrest for the murder of JFK, the New Orleans FBI took every book Oswald had ever checked out of the library during his stay there and never returned them.

# BODIES, BURIALS AND BETRAYAL

Although it had been speculated on almost immediately after the JFK assassination, the first major publicity regarding this twist of the plot came in 1976 with Michael Eddowes' book: *November 22; How They Killed Kennedy* (later re–issued as *The Oswald File*). Eddowes, a British author, maintained that the real Lee Harvey Oswald was either shot dead in New Orleans (by Jack Ruby) the day before Oswald's CIA double set sail for Europe, or was apprehended by Soviet officials upon arrival in the Soviet Union. Either way, claims Eddowes, the man we saw on television that terrible weekend was not the bona fide Oswald, but a Soviet substitute 'assassin', whose initial target had been Richard Nixon (Kennedy only won the 1960 election by the narrowest of margins; Eddowes maintains that the Soviets had trained their 'Oswald' to dispose of Nixon when he had defeated Kennedy. After JFK won the election their assassin was used to eliminate Kennedy). Eddowes spent many years immersed in the 'evidence' that 'Oswald' was, indeed, a Soviet plant and became totally convinced that Kennedy was murdered on orders from the KGB.

Eddowes cited many reasons for his conclusions:

1) Lee Harvey Oswald's Marine service records show a vaccination scar on his right arm along with other scars. After the murder of the alleged assassin, the Dallas autopsy report noted no such scars and the other scars had apparently moved to other parts of the arm.

2) At least eleven documents give Marine Oswald's height as 5'11" while 13 documents (including the Dallas autopsy report) show 'Oswald's' height to be 5'9" following his return to the United States.

3) FBI Director J Edgar Hoover expressed the possibility that

somebody may have been using the identity of Lee Oswald in the United States whilst the 'real' Oswald was in the Soviet Union.

4) The assassin's own widow, Marina, believed that her future husband was a Russian when they first met at a dance in Minsk.

5) Oswald had a mastoidectomy operation behind his left ear when a child. There was no mention of this scar in the Dallas autopsy report.

Dallas researcher Gary Mack presented audio tapes of Oswald to language experts, who were not told the identity of the person on the tape, and they all agreed that the person on the tape had 'acquired' the English vocabulary and accent later in life.

George and Jeanne de Mohrenschildt, a White Russian couple who befriended the Oswalds on their return to the United States, remarked how good Oswald's English was.

Oswald's family also saw changes in him. Lee's brother Robert told the Warren Commission in 1964 that he thought Oswald 'had changed to the extent that he had lost a considerable amount of hair [and that] his hair had become more kinky in comparison with his naturally curly hair prior to his departure to the Soviet Union. [Lee] appeared the first couple of days upon his return to be rather tense and anxious.'

This author does not find that unreasonable; Oswald had defected and maintained that he would give the Soviet authorities any information regarding his Marine Corps tour of duty they requested. It must be remembered that Oswald had worked at the top secret Marine/CIA base in Atsugi, Japan, as a radar operator there and had seen and spoken with pilots of the infamous U-2 spy plane. After returning home, it is not unreasonable to assume that Oswald, whoever he was, would have been prosecuted and jailed by the United States Government. That he was not, is another mystery.

Robert Oswald also noticed that his brother's complexion had changed. Before going to the Soviet Union, Lee, states his older brother, 'had always been of fair complexion. Upon his return, he was 'rather ruddy at this time – you might say it appeared like an artificial suntan that you get out of a bottle, but very slight. In other words, a tint of brown to a tint of yellow [and he] appeared to have picked up an accent.'

Oswald's stepbrother, John Pic, told the Warren Commission that he would never have recognised him; that he was 'much thinner' than when he had seen him last and that 'he didn't have as much hair.' Pic spoke of Lee's face being different that his eyes were 'set back his face was rounder and he had a bull neck.' Oswald introduced Pic to a visitor as his 'half-brother', something Lee had never done before. Pic went on record as saying that the 'Lee Harvey Oswald I met in 1962 was not the same Lee Harvey Oswald I knew ten years previously.' John Pic had not seen his brother from age 12. Again, this author does not find it unreasonable that 'Lee' had changed considerably in the decade from age 12 to 22, literally from a boy to a man.

On 10 January 1979, Eddowes, armed with all this 'evidence', went to a Texas court and asked that the grave of Lee Harvey Oswald be opened and a new autopsy be performed on the remains of whoever it was that occupied the coffin therein.

It didn't take long for Eddowes to run into problems; Lee Oswald had been murdered in Dallas County and buried in Tarrant County. The political posturing produced by Eddowes' request caused an unprecedented furore.

It would seem, however, that Eddowes was not the first person to want Oswald exhumed. A Warren Commission document declassified in 1975 revealed that the CIA were suspicious about the identity of whoever it was in the grave and wanted the grave opened as far back as 1964.

On 13 March 1964, Commission staff member W. David Slawson composed a memorandum regarding a letter from FBI Director Hoover he had received on 26 February 1964. In the letter, Hoover expressed an interest in the scar on Oswald's left wrist (probably referring to the scar Oswald inflicted upon himself in his 'suicide' attempt just after he arrived in the Soviet Union in 1959). The FBI, however, were reluctant to exhume the body. Slawson went on to say that, whilst Oswald was recuperating in the hospital after the defector's suicide attempt, he may have been brainwashed by Soviet officials.

In 1967 Oswald's mother added that 'now would be the time to exhume this boy's body and see if he has these scars.' She, too, was concerned about who was lying in that grave. Mrs Oswald told the Warren Commission that her son had lost a lot of hair and was 'very, very thin' after he returned from his stay in the Soviet Union.

Nothing was done and, as far as can be ascertained, no exhumation was carried out at that time.

Following Eddowes' more recent request, Dallas County authorised the exhumation, but could not convince the Tarrant County officials it was the right thing to do. In the summer of 1980, the assassin's widow, Marina also supported Eddowes and was in favour of an exhumation. Still Eddowes was stonewalled. Then, as it looked likely that Eddowes was to have his wish, Robert Oswald, Lee's elder brother, won an injunction against the exhumation on the premise that it would cause the Oswald family much anguish. The case was argued that, if the body were the real Lee Oswald, then the Oswald family already knew that he was dead. If the body were not Oswald and somebody else, would this not finally exonerate Lee Oswald in the eyes of the world?

Finally, on 20 August 1981, Marina Oswald Porter filed a suit in favour of the exhumation. Robert Oswald said he could no longer afford to fight against the exhumation in the courts and did not appeal. On 4 October 1981 Lee Harvey Oswald's grave was opened.

The body was taken from Rose Hill Cemetery to Baylor Medical Centre in Dallas. The teeth of the corpse were compared with Oswald's dental charts from the Marines. After almost four hours of examination, the head of the team, Dr Norton, made this announcement, 'Beyond any doubt, and I mean any doubt, the individual buried under the name Lee Harvey Oswald in rose Hill Cemetery is in fact Lee Harvey Oswald.'

Minor discrepancies were found between the corpse's teeth and the dental charts, but the examiners were satisfied that enough similarities were present to identify the body as that of Lee Harvey Oswald. In answer to Eddowes' main question, the team also told of a hole behind the right ear of the corpse, evidently the results of Oswald's mastoidectomy. The body was returned to the grave, where it remains to this day.

That, however, was not the end of the story. The people who had prepared Oswald for burial, undertakers Paul Groody and Alan Baumgartner had been summoned by Marina Oswald to the examination as witnesses and to recount the authenticity of various rings Marina had placed on the corpse back in 1963. They both confirmed that the rings were in the correct place, to the best of their knowledge. Then, they noticed that the skull of the corpse was in one piece. At autopsy, a craniotomy is performed; the top of the skull is removed to enable the pathologist to view the brain. The weight of Oswald's brain was recorded in the autopsy report, so there is no doubt that the craniotomy was carried out. Groody said, 'I put the skull back together and sewed back the scalp myself'

Both men, on viewing the corpse in 1981, saw no signs that a craniotomy had been performed on that particular corpse. If that were so, then the body buried in 1963 was not the same as the body that lay in the grave now and had just been exhumed. Anomalies regarding the exact height of the body buried in Rose Hill Cemetery and those of the Oswald who left the Marines are covered later.

Groody went on to say how he had over embalmed the body of Oswald. Somewhat morbidly, he had decided back in 1963 that somebody, at sometime, would want to take a look at the corpse one last time. He described how the body was then placed in an airtight cement vault. Groody was convinced that the body of whoever it was in that grave should look exactly the same as it did in 1963. When the workers opened the grave, however, the vault was already shattered and the seal of the coffin broken. Air had reached the interior of the coffin resulting in the body deteriorating to a skeleton.

The vault may have been disturbed when Oswald's mother was buried next to her son in 1981, of course. But could Oswald's grave have been disturbed and interfered with by choice at that same time? As Marguerite Oswald was being interred, a canopy surrounded both graves. Could there have been a substitution of bodies while Marguerite Oswald's body was being laid to rest?

Marina herself had been asked, way back in 1964, to sign papers to authorise an electronic security system at the Oswald grave. Marina is almost certain that the body was removed after she signed those papers. In 1963, Marina could speak little English, much less read it and she today wonders if one of the many documents she signed during that stressful time was permission to remove the body. No electronic alarm system was put around Oswald's grave as far as anyone is aware.

Once the issue of the craniotomy was raised, Marina Oswald, the only person to hold a copy of the video (produced by Hampton Hall, the son of a prominent Texas state politician) of the second autopsy on her husband, invited her friend and personal physician to view the video film and lay to rest the issue of the craniotomy. The friend and physician also noted no evidence of the craniotomy.

Four years later, it was reported in a forensic journal that there had in fact been a craniotomy and that mummified flesh had shrouded the cut in the skull.

Not unreasonably, researchers were far from happy with this report. They turned to Marina for the video. She did not have it. Hall had kept the video in his possession and, because of the passage of time, had decided that the video now belonged to him.

Marina was forced to take Hall to court in February 1984 in an effort to have the tape she commissioned returned to her possession. By mid 1986, the parties had settled out of court and

Hall had promised to return the tape. To this author's knowledge, the tape has not yet been returned.

Oswald's Marine records cast a certain amount of doubt as to exactly where he really was at several points in his military service career. This could, of course be just a bureaucratic error, but the possibility of two Oswald's begins at this point and warrants further examination.

Many researchers believe this puts forward the idea that another 'Oswald' was being trained for the mission in Russia and the real Oswald was acting as the bogus 'Oswald's' cover. The 'real' Oswald, the patriotic Oswald many of his Marine colleagues speak of, could have been approached, told of the plan and willingly gone along with it. Eddowes suggests that the 'real' Oswald was murdered in New Orleans by Jack Ruby and at that time the substitution was made, by which time the 'real' Oswald would be past caring. If the Oswald who returned to the United States was a Soviet agent, he wouldn't have had much defence against his captors. He would have been almost as good a patsy as the 'real' Oswald, considering that the 'assassin' was silenced, again by Jack Ruby, two days after the assassination of Kennedy.

Strangely, Eddowes (a former British intelligence officer) treated the evidence that Kennedy was shot by someone other than Oswald the same way that the Warren Commission and the *House Select Committee on Assassinations* had. He ignored it.

A closer look at that same evidence supports the fact that the man buried in Rose Hill Cemetery, Dallas, (whether he be Lee Harvey Oswald, patsy and former American Marine defector, or even a Soviet KGB agent substituted during the real Oswald's stay in the Soviet Union), could not have killed President John F Kennedy.

The late Jack White, a Fort Worth, Texas advertising agency art director, has applied his photographic skills to the Kennedy assassination photographs for many years. He has argued that the photographs of Lee Oswald holding the alleged murder rifle are fakes, not very good ones at that and that the rifle being removed from the Book Depository following JFK's assassination was not the one presented in evidence, suggesting a substitution. White also believes photographs of 'Oswald' taken in the Soviet Union prove that the man who returned was not the Lee Oswald who defected.

White also worked as a consultant with the *House Select Committee on Assassinations* in 1978 and whilst working for that Committee was subjected to an horrendous grilling in front of the panel regarding his work on the Oswald 'backyard' photos. One newspaper reported that 'it marked the first time in more than a week of public hearings that any witness was placed in such a trial-like atmosphere.' The Committee attacked White for his lack of knowledge about state-of-the-art computer techniques. Their intent, clearly, was to subject independent researchers to ridicule. The fact that White was working for the Committee seemed to escape their attention. For the record, White believes that the man who returned from the Soviet Union in 1962 was a Soviet agent posing as Lee Harvey Oswald.

# CRYPTONYMS, TESTIMONY AND THE TRUTH

On 22 March 1978, former CIA accountant James B Wilcott swore under oath before the *House Select Committee on Assassinations* (HSCA) that he believed that Lee Harvey Oswald was a 'regular employee' of the Central Intelligence Agency, and that he believed Oswald received 'a full-time salary for agent work for doing CIA operational work'. He also testified that he was told by another CIA employee that money he (Wilcott) had personally disbursed was for 'the Oswald project or for Oswald'.

The full text of Wilcott's testimony was kept out of the public's eye for two decades. Redactions are shown as [] in Wilcott's testimony. The following is taken from an article written by researcher Jim Hargrove.

It should be noted that the HSCA Report briefly and somewhat inaccurately summarized Wilcott's testimony and then pointedly tried to discredit it. The HSCA stated that, 'In an attempt to investigate Wilcott's allegations, the committee interviewed several present and former CIA employees selected on the basis of the position each had held during the years 1954-64. Among the persons interviewed were individuals whose responsibilities covered a broad spectrum of areas in the post abroad, including the chief and deputy chief of station, as well as officers in finance, registry, the Soviet Branch and counterintelligence.

'None of these individuals interviewed had ever seen any documents or heard any information indicating that [Lee Harvey] Oswald was an agent [of the CIA]. This allegation was not known by any of them until it was published by critics of the Warren Commission in the late 1960's. Some of the individuals, including a chief of counterintelligence in the Soviet Branch, expressed the belief that it was possible that Oswald had been recruited by the

Soviet KGB during his military tour of duty overseas, as the CIA had identified a KGB program aimed at recruiting US military personnel during the period Oswald was stationed there. An intelligence analyst whom Wilcott had specifically named as having been involved in a conversation about the Oswald allegation told the committee that he was not in the post abroad at the time of the assassination [of JFK]. A review of this individual's office of personnel file confirmed that, in fact, he had been transferred from the post abroad to the United States in 1962. The chief of the post abroad from 1961 to 1964 stated that had Oswald been used by the Agency he certainly would have learned about it. Similarly, almost all those persons interviewed who worked in the Soviet Branch of that station indicated they would have known if Oswald had, in fact, been recruited by the CIA when he was overseas. These persons expressed the opinion that, had Oswald been recruited without their knowledge, it would have been a rare exception contrary to the working policy and guidelines of the post abroad.

'Based on all the evidence, the committee concluded that Wilcott's allegation was not worthy of belief.'

This researcher, and many others, have long held the opinion that Oswald's travel to and from the Soviet Union show that Oswald was some sort of agent for the United States Government.

Wilcott's testimony appears here in full:

# EXECUTIVE SESSION
## Assassination Of President John F. Kennedy
### Wednesday, March 22, 1978

House of Representatives, John F Kennedy Subcommittee of the Select Committee on Assassinations, Washington, D. C.

*The subcommittee met at 10:20 a.m., pursuant to notice, in room 2344 of the Rayburn Office Building, the Honorable Richard Preyer (Chairman of the subcommittee), presiding.*

*Present:* Representatives Preyer (presiding), Dodd and Sawyer.

*Also Present:* Michael Goldsmith, Counsel, and Gary Cornwell, Counsel.

*Also Present:* Elizabeth Berning, Chief Clerk, and Charles Berk, Betsy Wolf and James Wolf.

*Mr Preyer:* Thank you for being here today, and I will call the subcommittee to order at this time. I will ask if you will stand and be sworn.

Do you solemnly swear that the evidence you are about to give before this subcommittee will be the truth, the whole truth and nothing but the truth, so help you God?

*Mr Wilcott:* I do.

*Mr Preyer:* I would like before we begin to read a written statement concerning the subject of the investigation.

We are operating under House Resolution 222, which mandates the Committee to conduct a full and complete investigation and study of the circumstances surrounding the assassination and death of President John F Kennedy, including determining whether the existing laws of the United States concerning the protection of the President and the investigatory jurisdiction and capability of agencies and departments are adequate in their provisions and enforcement; and whether there was full disclosure of evidence and information among agencies and department of the United States Government and whether any evidence or information not in the possession of an agency of department would have been of assistance in investigating the assassination and why such information was not provided or collected by that agency or department, and to make recommendations to the House if the Select Committee deems it appropriate for the amendment of existing legislation or the enactment of new legislation.

That is what we are attempting to accomplish, which is quite a big order.

We appreciate your being here today, Mr Wilcott.

*(Whereupon, a recess was taken while the members of the Committee went to the floor of the House for a vote.)*

*Mr Preyer:* We will come to order. We will resume the session, and I will recognise Counsel to begin his questioning.

## TESTIMONY OF JAMES B WILCOTT, A FORMER EMPLOYEE OF THE CENTRAL INTELLIGENCE AGENCY

*Mr Goldsmith:* For the record, would you please state your name and address and occupation?

*Mr Wilcott:* My name is James B Wilcott. My address is 2761 Atlantic Street, in Concord, and my occupation is electronic technician.

*Mr Goldsmith:* Where is Concord located?

*Mr Wilcott:* It is a little bit east of Oakland, California.

*Mr Goldsmith:* Have you received a copy of the Committee's rules?

*Mr Wilcott:* Yes.

*Mr Goldsmith:* And a copy of the relevant House Resolutions?

*Mr Wilcott:* Yes.

*Mr Goldsmith:* And, Mr Wilcott, is it true that you are a former employee with the CIA and that you are here today testifying voluntarily without a subpoena?

*Mr Wilcott:* Yes.

*Mr Goldsmith:* During what years did you work for the CIA?

*Mr Wilcott:* I worked from the years May of 1957 to April of 1966.

*Mr Goldsmith:* And in what general capacity did you work with the CIA?

*Mr Wilcott:* All in the finance — in accounting all of the time.

*Mr Goldsmith:* How did you become employed with the CIA?

*Mr Wilcott:* I was recruited from the school in Syracuse New York, where I was taking a course in accounting and business administration.

*Mr Goldsmith:* Very generally now, what were your responsibilities as a finance employee with the agency?

*Mr Wilcott:* Well, from May of 1957 to January of 1960...

*Mr Goldsmith:* ...excuse me, just answer the question very generally, without referring to anything right now, and please describe generally what your responsibilities were as a finance officer.

*Mr Wilcott:* My responsibilities were primarily record keeping and disbursing of funds.

*Mr Goldsmith:* Mr Wilcott, are you here with Counsel today?

*Mr Wilcott:* Yes, I am.

*Mr Goldsmith:* Would your Counsel identify himself for the recorder?

*Mr Schaap:* My name is William Schaap, S–c–h–a–a–p (spelling), and I am an Attorney here in Washington. I will give my card to the Committee.

*Mr Goldsmith:* Mr Wilcott, did I ask you to prepare a list indicating the dates that you were employed with the CIA and where you were stationed?

*Mr Wilcott:* Yes, you did.

*Mr Goldsmith:* Did you prepare such a list?

*Mr Wilcott:* Yes, I did.

*Mr Goldsmith:* Do you have that list with you?

*Mr Wilcott:* Yes. I do.

*Mr Goldsmith:* Referring to that list, would you tell the Committee where you were stationed during your period with the CIA?

*Mr Wilcott:* Certainly, from May of 1957 to January of 1960, I was in the pre-fab building on the Potomac in finance. During the period, it was unvouchered funds, and my duties were general accounting, and my rate in status was GS-5. From about January of 1960 to about June of 1960, I was transferred to Finance Field Payroll, also, in this same building, on the Potomac. This was making payments and keeping pay records.

From June of 1960 to June of 1964, I was stationed at [] Station, and my primary duty was finance and cash disbursements. This was all cash payments and record keeping for the station. And during that period, I had been promoted GS-7 and also gained a career status. From June of 1964 to about December of 1964, I was at Roseland. This was just prior to moving to Langley, in finance, and my duties there were policing accounts, and included auditing of special accounts.

From January of 1965 to about March of 1965, I was at Langley in the same area, in finance, policing accounts and auditing of special accounts, and I was promoted up to GS-9. From April of 1965 to April of 1966, I was at Miami Station in finance, and I was handling the staff payroll. This was preparing and reconciling payrolls.

In April of 1966, I resigned from the CIA.

*Mr Goldsmith:* I take it, from your testimony, that in November of 1963, you were stationed in [] Station, is that correct?

*Mr Wilcott:* That is right.

*Mr Goldsmith:* Drawing your attention to the period immediately after the assassination of President Kennedy, at that time, did you come across any information concerning Lee Harvey Oswald's relationship with the CIA?

*Mr Wilcott:* Yes, I did.

*Mr Goldsmith:* And will you tell the Committee what that relationship was?

*Mr Wilcott:* Well, it was my understanding that Lee Harvey Oswald was an employee of the agency and was an agent of the agency.

*Mr Goldsmith:* What do you mean by the term 'agent'?

*Mr Wilcott:* That he was a regular employee, receiving a full-time salary for agent work for doing CIA operational work.

*Mr Goldsmith:* How did this information concerning Oswald first come to your attention?

*Mr Wilcott:* The first time I heard about Oswald being connected in any way with CIA was the day after the Kennedy assassination.

*Mr Goldsmith:* And how did that come to your attention:

*Mr Wilcott:* Well, I was on day duty for the station. It was a guard–type function at the station, which I worked for overtime. There was a lot of excitement going on at the station after the Kennedy assassination. Towards the end of my tour of duty, I heard certain things about Oswald somehow being connected with the agency, and I didn't really believe this when I heard it, and I thought it was absurd. Then, as time went on, I began to hear more things in that line.

*Mr Goldsmith:* I think we had better go over that one more time. When, exactly, was the very first time that you heard or came across information that Oswald was an agent?

*Mr Wilcott:* I heard references to it the day after the assassination.

*Mr Goldsmith:* And who made these references to Oswald being an agent of the CIA?

*Mr Wilcott:* I can't remember the exact persons. There was talk about it going on at the station, and several months following at the station.

*Mr Goldsmith:* How many people made this reference to Oswald being an agent of the CIA?

*Mr Wilcott:* At least there was at least six or seven people, specifically, who said that they either knew or believed Oswald to be an agent of the CIA.

*Mr Goldsmith:* Was Jerry Fox one of the people that made this allegation?

*Mr Wilcott:* To the best of my recollection, yes.

*Mr Goldsmith:* And who is Jerry Fox?

*Mr Wilcott:* Jerry Fox was a Case Officer for his branch the Soviet Russia Branch, [deleted] Station, who purchased information from the Soviets.

*Mr Goldsmith:* Mr Wilcott, did I ask you to prepare a list of CIA Case Officers working at [that] Station in 1963?

*Mr Wilcott:* Yes, you did.

*Mr Goldsmith:* Did you prepare such a list?

*Mr Wilcott:* Yes, I did.

*Mr Goldsmith:* Is that list complete and does it have every CIA Case Officer who worked [that station] in 1963?

*Mr Wilcott:* Oh, no. It doesn't have every one. It has every one that I can remember.

*Mr Goldsmith:* Did you bring that list with you today?

*Mr Wilcott:* Yes, I did.

*Mr Goldsmith:* Were any of these people on your list possible subjects who made references to Oswald being a CIA agent?

*Mr Wilcott:* Yes.

*Mr Goldsmith:* Would you read the list to the Committee?

*Mr Wilcott:* Yes.

*Mr Goldsmith:* Only of Case Officers.

*Ms. Berning:* I think we ought to state that the record shows that Mr Sawyer is a member of the Kennedy Subcommittee.

*Mr Preyer:* We will.

*Mr Goldsmith:* Upon your memory and the list that your brought with you today, will you tell the Committee the names of the CIA Case Officers who you remember working [that station] in 1963?

*Mr Wilcott:* Yes. There was [] Branch, who had [] cover. Jerry Fox, SR Branch, Soviet Russia Branch.

*Mr Goldsmith:* Excuse me, please proceed very slowly.

*Mr Wilcott:* Jerry Fox, SR Branch, Reid Dennis, Chief of Soviet Satellite Branch; and [], China Branch, and he also had a cover.

(Some testimony excluded here by this author).

*Mr Goldsmith:* Do you remember which of these individuals if any, made the specific allegation or reference that Oswald was an agent?

*Mr Wilcott:* It has been 15 years, and I can't remember specifically who said what, but certainly I am sure that Jerry Fox, for instance, had at least made some mention of it.

*Mr Goldsmith:* At the time that this allegation first came to your attention, did you discuss it with anyone?

*Mr Wilcott:* Oh, yes. I discussed it with my friends and the people that I was associating with socially.

*Mr Goldsmith:* Who were your friends that you discussed this with?

*Mr Wilcott:* [] George Breen, Ed Luck, and [].

*Mr Goldsmith:* Who was George Breen?

*Mr Wilcott:* George Breen was a person in Registry, who was my closest friend while I was in [].

*Mr Goldsmith:* Was he a CIA employee?

*Mr Wilcott:* Yes, he was.

*Mr Goldsmith:* And would he corroborate your observation that Oswald was an agent?

*Mr Wilcott:* I don't know.

*Mr Goldsmith:* At the time that this allegation first came to your attention, did you learn the name of Oswald's Case Officer at the CIA?

*Mr Wilcott:* No.

*Mr Goldsmith:* Were there any other times during your stay with the CIA at [that] Station that you came across information that Oswald had been a CIA agent?

*Mr Wilcott:* Yes.

*Mr Goldsmith:* When was that?

*Mr Wilcott:* The specific incident was soon after the Kennedy assassination, where an agent, a Case Officer – I am sure it was a Case Officer – came up to my window to draw money, and he specifically said in the conversation that ensued, he specifically said, 'Well, Jim, the money that I drew the last couple of weeks ago or so was money either for the Oswald project or for Oswald.'

*Mr Goldsmith:* Do you remember the name of this Case Officer?

*Mr Wilcott:* No, I don't.

*Mr Goldsmith:* Do you remember when specifically this conversation took place?

*Mr Wilcott:* Not specifically, only generally.

*Mr Goldsmith:* How many months after the assassination was this?

*Mr Wilcott:* I think it must have been two or three omths (sic) after the assassination.

*Mr Goldsmith:* Do you remember where this conversation took place?

*Mr Wilcott:* It was right at my window, my disbursing cage window.

*Mr Goldsmith:* Did you discuss this information with anyone?

*Mr Wilcott:* Oh, yes.

*Mr Goldsmith:* With whom?

*Mr Wilcott:* Certainly with George Breen, [] the circle of social friends that we had.

*Mr Goldsmith:* How do you spell [] last name?

*Mr Wilcott:* [] (spelling).

*Mr Schaap:* For the record, I have made a list of all of these spellings of the names which have been mentioned, which I will give to the stenographer so that he will have them correctly.

*Mr Goldsmith:* Did this Case Officer tell you what Oswald's cryptonym was?

*Mr Wilcott:* Yes, he mentioned the cryptonym specifically under which the money was drawn.

*Mr Goldsmith:* And what did he tell you the cryptonym was?

*Mr Wilcott:* I cannot remember.

*Mr Goldsmith:* What was your response to this revelation as to what Oswald's cryptonym was? Did you write it down or do anything?

*Mr Wilcott:* No; I think that I looked through my advance book – and I had a book where the advances on projects were run, and I leafed through them, and I must have at least leafed through them to see if what he said was true.

*Mr Goldsmith:* And are you saying then that you attempted to investigate this allegation?

*Mr Wilcott:* No, I am not saying that. It was more of a casual kind of thing, to my way of thinking.

*Mr Goldsmith:* Did you check your cash disbursement files?

*Mr Wilcott:* Not the files, no.

*Mr Goldsmith:* I am not sure I am following, then, what specifically you did check.

*Mr Wilcott:* It was a book that I had. At the end of the day we would list all of the advances that were made in an advance book. It was just a three-ring binder, and we would list down the advances by cryptonym and the amounts and then reconcile that with the daily disbursements.

*Mr Goldsmith:* How long were these records maintained?

*Mr Wilcott:* They were maintained on a thirty-day basis, and then they were closed off at the end of the month.

*Mr Goldsmith:* So, does that mean you were able to check back only thirty days from the time that you were given this information?

*Mr Wilcott:* Yes.

*Mr Goldsmith:* I realize this is testimony 15 years after the fact. However, if you received this information two or three months after the assassination, at a time that Oswald was already dead and had been dead for two or three months, what purpose would have been served by checking records that were only 30 days old? Do you follow the question?

*Mr Wilcott:* No.

*Mr Goldsmith:* Well, in other words, if you got the information three months after the assassination, Oswald had already been dead for three months, is that right?

*Mr Wilcott:* Yes.

*Mr Goldsmith:* Answer 'yes' or 'no' for the recorder.

*Mr Wilcott:* Yes.

*Mr Goldsmith:* You testified that your records were only kept for thirty days, is that correct?

*Mr Wilcott:* Yes.

*Mr Goldsmith:* Then, by checking your records, which only went back thirty days, isn't it true that you wouldn't have gotten any information concerning Oswald anyway because Oswald had already been dead for one or two months?

*Mr Wilcott:* That is true.

*Mr Goldsmith:* So, then, really, no purpose would have been served by checking those records?

*Mr Wilcott:* That is right.

*Mr Goldsmith:* And did you check any other records?

*Mr Wilcott:* No.

*Mr Preyer:* I understand this might be a good place for us to break and go and vote, so that we will take another recess for about ten minutes. I am sorry.

(Whereupon, a recess was taken while the members of the Committee went to the floor of the House for a vote.)

*Mr Preyer:* The Committee will resume.

*Mr Goldsmith:* Mr Wilcott, you indicated that after receiving this information concerning Oswald's cryptonym, you went back to check some files, is that correct?

*Mr Wilcott:* Not really files; it was my book.

*Mr Goldsmith:* Your book.

*Mr Wilcott:* I flipped through it.

*Mr Goldsmith:* What is the name of the book?

*Mr Wilcott:* It was my Request for Advance Book.

*Mr Goldsmith:* And for purposes of clarification, now, if Oswald was already dead at the time that you went to this book, why did you go back to examine the book?

*Mr Wilcott:* Well, I am sorry – if Oswald was what?

*Mr Goldsmith:* At the time you went to look at the book, Oswald was already dead is that correct?

*Mr Wilcott:* That is right.

*Mr Goldsmith:* Why did you go back to look at the book?

*Mr Wilcott:* Well, the payments that were made especially to substations like Oswald's was operated it was a sub-station of the [] station, and they had one in [] and they had one in [] and it may be six months or even a year after the initial allocation that the final accounting for those funds were submitted, and they would operate out of revolving funds or out of their own personal funds in many cases.

*Mr Goldsmith:* So, is your testimony then that even though Oswald was already dead at that time, the book might have contained a reference to either Oswald or the Oswald project and that that reference would have been to a period six months or even a year earlier, is that correct?

*Mr Wilcott:* That is correct.

*Mr Goldsmith:* Mr Wilcott, how long were these advance books retained?

*Mr Wilcott:* They were retained for approximately one year by the finance office, approximately one to two years, and were destroyed at the time of audit.

*Mr Goldsmith:* So that they would be routinely destroyed at the time of auditing?

*Mr Wilcott:* Yes.

*Mr Goldsmith:* Did you check any of the earlier books?

*Mr Wilcott:* No, I didn't, as far as the Oswald cryptonym was concerned; no, I didn't.

*Mr Goldsmith:* So basically, you checked only one of the advance books, is that correct?

*Mr Wilcott:* My current one that I had on my counter.

*Mr Goldsmith:* And when you testified earlier that you learned Oswald's cryptonym, by that do you mean that you learned both Oswald's personal cryptonym and his project cryptonym, or was it one of the two?

*Mr Wilcott:* Well, it was just a cryptonym, and it could refer to a person, or it could refer to something else and I would have no way of knowing what a cryptonym referred to.

*Mr Goldsmith:* So, when the officer told you — strike that. So, when the Case Officer made reference to a cryptonym you didn't know whether the cryptonym referred to Oswald specifically or to a project in which Oswald had been involved is that correct?

*Mr Wilcott:* Yes, sir.

*Mr Goldsmith:* Mr Wilcott, assuming that Oswald had been employed as an agent by the CIA, would there have been a reference to that fact in the CIA's cash disbursement file?

*Mr Wilcott:* No.

*Mr Goldsmith:* Why not?

*Mr Wilcott:* Anything they had there would have — sometimes they used as many as two or three different cryptonyms and they would have — it all depended on how far they wanted to isolate it from the original source, from the original source as to where the project was run.

*Mr Goldsmith:* But as a matter of routine, would the CIA cash disbursement files refer to the cryptonym of either the person or the project that is receiving funds?

*Mr Wilcott:* Yes, I am sure somewhere.

*Mr Goldsmith:* As a matter of routine, there would be that reference? Do you believe that there was such a reference to Oswald?

*Mr Wilcott:* Yes, I do, and I believe there was such a reference.

*Mr Goldsmith:* Well, if I understand you correctly, then, your answer now was somewhat different from what you testified earlier. And I will ask the question again, okay?

*Mr Wilcott:* Yes.

*Mr Goldsmith:* Assuming that Oswald was an agent for the CIA, would the agency's cash disbursement files have referred to either Oswald or to his cryptonym?

*Mr Wilcott:* Yes.

*Mr Goldsmith:* And you have had access to the cash disbursement files at [] Station?

*Mr Wilcott:* Yes, for a limited period.

*Mr Goldsmith:* Were you ever able to check those particular files?

*Mr Wilcott:* I was able to but I never did.

*Mr Goldsmith:* So, you never checked the cash disbursement files to see if any reference was made there to Oswald's cryptonym, is that correct?

*Mr Wilcott:* That is right. It was only my personal files – my internal files, prior to the end of the month.

*Mr Goldsmith:* I understand. How long were the [] cash disbursement files or records retained?

*Mr Wilcott:* The details approximately two years. We had accountings, or we had audits about every two years, and then the files that I kept the requests for advances, the details of the accountings that were done usually on a monthly basis by the [] Station Branches, would be destroyed and then they would be—and, in fact, I helped destroy them.

*Mr Goldsmith:* Are you saying, then, that the cash disbursement files as a matter of routine would be periodically destroyed? (sic)

*Mr Wilcott:* Yes.

*Mr Goldsmith:* Do you know whether CIA Headquarters would have had either copies or originals of the cash disbursement files?

*Mr Wilcott:* They would have summaries of some sort.

*Mr Goldsmith:* Would those summaries be destroyed as a matter of routine, to your knowledge?

*Mr Wilcott:* I really don't know.

*Mr Goldsmith:* Were you ever able to find any indication in any of the [] Station's records that Oswald was, in fact, a CIA agent?

*Mr Wilcott:* Well, I never really looked.

*Mr Goldsmith:* To your knowledge, would any records at CIA Headquarters document that Oswald was a CIA agent?

*Mr Wilcott:* I believe they would at one time. Whether they are there now or not is hard to say.

*Mr Goldsmith:* Do you have any personal knowledge that any records at CIA Headquarters were ever destroyed?

*Mr Wilcott:* No.

*Mr Goldsmith:* Do you have any knowledge of any record of the CIA at the [] Station ever being destroyed out of the ordinary course of business, not as a matter of routine?

*Mr Wilcott:* Yes.

*Mr Goldsmith:* To your personal knowledge, CIA records [] were destroyed?

*Mr Wilcott:* Destroyed or changed.

*Mr Goldsmith:* Could you give an example of that?

*Mr Wilcott:* Yes. Let us say, for instance, that there was a certain project going on, and the project was one that became known that this project was being carried out – and we call it 'flaps' – and the Case Officer in charge might get word that somebody from headquarters was coming to review the files to investigate the flap. Well, they would go through the files and take out anything that they thought was, say, indicative of how this flap occurred and change the files.

For instance, in accounting, when we had our audits, for instance, in most of the audits, he would call up somebody – let's say in China Branch – and say, 'I know you were having problems with this, would you like to look it over before the auditors come?', and they might look it over and retype the accounting for funds for their project and, you know, make changes that they might think were in their interest to do.

*Mr Goldsmith:* Did you ever actually Xerox records being destroyed or changed?

*Mr Wilcott:* Yes, I did.

*Mr Goldsmith:* And have you just described one of those instances to us?

*Mr Wilcott:* Yes.

*Mr Goldsmith:* Mr Wilcott after leaving the [] Station, was there any other time when you came across any information that indicated that Oswald was a CIA agent?

*Mr Wilcott:* In conversation.

*Mr Goldsmith:* Is the answer to that 'yes'?

*Mr Wilcott:* Yes.

*Mr Goldsmith:* When did that occur?

*Mr Wilcott:* From the time I left I talked at various times, especially at parties and things like that, on social occasions, with people at headquarters and with people at my station, and we would converse about it and I used to say things like, 'What do you think about Oswald being connected with the CIA?', and things like that.

*Mr Goldsmith:* What was their response?

*Mr Wilcott:* The response was, among quote a few people 'Oh, well, I am sure he was.'

*Mr Goldsmith:* What were these people's names?

*Mr Wilcott:* Well, George Breen, again, after we came back from [], for instance, [] was a person that I knew before I had gone to [] Station, and I met with him, and I had dinner at his house with his wife and my wife.

*Mr Goldsmith:* Just give us their names. Anyone else?

*Mr Wilcott:* Not that I can recall.

*Mr Goldsmith:* So, it is your testimony that, once you left the [] station, people, both at headquarters, in Langley, and at the Miami Station, made references to Oswald being an agent, is that correct?

*Mr Wilcott:* Yes, in a speculative manner.

*Mr Goldsmith:* How many people have you spoken to that said that Oswald was an agent of the CIA, to the best of your recollection?

Mr Schaap. Do you mean, how many people who were in the CIA or how many people in the general population?

*Mr Goldsmith:* How many people in the CIA?

*Mr Wilcott:* With any degree of certainty, other than just speculation, I would say, six or seven with some degree of certainty.

*Mr Goldsmith:* Do you have a personal opinion as to how or for what purpose the CIA might have handled any projects that involved Lee Harvey Oswald?

*Mr Wilcott:* I am sorry?

*Mr Goldsmith:* Do you have an opinion as to how the CIA might handled any projects involving Oswald and for what purpose they might have used Oswald?

*Mr Wilcott:* Yes, I have opinions.

*Mr Goldsmith:* What is that opinion?

*Mr Wilcott:* I believe that Oswald was a double agent, was sent over to the Soviet Union to do intelligence work, that the defection was phoney and it was set up and that I believe that Marina Oswald was an agent that had been recruited sometime before and was waiting there in Tokyo for Lee Harvey Oswald.

*Mr Goldsmith:* What is the basis for that opinion?

*Mr Wilcott:* The basis for that is discussions that I had with people at the [] Station. Those are discussions with people who gave the indication that there was every certainty that Oswald was an agent of CIA, run out of [] Station, and that he was freed from Russia there in the final courses in Russia and was trained by CIA people at Atsugi.

*Mr Goldsmith:* However, your testimony is that you spoke to only six people as an estimate who indicated that Oswald was a CIA agent – and when I say six people, I mean six CIA people, is that correct?

*Mr Wilcott:* There were more people than that that believed it, and six people with any degree of certainty that, you know, I felt from what they were saying that they either had some kind of

168

substantial knowledge, or they had talked to somebody who had some knowledge.

*Mr Goldsmith:* How many people from the CIA did you speak to who speculated that Oswald was an agent?

*Mr Wilcott:* Dozens, literally dozens.

*Mr Goldsmith:* Do you have any explanation for why none of these people have come forward with this story?

*Mr Wilcott:* Yes.

*Mr Goldsmith:* What is that explanation?

*Mr Wilcott:* I have been trying to talk about this thing and other things for the last ten years. I found it very, very difficult to talk about these things that I think ought to be talked about, very difficult. I talked to reporters from various papers, and I talked to people in other forms of meetings, and to me it is not surprising at all. I think, or I am certain, in my own mind, that, if these people were approached that some of these people.

*Mr Goldsmith:* Why has it been difficult?

*Mr Wilcott:* Well, it has been difficult because people don't want to get involved, and people were scared. I was scared until the Carter Administration. I was really scared to go to the Government and talk about any of these things.

*Mr Goldsmith:* Did you bring your allegation to the attention of the Warren Commission?

*Mr Wilcott:* No, I didn't.

*Mr Goldsmith:* And what is the reason for that?

*Mr Wilcott:* I really didn't think that the Warren Commission was out to really get at the facts, and I am not saying that they purposely did anything, because I don't know, and maybe they did or maybe they didn't, but certainly, they didn't impress me as really trying to scrutinize the evidence that there was. And the security that there is in the Government didn't strike me as the kind of security that would keep me from getting attacked in some way, if someone wanted to do it.

*Mr Goldsmith:* How did you know, in 1963, what type of security precautions the Warren Commission had for conducting its investigation?

*Mr Wilcott:* I don't understand.

*Mr Goldsmith:* You have indicated that you were not inclined to go to the Warren Commission because you were concerned about their security?

*Mr Wilcott:* Yes.

*Mr Goldsmith:* Did you have any basis for thinking that their security was poor?

*Mr Wilcott:* In 1963, I wasn't thinking that much about it.

*Mr Goldsmith:* So, it never really came forward for you to go to the Warren Commission, did it?

*Mr Wilcott:* Not until after I left the agency.

*Mr Goldsmith:* When was the first time that you alleged in public that Oswald was a CIA agent.

*Mr Wilcott:* In 1968.

*Mr Goldsmith:* So, you first came across this information in November of 1963, is that correct?

*Mr Wilcott:* That is correct.

*Mr Goldsmith:* And the first time you alleged in public this allegation was in 1968?

*Mr Wilcott:* That is correct.

*Mr Goldsmith:* Why did you wait five years?

*Mr Wilcott:* We thought every year, my wife and I and the friends that we had – we said, 'Well, this is one thing that they aren't going to keep a lid on.' And we thought every year it was going to be coming out, and especially I didn't think that since what I had heard was all hearsay that I would never have seen Oswald or anything like that – this is not the kind of thing that would be used for even something like the Warren Commission, and they would have to have something more substantial than that to go on, aside from the fact that I never would have done it in the CIA, being a very risky thing to do with the CIA.

*Mr Goldsmith:* Is it fair to say that the CIA is an operation that runs itself on a 'need–to–know' basis? Would you tell the Committee what the 'need-to-know' principle is?

*Mr Wilcott:* It is based on the principle that only those persons who are involved in a project or involved in operation – and even things that would not seem to be at all in any way secret – only those people should know about it and nobody else should know about it, and that was a 'need-to-know' basis.

*Mr Goldsmith:* If the agency, in fact, was run on the 'need-to-know' basis, how would you account for so many people supposedly knowing that Oswald was an agent?

*Mr Wilcott:* The 'need-to-know' principle was not all that we followed, and just about every one of the big projects that the agency was involved in, information leaked out, and we especially within the CIA knew about it, and someone would go to a party and have a little bit too much to drink and start saying things that they really shouldn't be saying to keep in mind what the 'need-to-know' principle was.

*Mr Goldsmith:* Why would anyone have shared this particular information with you?

*Mr Wilcott:* Especially after Kennedy's assassination, there was a great deal of very, very serious discontent with CIA, and the morale at the station had dropped considerably, and we heard some very, very bitter denunciations of CIA and the projects that they were undertaking.

*Mr Goldsmith:* I am not sure that that is responsive. Why would anyone share the information that Oswald was an agent with you, Mr Wilcott?

*Mr Wilcott:* I don't know how to answer that.

*Mr Schaap:* Excuse me.

(The witness conferred with his Counsel.)

*Mr Goldsmith:* Do you have anything to add in response to that question?

*Mr Wilcott:* Yes, I was on security duty, and on security duty, agents were coming in and out of the station, and I pulled a lot of security duty, three and four nights right in a row, and pulled as much as 24 hours on weekends, and an agent would come back from meeting with somebody and he would be waiting for his wife to pick him up or would be waiting for a call from one of the indigenous agents that he was running and a lot of times conversations would be talked.

And I think that is why I probably heard a lot more things than other people did, for instance, than my wife did, because of that situation.

*Mr Goldsmith:* Mr Wilcott, when did you leave the agency?

*Mr Wilcott:* I left the agency in April of 1966 for the Miami Station.

*Mr Goldsmith:* I am sorry, I didn't hear.

*Mr Wilcott:* – to the Miami Station.

*Mr Goldsmith:* And were you dismissed by the agency or did you resign?

*Mr Wilcott:* I resigned.

*Mr Goldsmith:* To your knowledge, did the CIA ever conduct an investigation into your allegation that Oswald was an agent?

*Mr Wilcott:* Not that I know of.

*Mr Goldsmith:* Did you ever bring your allegation to the attention of anyone in the CIA?

*Mr Wilcott:* No.

*Mr Goldsmith:* Can you give the Committee the names of any persons who might corroborate your allegation?

*Mr Wilcott:* All of the people that we mentioned in the case.

*Mr Goldsmith:* And finally, as I said at the beginning is it fair to say that you are here voluntarily today?

*Mr Wilcott:* Yes, it is.

*Mr Goldsmith:* And you testified without any reservation?

*Mr Wilcott:* Yes.

*Mr Goldsmith:* And your testimony has been truthful and candid?

*Mr Wilcott:* Yes.

*Mr Goldsmith:* I have nothing further, Mr Chairman.

*Mr Preyer:* I will ask a few questions. Why this information would come out to a CIA station [] rather than some other part of the world is, I assume, because Oswald was trained in Japan, according to your belief. He was in the military service over there, and so you feel he was a double agent who was trained while he was in the military by the CIA, and you mentioned he was given a Russian course. And do you know for a fact that he was given Russian courses?

*Mr Wilcott:* No; I know for a fact, or I know from hearsay, and I believe it to be true from the circumstances how this conversation came up and so on.

*Mr Preyer:* Well, that is the other question that I want to be very sure on. I think you are making some important allegations here, and you have been very helpful in giving some witnesses' names through which we might be able to corroborate it, but I think it is very important that we know clearly how much of this was cocktail party talk and how much was shop talk and how much was speculation and rumor and how much was hard fact.

You mentioned the day after the assassination you talked to someone at the station about it. Did he say to you, 'I think Oswald was a CIA agent,' or did that first person say to you that he was a CIA agent? Can you recall whether the tone of it was rumor or shop talk or was the tone of it that 'this is true'?

*Mr Wilcott:* Well, sir, the day after the assassination I don't think that there was any of that kind of talk. The day after, perhaps, two or three weeks after, the kind of talk was that CIA was somehow connected.

*Mr Preyer:* That was shop talk, speculation, I gather; people were saying that the CIA is somehow connected with it.

*Mr Wilcott:* Well, I believed it to be a little more than speculation, that the source at least of this kind of talk was, I believe, to be something more serious than speculation.

*Mr Preyer:* It was your conclusion from that talk that some of these people might have knowledge that he was a CIA agent rather than that they were speculating about it?

*Mr Wilcott:* Yes, sir.

*Mr Preyer:* And you did mention the case officer who came in and told you that the money he had drawn out a few weeks earlier was drawn out for Oswald?

*Mr Wilcott:* Yes, sir.

*Mr Preyer:* He stated that as a fact and not that he believed it was drawn out for Oswald or it could have been or something like that?

*Mr Wilcott:* It was stated as a fact — Oswald or the Oswald project.

*Mr Preyer:* How many people were at the station in [] approximately?

*Mr Wilcott:* I believe our full strength was around [] and we never actually had that many, I don't think. It was about [] I think, was our actual roster was.

*Mr Preyer:* And Miami, was that comparable in size?

*Mr Wilcott:* No, sir; that was a smaller station.

*Mr Preyer:* So that in [], you indicated, six or seven people talked to you and were, as I understood it, rather definite about the Oswald connection?

*Mr Wilcott:* Yes, sir.

*Mr Preyer:* And dozens of others talked to you in a general, speculative manner?

*Mr Wilcott:* Yes, sir.

*Mr Preyer:* Why did you resign from the CIA?

*Mr Wilcott:* My wife and I came to believe that what the CIA was doing couldn't be reconciled to basic principles of democracy or basic principles of humanism.

*Mr Preyer:* It had no relation to your performance?

*Mr Wilcott:* No, sir; I think I had good performance reviews right up to the time that I left.

*Mr Preyer:* I believe you have written an article about this, an unpublished article.

*Mr Wilcott:* Yes.

*Mr Preyer:* And have you made that available to us?

*Mr Wilcott:* Yes, I have.

*Mr Preyer:* Thank you. I have no further questions.

*Mr Sawyer:* Do you distinguish between an agent and a paid informant or do you use those terms interchangeably?

*Mr Wilcott:* Well, sir, I think of an agent as an actual employee of the Agency; we called them indigenous agents [] who were agents that were on a regular salary by the case officer who was running an agent, and then there were a lot of one-time informers or maybe one or two or three-time informers that were paid like maybe $50 or so to attend a meeting of a political party or something of that nature.

*Mr Sawyer:* When you refer to Oswald as an agent, you are referring to the extent you have – as an agent as opposed to a paid informer, in effect?

*Mr Wilcott:* Yes; it is my belief that he was a regular agent and this was a regular project of the Agency to send Oswald to the Soviet Union.

*Mr Sawyer:* Now, did the [] station have any jurisdiction over the Russian operation or within the Soviet Union?

*Mr Wilcott:* Yes, sir. That was the SR branch which had all of the projects having anything to do with the Soviet Union.

*Mr Sawyer:* It went through the [] station?

*Mr Wilcott:* Well, that was just those that were assigned to [] and those projects that were assigned to []. Every station was divided up – at least every class station was divided up into areas, where we would have a China branch, Korea branch and [] branch and SR branch and SR satellite.

*Mr Sawyer:* I noticed in some of the information we are provided you say that following your leaving the CIA in 1967 or thereabouts, for a period of some three years or so, you were harassed by the CIA and the FBI and sabotaged, as I recollect it.

*Mr Wilcott:* Yes, sir; I believe that happened.

*Mr Sawyer:* Could you tell us what those things consisted of?

*Mr Wilcott:* I think the most significant thing that can be actually substantiated is the circumstances surrounding my employment with the community renewal program in Utica, and I was the finance analyst for the community renewal program in Utica. One day Frank O'Connor, the director of the program, called me into his office and he said that he had had a discussion with the public safety commissioner and that the public safety commissioner told him that my phone was bugged, that my house was under surveillance and that a Federal indictment was coming down on me at any time, that he had talked to the mayor and the mayor decided not to fire me but asked me to sign a resignation form which he would date the day previous to the date that the Federal indictment came down.

*Mr Sawyer:* Who told this to the community development people?

*Mr Wilcott:* My boss, Frank O'Connor said that this was told him by the public safety commissioner and that the FBI had told the public safety commissioner.

*Mr Sawyer:* Who is the public safety commissioner?

*Mr Wilcott:* I don't remember his name now offhand.

*Mr Sawyer:* Was he in Utica?

*Mr Wilcott:* Yes. The mayor, Mr Sawyer, was Dominic Casaro. He was the mayor at that time.

*Mr Sawyer:* Were there any other instances of harassment?

*Mr Wilcott:* Yes, there were several other incidents that I believe could possibly be somehow connected with CIA.

*Mr Sawyer:* What were they?

*Mr Wilcott:* Well, they were such incidents as the FBI agent that was working with a group – and this was an established fact that this person was an FBI agent and that he was working with the group that I was working with an anti-war group and, to my mind, there is a very great likelihood that this person was there to neutralize me, as the CIA term went.

*Mr Sawyer:* What did he do – anything?

*Mr Wilcott:* Well, I would get calls and they would say 'We know all about you,' shooting a machine gun into the phone, and hang up, and I would get notes written in snow or my windshield and I had slips of paper left under my windshield and this sort of thing.

*Mr Sawyer:* What would they say?

*Mr Wilcott:* They were extremely vulgar and I don't think that I should give the full context of them.

*Mr Sawyer:* What was the gist of them?

*Mr Wilcott:* Well, it was 'We all know all about you' and signed 'The Minutemen' or some very vulgar remarks and 'We know all about you and signed 'Minutemen.''

*Mr Sawyer:* What was the name of the FBI agent who you think infiltrated this antiwar group?

*Mr Wilcott:* Gordon Finch.

*Mr Sawyer:* He was in Utica also?

*Mr Wilcott:* Yes.

*Mr Sawyer:* What were some other instances?

*Mr Wilcott:* Well, my tires were slashed and damage done to my car and I believe sugar poured in the gas tank, and whether this was actually CIA or not I have no way of knowing, and it could also have been just for harassment as a result of anti-war activities but I think there is also a possibility that it could have been attempts to intimidate me into talking about the CIA.

*Mr Sawyer:* Are there any others that you can specifically identify as coming from the CIA or FBI?

*Mr Wilcott:* I don't confirm any of them except with the community renewal program as coming from there and I am suspicious that many of the other things that happened may have had as its source the CIA.

*Mr Sawyer:* Well, what were your anti–war activities that you refer to?

*Mr Wilcott:* We had – in Utica there was a group called the Vietnam Educational Council, which was informed people, formed to inform people as to what was going on in Vietnam, and we didn't feel that there was coverage enough in the media as to what was going on, and the purpose of the Vietnam Educational Council was to inform people as to what was going on. I was on the executive committee along with doctors and lawyers and some of the most respected people in the community.

*Mr Sawyer:* How long were you associated with that?

*Mr Wilcott:* Approximately two years, sir.

*Mr Sawyer:* Thank you. That is all I have.

*Mr Dodd:* I have just a couple of questions. First of all I apologize for having to run in and out during your testimony and some of this you may have already covered; and, if you have, then I will not proceed with it. But I was intrigued – and it may have been in the transcription but you were in [] as financial disbursement officer–is it your testimony that you were told by a case officer that you had disbursed funds for an Oswald project?

*Mr Wilcott:* Yes, sir.

*Mr Dodd:* Am I to believe by that that you were not aware at the time you made the disbursement that it was, in fact, an Oswald project?

*Mr Wilcott:* That is correct, sir.

*Mr Dodd:* It would have been a cryptonym and he was telling you, you had, in fact, made a disbursement?

*Mr Wilcott:* Yes sir.

*Mr Dodd:* And this would have been, now, shortly after the assassination?

*Mr Wilcott:* Yes, sir.

*Mr Dodd:* Talking about hours afterwards or a day afterwards?

*Mr Wilcott:* It was at least a matter of weeks and perhaps as much as three months after.

*Mr Dodd:* After the assassination actually occurred?

*Mr Wilcott:* Yes.

*Mr Dodd:* When you were told all of this?

*Mr Wilcott:* Yes.

*Mr Dodd:* And it includes the information that Oswald was an agent?

*Mr Wilcott:* Yes, sir.

*Mr Dodd:* Was he described as an agent to you or was he described as an operative or a paid informant?

*Mr Wilcott:* No, sir; he was described to me as an agent and I was led to believe, from the conversations, that he was an agent.

*Mr Dodd:* As a point of information, are people who work within the Agency fairly careful in their language in describing what the category of certain people are who work for the Agency?

*Mr Wilcott:* Generally so, I would say, at that time.

*Mr Dodd:* And it is your clear recollection that he was described as an agent?

*Mr Wilcott:* Yes, sir.

*Mr Dodd:* And the information given you occurred sometime three months after the actual assassination. That would have put it into 1964?

*Mr Wilcott:* Yes, sir, early 1964.

*Mr Dodd:* When did you leave to go back?

*Mr Wilcott:* June of 1964.

*Mr Wilcott:* So it was sometime between February and June of 1964?

*Mr Wilcott:* Or perhaps January.

*Mr Dodd:* In 1964, of course, the Vietnam war was going on and Lyndon Johnson was now president. And when did you begin to develop attitudes of dissatisfaction with the Agency and its reaction and attitudes toward what you described as undemocratic principles and a lack of humanism?

*Mr Wilcott:* Well, actually even prior to the Kennedy assassination, my wife and I both became disturbed about the stories that we kept hearing about things, control of newspapers and so on.

*Mr Dodd:* How long had you been married by the way?

*Mr Wilcott:* We were married in 1954, sir.

*Mr Dodd:* And you and your wife both went to work for the CIA about the same time?

*Mr Wilcott:* Yes, sir.

*Mr Dodd:* In 1957?

*Mr Wilcott:* Yes, sir.

*Mr Dodd:* Am I to presume that you told your wife of the conversation you had with this case officer at the time it occurred?

*Mr Wilcott:* Yes, sir.

*Mr Dodd:* And she was aware of it from 1964 up until 1968 –

*Mr Wilcott:* Yes, sir.

*Mr Dodd:* – when you decided to release that information?

*Mr Wilcott:* Yes, sir.

*Mr Dodd:* And your dissatisfaction with the Agency and with the course of American government preceded the actual assassination of President Kennedy?

*Mr Wilcott:* Well, with the Agency, yes, sir.

*Mr Dodd:* And this was a view shared by you and your wife –

*Mr Wilcott:* Yes, sir.

*Mr Dodd:* – at that time?

*Mr Wilcott:* Yes.

*Mr Dodd:* Did anyone else at the Agency know of your views at the Agency and did you communicate with other people about your dissatisfaction?

*Mr Wilcott:* Yes.

*Mr Dodd:* Would you care to tell us any of the names of people whom you communicated with?

*Mr Wilcott:* Particularly George Breen and [] to a lesser extent.

*Mr Dodd:* I am a little confused, I suppose, Mr Wilcott, did you vote for President Kennedy?

*Mr Wilcott:* Yes, sir, I did.

*Mr Dodd:* You liked him?

*Mr Wilcott:* Very much.

*Mr Dodd:* I am just a little confused, I guess, over your reaction. Here, by your own testimony, you were supportive of the President, and certainly the most significant tragedy, I think, probably in the last 15 years or 20 years was the assassination of President Kennedy, and you are told by some who worked for the Agency that Oswald was a CIA agent and you already were dissatisfied with the actions of the Agency and you are told this in 1964 and yet it takes four years, or two years, after you had left the Agency, recognizing the tremendous import and significance of that, and I am terribly confused as to why you decided to keep that information to yourself and to your wife.

*Mr Wilcott:* I was afraid quite frankly.

*Mr Dodd:* You may have covered this as well, Mr Chairman, and, if you have, I will drop the question. But you apparently indicated that you feel there was a direct connection between the Bay of Pigs operation and the assassination of the President. Did you cover this ground? Did you want to do this or intend to proceed with that line of questioning?

*Mr Goldsmith:* I did not intend to get into that area.

*Mr Dodd:* Just one second, then. Mr Wilcott, maybe we can expedite this somewhat by asking you this: Do you have any first-hand knowledge or information as to a link between the failed Bay of Pigs operation and the assassination of John Fitzgerald Kennedy?

*Mr Wilcott:* No, sir.

*Mr Dodd:* I have no further questions.

*Mr Cornwell:* In the conversations which you have described occurring within a period of one, two or three months after the assassination with other CIA employees and officers, did they suggest in those conversations to you that their employment, the CIA's employment, of Oswald had any relation to the assassination or only that it related to the events you have already described – namely, the training of him in Atsugi in the Russian language and the sending of him to Russia and using of him as a double agent and that sort of thing?

*Mr Wilcott:* I am sorry, sir; I lost the thread of your question.

*Mr Cornwell:* In the conversations you had with other CIA employees, the six or seven persons who purported to have good information about the use of Oswald as an agent, did any of those people say anything to you which suggested that the CIA had some role in the assassination of President Kennedy?

*Mr Wilcott:* Yes, sir.

*Mr Cornwell:* What did they say along those lines?

*Mr Wilcott:* Along those lines they said things like, well, that Oswald couldn't have pulled the trigger, that only CIA could have set up such an elaborate project and there was nobody with the kind of knowledge or information that could have done this, and this was more in the speculative realm.

As far as that they actually said, they said they were having trouble with Oswald and that there was dissatisfaction with Oswald after he came back from the Soviet Union, and they would say things like 'Well, you know this was the way to get rid of him – to get him involved in this assassination thing and put the blame on Cuba as a pretext for another invasion or another attack against Cuba.'

That was the kind of things that people said. How much exact knowledge they had it is impossible for me to say. I believe it was more in a speculative realm.

*Mr Cornwell:* At several points in your testimony you have stated there were six or seven persons, and on each occasion you raised the extent of their knowledge as 'knew' or 'believed'. Apart from the one officer who said to you that you had paid monies with respect to Oswald's cryptonym, what were the other six or seven persons' purported connection with Oswald and the Agency's relation to him?

*Mr Wilcott:* They never revealed that to me, sir, as far as their relations with Oswald.

*Mr Cornwell:* Do you have any knowledge, based upon your tenure [] as to who would have trained Oswald in the Russian language if that occurred?

*Mr Wilcott:* No, sir.

*Mr Preyer:* Let me interrupt. I am afraid we are going to have to leave to make this vote right now. I will be back in about 10 minutes.

*(Whereupon, a brief recess was taken.)*

*Mr Preyer:* The committee will resume. Did you have further questions?

*Mr Cornwell:* The cryptonym – did you write it down at any point?

*Mr Wilcott:* I may have, sir, and I can't remember exactly for sure. It seems to me that I recall jotting it on a little pad, that I had at my gate, and I did that with cryptonyms from time to time for something – we would want to check back into their accounting for something.

*Mr Cornwell:* Is there any chance that that record still exists?

*Mr Wilcott:* I doubt it, sir.

*Mr Cornwell:* Your best memory is, you wrote it on a note pad, is that correct?

*Mr Wilcott:* That is true, sir.

*Mr Cornweil:* What routinely was done with such note pads?

*Mr Wilcott:* Usually I threw them away at the end of the day or once in a while I would put it in – I had a little folder where I kept personal things and it is possible I could have put it in there, but certainly it would have been destroyed when I left.

*Mr Cornwell:* Do you recall whether or not you used that in the process of looking through the 30-day book you described?

*Mr Wilcott:* I can't remember, sir.

*Mr Cornwell:* It was not normally part of your duties or the scope of the knowledge that you routinely acquired on your job, as I understand it, for you to know what the cryptonyms meant; is that correct?

*Mr Wilcott:* That is correct, sir.

*Mr Cornwell:* However, I take it from the fact that, as you describe it, it wasn't always applied, that occasionally you did learn something about the identities of the persons or projects that the cryptonyms referred to; is that correct?

*Mr Wilcott:* That is true.

*Mr Cornwell:* When this cryptonym was given to you by the officer, did any part of it ring any familiar note with you? Did you recognize any part of it, the first two letters or the last portions of it, as referring to any geographic area or any type of activity or anything like that?

*Mr Wilcott:* No, sir, not that I can recall.

*Mr Cornwell:* Had you ever run into any similar cryptonym?

*Mr Wilcott:* Yes, sir.

*Mr Cornwell:* In other words, that is, the first two letters or the last ones would have been the same as this?

*Mr Wilcott:* Yes, sir; it was a cryptonym that I was familiar with, that it must have been at least two or three occasions that I had remembered it and it did ring a bell, yes.

*Mr Cornwell:* Do you remember anything about it?

*Mr Wilcott:* Not at this time. I can't remember what it was.

*Mr Cornwell:* All you can recall is that, when you heard it, that was not the first occasion on which you had seen it or heard it?

*Mr Wilcott:* That is correct, sir.

*Mr Cornwell:* Why did you leave the CIA?

*Mr Wilcott:* My wife and I both left the CIA because we became convinced that what CIA was doing couldn't be reconciled to basic principles of democracy or basic principles of humanism.

*Mr Cornwell:* Is that the only reason?

*Mr Wilcott:* The principal reason —

*Mr Cornwell:* Let me rephrase it. Was there any dispute between you and the Agency?

*Mr Wilcott:* No, sir.

*Mr Cornwell:* Did they request that you leave?

*Mr Wilcott:* No, sir, they did not.

*Mr Cornwell:* Did any event cause any disagreement between you and the Agency?

*Mr Wilcott:* No, sir.

*Mr Cornwell:* Had you done anything or said anything engaged in any activity which became of concern to them?

*Mr Wilcott:* No, sir. I had been involved at one point with a group civil rights group, and they had investigated it and said that there was no wrong doing on my part as far a this association with the civil rights group.

*Mr Cornwell:* What group was it?

*Mr Wilcott:* This was SNIC, the Student Nonviolent Coordinating Committee before they became a black power group.

*Mr Cornwell:* What, if any, investigation did the Agency do with respect to that?

*Mr Wilcott:* They called me up to chief of security, the agent security, and they interviewed me on the association that I had had with the group, and then they gave me a polygraph – in fact, two polygraphs – concerning my association with the group of people that I met with the group.

*Mr Cornwell:* Did they tell you whether or not you passed the polygraphs?

*Mr Wilcott:* Yes, they did. They told me that I had passed both of those.

*Mr Cornwell:* It is your testimony, as I understand it, the first time that you spoke about the Oswald agency matter outside of the CIA was after you left the CIA; is that correct?

*Mr Wilcott:* That is true, sir.

*Mr Cornwell:* On that occasion to whom did you speak?

*Mr Wilcott:* When I first started speaking, both my wife and I discussed it and we felt that we should be speaking out about not only Oswald but some other things. They way that we did this was to contact as many people all at once and we figured this would be our best protection, that the more people that knew about it, the more protection it would be for us.

*Mr Cornwell:* What type of people were they?

*Mr Wilcott:* Most of the people were involved in the civil rights movement or in the anti-war movement in 1968.

*Mr Cornwell:* How many of them were newspaper or magazine reporters or involved in at least the news business ?

*Mr Wilcott:* None initially. The first contact I had with any reporter or any newspaper people or any media people was with Glad Day Press.

*Mr Cornwell:* What year was that?

*Mr Wilcott:* That was late '68 or perhaps early 1969.

*Mr Cornwell:* You had signed a secrecy oath while you were employed with the Agency?

*Mr Wilcott:* Yes, sir.

*Mr Cornwell:* Did you – at the time you made the decision to discuss outside of the Agency this matter, did you focus on the secrecy oath problem?

*Mr Schaap:* Mr Chairman, I would like to interpose, I guess, an objection, although I would like to make it more in the nature of a request, that I have some problems in terms of advising my client with respect to possibly self-incrimination, that I would not advise him to go into questions of his specific knowledge of the oath and the application to what he did other than the fact that he has told you, which is a fact, that he did sign the oath; but to go into his mental processes as to whether he felt what he was then doing related to the oath in a particular way, I would request that those questions not be asked on the grounds that they may violate either his First Amendment rights or his Fifth Amendment rights, if that would be all right. If you have something–

*Mr Cornwell:* Perhaps I can rephrase the question and get more pointedly what I need without running into the problem that you see.

Did you contact any CIA officer or employee with respect to the secrecy oath and discuss with them whether or not you should be permitted to discuss these matters outside of the Agency?

*Mr Wilcott:* No, sir, I did not.

*Mr Cornwell:* To your knowledge, when was the first point in time at which your extra-agency discussions on this subject matter came to the attention of the Agency, if ever?

*Mr Wilcott:* I have no idea, sir.

*Mr Cornwell:* At what point in time did your discussions outside of the Agency first become a matter of publication in a newspaper or magazine or on television?

*Mr Wilcott:* In December of 1975, in the little magazine called The Pelican at the University of California, and an interview was conducted by a reporter from that magazine.

*Mr Cornwell:* And would that – at least in part – would that interview have contained your resume of the Oswald agency matter, your statements about that matter?

*Mr Wilcott:* Very briefly it did, yes, in what was finally published.

*Mr Cornwell:* That is, that subject matter, your statement on the Oswald agency matter, be printed or otherwise publicized in a news publication, radio or TV or anything like that on any other occasion?

*Mr Wilcott:* Yes, sir.

*Mr Cornwell:* When was that?

*Mr Wilcott:* On two other occasions, I was on KPOO Radio in San Francisco and I discussed in detail, in quite a bit of detail, the speculations and also the incident of the case officer contacting me at the window.

*Mr Cornwell:* What year was that?

*Mr Wilcott:* That was November of 1977.

*Mr Cornwell:* Last November?

*Mr Wilcott:* Yes.

*Mr Cornwell:* On any other occasion?

*Mr Wilcott:* Yes sir; at Oakland Technical High School, at the invitation of–the social department asked me if I wanted to speak and I said yes, and so I spoke to two classes at Oakland Technical High School. This was about, I believe – about October of 1975.

*Mr Cornwell:* On any other occasions?

*Mr Wilcott:* Not publicly. I spoke to groups in their homes and I spoke to groups in the Peace and Freedom Party and I was with the Peace and Freedom Party for several years.

*Mr Cornwell:* But your testimony or your statements on the subject hadn't been made a matter of publicity on any other occasion?

*Mr Wilcott:* Not to my knowledge.

*Mr Cornwell:* Has any representative of the Agency or anyone who you believed might be a representative of the Agency ever come to you and discussed these matters?

*Mr Wilcott:* Not directly, no, sir.

*Mr Cornwell:* I have no further questions.

*Mr Preyer:* Under our committee rules, Mr Wilcott, a witness is entitled, at the conclusion of the questioning, to make a five minute statement if he wishes or to give a fuller explanation of any of his answers; so that at this time we make that five minutes available to you if you care to elaborate or say anything further.

*Mr Wilcott:* I don't really have anything and maybe I would just like to say I think it is time we got this thing cleared up; and I think for the good of the country and for good of the people I think it is really time that all of the facts were brought out and the people really get the facts.

*Mr Preyer:* Thank you. We appreciate that, and if at any time you think of any further way in which your testimony can be corroborated or the name of any other CIA man or any record or anything of that sort that might be available we hope you will get in touch with us and let us know about it.

*Mr Wilcott:* Surely, sir.

*Mr Preyer:* Thank you very much and we appreciate you and Mr Schaap being with us today, and the hearing will stand in recess.

*(Whereupon, at 12:55 p.m. the subcommittee recessed)*

## Aristocrats, Agencies and Espionage

Another mysterious player in the Oswald tale is one George de Mohrenschildt. Born in Mozyr in Tsarist Russia on 17 April 1911, barely six years before the Russian revolution. de Mohrenschildt was a petroleum geologist and professor who befriended Lee Harvey Oswald in Dallas during the summer of 1962 and maintained that friendship until Oswald's death, two days after Oswald's alleged assassination of President John F Kennedy. de Mohrenschildt was acquainted with the Bush family; George H W Bush had roomed with de Mohrenschildt's nephew, Edward G Hooker, at Phillips Academy in Andover, Massachusetts. He was also acquainted with the Bouvier family, including Jacqueline Bouvier Kennedy, JFK's wife, when she was still a child. His testimony before the Warren Commission investigating the assassination was one of the longest of any witness.

De Mohrenschildt emigrated to the United States in May 1938. Upon his arrival, British intelligence reportedly told the United States government that they suspected he was working for German intelligence. By some accounts, he was under FBI surveillance for a time. de Mohrenschildt was hired by the Shumaker company in New York City, which also employed a man named Pierre Fraiss who had connections with French intelligence. According to de Mohrenschildt, he and Fraiss, among their other duties, gathered information about people involved in 'pro-German' activities, such as those bidding for US oil leases on behalf of Germany before the US became involved in the Second World War. de Mohrenschildt testified that the purpose of their data-collection was to help the French out-bid the Germans.

De Mohrenschildt spent the summer of 1938 with his older brother Dimitri von Mohrenschildt on Long Island, New York.

Dimitri was a staunch anti-Communist and member of the OSS and one of the founders of the CIA's Radio Free Europe and Amcomlib (aka, Radio Liberty) stations. His contacts included top officials of the CIA. Dimitri died at the age of 100 in 2002.

While in New York, de Mohrenschildt became acquainted with the Bouvier family, including the young Jackie, the future wife of Senator John F Kennedy. Jackie grew up calling de Mohrenschildt 'Uncle George' and would sit on his knee. George would also became a close friend of Jackie's aunt Edith Bouvier Beale.

De Mohrenschildt dabbled in the insurance business from 1939 to 1941, but failed to pass his broker's examination. In 1941, he became associated with Film Facts in New York, a production company owned by his cousin Baron Maydell who was said to have pro-Nazi sympathies. de Mohrenschildt denied any Nazi sympathies of his own, claiming he helped raise money for the Polish resistance. de Mohrenschildt made a documentary film about resistance fighters in Poland. However, when the United States entered the Second World War, his application to join the Office of Strategic Services (OSS) was rejected. According to a memo by former CIA director Richard Helms, de Mohrenschildt 'was alleged to be a Nazi espionage agent.'

De Mohrenschildt received a master's degree in petroleum geology from the University of Texas in 1945.

Following the end of Second World War, de Mohrenschildt moved to Venezuela where he worked for Pantepec Oil, a company owned by the family of William F Buckley (In 1951 Buckley was recruited into the CIA; Although Buckley served the agency for only two years, he spent one year in Mexico City working as a political action specialist in the elite Special Activities Division for E Howard Hunt. These two officers remained lifelong friends.)

De Mohrenschildt became a US citizen in 1949. Three years later, de Mohrenschildt settled in Dallas, Texas and took a job with oilman Clint Murchison as a petroleum geologist.

Described as sophisticated and articulate, de Mohrenschildt

became a respected member of the Russian émigré community in Dallas. George Kitchel, one of de Mohrenschildt's long time 'oil' friends, told the FBI that de Mohrenschildt counted among his good friends Texan oil barons Clint Murchison, Madeleine Brown (an advertising executive who claimed to have had an on going affair and a son with President Lyndon B Johnson, Brown said that she attended a party at Murchison's Dallas home on 21 November 1963, the evening prior to the assassination. In attendance, were Lyndon Johnson as well as other famous, wealthy, and powerful individuals including, FBI Director J Edgar Hoover, Richard Nixon, H L Hunt and John McCloy. Madeleine Brown said that Johnson met privately with several of the men after which he told her: 'After tomorrow, those goddamn Kennedys will never embarrass me again. That's no threat. That's a promise.'), HL Hunt, John Mecom, and Sid Richardson.

De Mohrenschildt also joined the right-wing Texas Crusade for Freedom whose members included Dallas Mayor Earle Cabell (Cabell was the brother of Charles Cabell, Deputy Director of Central Intelligence until he was forced to resign by President Kennedy in the wake of the Bay of Pigs invasion), Harold Byrd (owner of the Texas School Book Depository) and Ted Dealey (the son of George Bannerman Dealey the long-time publisher of The *Dallas Morning News* and the man who had crusaded for the redevelopment of a particularly blighted area near downtown Dallas. When the redevelopment, involving a large square located at the intersection of three major avenues, was completed, it was named Dealey Plaza in his honor. Ted Dealey approved the publication of a full page, paid advertisement critical of President Kennedy that ran in The *Dallas Morning News* the morning of 22 November 1963, the day President Kennedy was assassinated.)

Sometime in 1957 de Mohrenschildt went to Yugoslavia to conduct a geological field survey for the US State Department sponsored International Cooperation Administration. While in Yugoslavia, he was accused by the authorities there of making drawings of military fortifications. Following his return to the United States, de Mohrenschildt was debriefed by the CIA, both in Washington and in Dallas. It should be noted that during this time, thousands of American citizens were routinely debriefed by the CIA after travelling to countries such as Yugoslavia, as de Mohrenschildt had done.

De Mohrenschildt married his fourth wife, Jeanne, in 1959. From late 1960 and into 1961, he and his wife toured Central America and the Caribbean, insisting that the trip was merely for pleasure. However, de Mohrenschildt submitted a written report of his trip to the US State Department, and a photograph shows de Mohrenschildt meeting with the American ambassador to Costa Rica.

Lee Harvey Oswald and his wife Marina were introduced to de Mohrenschildt in the summer of 1962 in Fort Worth, Texas. de Mohrenschildt had heard of the Oswalds from one of the Russian speaking group of émigrés in the Dallas-Fort Worth area. George and Jeanne befriended them, tried to help them as best they could, and introduced them to the Russian community in Dallas. In his Warren Commission testimony in 1964, de Mohrenschildt stated that he believed he had discussed Oswald with J Walton Moore, who de Mohrenschildt described as 'a Government man, either FBI or Central Intelligence'. (According to a CIA classified document, obtained by HSCA, Moore was an agent of the CIA's Domestic Contacts Division in Dallas.) de Mohrenschildt asserted that shortly after meeting Oswald, he had asked Moore and Fort Worth attorney Max E Clark about Oswald to reassure himself that it was 'safe' for the de Mohrenschildts to assist Oswald. de Mohrenschildt testified to the Warren Commission that he told that Oswald 'seems to be OK' and that 'he is a harmless lunatic'. However, de Mohrenschildt was not exactly sure who it was who told him this. When interviewed in 1978 by the HSCA, Moore denied that de Mohrenschildt had asked for his permission to contact Oswald.

In October of 1962, de Mohrenschildt told Lee Oswald, who had just lost his job in Fort Worth, that he would have a better chance of finding work in Dallas. Oswald was then hired by the Dallas photographic firm of Jaggars-Chiles-Stovall. George de Mohrenschildt's wife and daughter would later say that it was George de Mohrenschildt who secured the job for Oswald at Jaggars-Chiles-Stovall.

On 14 April 1963, George de Mohrenschildt and his wife visited the Oswalds' apartment. As Oswald's wife Marina was showing Jeanne around the apartment, they discovered Oswald's rifle leaning against the wall inside a closet. Jeanne told George that Oswald had a rifle, and George joked to Oswald, 'Were you the one who took a pot-shot at General Walker?' In reaction to his question, George de Mohrenschildt said that Oswald 'smiled at that.' The Warren Commission concluded that on 10 April 1963, Oswald had attempted to kill Walker. (General Edwin Walker was a right wing activist who George de Mohrenschildt said he 'knew that Oswald disliked').

In March 1963, de Mohrenschildt received a Haitian government contract for $285,000 to set up an industrial enterprise with other investors, which included surveying oil and geological resources on the island. In May, he met in Washington DC with CIA and Army intelligence contacts to further his Haitian connections. de Mohrenschildt moved to Haiti in June. He never saw Oswald again. de Mohrenschildt testified before the Warren Commission in April 1964.

De Mohrenschildt returned to Dallas in 1967. New Orleans District Attorney Jim Garrison interviewed George and Jeanne de Mohrenschildt as part of Garrison's prosecution of Clay Shaw. Garrison said that both de Mohrenschildts insisted that Oswald had been the scapegoat in the assassination of President Kennedy. Garrison concluded from his conversation with the de Mohrenschildts that George de Mohrenschildt had been one of Oswald's unwitting 'baby-sitters' 'assigned to protect or otherwise see to the general welfare of [Oswald].'

No credible evidence has been provided that establishes that de Mohrenschildt was in the employ of the CIA, or that he managed Oswald under the agency's direction.

On 17 September 1976, the CIA requested that the FBI locate de Mohrenschildt, because he had 'attempted to get in touch with the CIA Director.' On 5 September 1976, de Mohrenschildt had written a letter to the Director of the Central Intelligence Agency, George H W Bush asking for his assistance. The letter said:

> 'You will excuse this hand-written letter. Maybe you will be able to bring a solution to the hopeless situation I find myself in. My wife and I find ourselves surrounded by some vigilantes; our phone bugged; and we are being followed everywhere. Either [the] FBI is involved in this or they do not want to accept my complaints. We are driven to insanity by the situation. I have been behaving like a damn fool ever since my daughter Nadya died from [cystic fibrosis] over three years ago. I tried to write, stupidly and unsuccessfully, about Lee H Oswald and must have angered a lot of people — I do not know. But to punish an elderly man like myself and my highly nervous and sick wife is really too much. Could you do something to remove the net around us? This will be my last request for help and I will not annoy you any more. Good luck in your important job. Thank you so much.'

George Bush wrote in reply:

> 'Let me say first that I know it must have been difficult for you to seek my help in the situation outlined in your letter. I believe I can appreciate your state of mind in view of your daughter's tragic death a few years ago, and the current poor state of your wife's health. I was extremely sorry to hear of these circumstances. In your situation I can well imagine how the attentions you described in your letter affect both you and your wife.

> 'However, my staff has been unable to find any indication of interest in your activities on the part of Federal authorities in recent

*years. The flurry of interest that attended your testimony before the Warren Commission has long subsided. I can only speculate that you may have become 'newsworthy' again in view of the renewed interest in the Kennedy assassination, and thus may be attracting the attention of people in the media. I hope this letter had been of some comfort to you, George, although I realize I am unable to answer your question completely.*

> *George Bush,*
> *Director of the Central Intelligence Agency.'*

On 9 November 1976, Jeanne had George committed to a mental institution in Texas, where she remained for three months. Jeanne had a notorised document listing George's four previous suicide attempts. In the affidavit she stated that George suffered from depression, heard voices, saw visions, and believed that the CIA and the Jewish Mafia were persecuting him.

On 29 March 1977, de Mohrenschildt gave an interview to author Edward Jay Epstein. George claimed that in 1962, Dallas CIA operative J Walton Moore had given him the go-ahead to meet Oswald. 'I would never have contacted Oswald in a million years if Moore had not sanctioned it,' de Mohrenschildt said to Epstein. 'Too much was at stake.' On the same day as the Epstein interview, de Mohrenschildt received a business card from Gaeton Fonzi, an investigator for the *House Select Committee on Assassinations*, telling him that he would like to see him. That afternoon, de Mohrenschildt was found dead from a shotgun blast to the head in a house where he was staying in Manalapan, Florida. The coroner's verdict was suicide.

On the day of de Mohrenschildt's death, Edward Jay Epstein, the author who had interviewed him that day, wrote the following diary entry (29 March 1977):

> *'David Bludworth, The State's Attorney, was a folksy, charming and savvy interrogator. He began by telling me that de Mohrenschildt*

*had put a shotgun in his mouth and killed himself at 3:45 p.m. There were no witnesses – and no one home at the time of the shooting. The precise time of his death was established by a tape-recorder, left running that afternoon to record the soap operas for the absent Mrs Tilton, and which recorded a single set of footfalls in the room and the blast of the shotgun, which was found on the Persian carpet next to him. No suicide note or other clue was found. He said I was probably the last person to talk to him. Then, he asked whether I had in my possession de Mohrenschildt's black address book. I replied 'No'. He politely rephrased the question, and asked me again–about a half-dozen times, whether I had the black book.'*

On 1 April 1977, Jeanne de Mohrenschildt gave the *House Select Committee on Assassinations* a photograph taken of Lee Harvey Oswald by his wife Marina. Oswald is seen standing in his Dallas backyard holding two newspapers and a rifle, and with a pistol on his hip. The existence of this print, while similar to others which had been found among Oswald's effects on November 23, 1963, was previously unknown. On the back was written 'To my friend George from Lee Oswald, and the date '5/IV/63' (5 April 1963)'. Also written on the photo were the words 'Copyright Geo de M' and a Russian phrase translated as 'Hunter of fascists, ha-ha-ha!' Handwriting specialists later concluded that the words, 'To my friend George' and Oswald's signature were written by Lee Harvey Oswald, but could not determine whether the rest was the writing of Lee Oswald, George de Mohrenschildt or Marina Oswald. Some historians have speculated the Russian line was written by Marina, in sarcasm. (George de Mohrenschildt in his memoir translated it as 'This is the hunter of fascists, ha, ha, ha!' and also assumed that Marina had written it sarcastically).

George de Mohrenschildt wrote later that he had missed Oswald's photograph in packing for the move to Haiti in May, 1963, and this was why he hadn't mentioned it to the Warren Commission. According to de Mohrenschildt, the photo was not found among his stored papers until his wife found it in 1967. When analyzed by the HSCA in 1977, this photo turned out to be a first generation print of the backyard photo already known to the Warren Commission as CE-133A, and which had probably been taken on 31 March 1963. But were any of the other 'backyard' photos genuine?

It seems unlikely to this author that a man such as George de Mohrenschildt, an anti-communist and successful business man, would give the 'pro-communist' nobody Lee Oswald the time of day, never mind take him under his wing and help him and his family. Was George de Mohrenschildt Oswald's intelligence 'babysitter' as has been suggested here and in other books and documents, or is this just another of the many 'coincidences' surrounding this case?

## BYRDS, BUILDINGS AND BADGES

David Harold Byrd was born in Detroit, Texas on 24 April 1900. In the 1930s he purchased the Texas School Book Depository building in Dallas. During this period Byrd became very interested in aviation and, in 1938, Texas Governor James Allred appointed him to the Texas Civil Aeronautics Commission. In September 1941 Byrd formed the Civil Air Patrol; during the Second World War Byrd he commanded an antisubmarine base for the Civil Air Patrol in Beaumont, Texas. Byrd also had a close relationship with Sam Rayburn, Lyndon Johnson and John Connally. As Byrd pointed out in his autobiography 'I'm an Endangered Species', 'Another goal was to reach a rapport with the politicians who ran things, especially at the seat of state government in Austin. [People like] Sam Rayburn, Morrie Sheppard, John Connally and Lyndon Johnson on the national scene were to become men I could go to any time that I wanted action, and so were a succession of Texas governors.'

Barr McClellan, author of 'Blood, Money & Power' points out that Byrd, along with Clint Murchison, Haroldson L Hunt and Sid Richardson, was part of the Big Oil group in Dallas. McClellan argues that 'Big Oil would be, during the fifties and into the sixties, what the OPEC oil cartel was to the United States in the seventies and beyond'. One of the main concerns of this group was the preservation of the oil depletion allowance. McClellan further states that the killing of Kennedy was paid for by oil magnates, including Murchison and Hunt; that the assassination of Kennedy allowed the oil depletion allowance to be kept at 27.5 percent. It remained unchanged during the Johnson presidency. According to McClellan, this resulted in a saving of over 100 million dollars to the American oil industry.

Byrd became involved in the Suite 8F Group, a collection of right-wing businessmen; members of the group included Lyndon B Johnson and John Connally.

In November 1963 Byrd left Texas to go on a two-month safari in Africa. While he was away President John F Kennedy was assassinated. Accused assassin Lee Harvey Oswald worked in Byrd's Texas School Book Depository building. Byrd was a member of the Dallas Petroleum Club and it has been alleged that it was here that he met with George de Mohrenschildt, David Atlee Phillips and George H W Bush. Author Richard Bartholomew suggested in 'Byrds, Planes, and an Automobiles' that Byrd knew David Ferrie via the Civil Air Patrol.

David Harold Byrd died in Dallas on 14 September 1986.

★

Yet another mysterious individual in the JFK assassination is one Roscoe White. White served in the United States Marine Corps with Lee Harvey Oswald and travelled from California to Japan on the same ship. The pair were stationed, at the same time, in the Marine Air Wing Number One at Japan's Atsugi Air Base. Atsugi was the home of the US top secret U-2 spy plane operation, and was also allegedly the base of operations for the CIA's mind-control programme codenamed MK/Ultra. Roscoe White attained a position as an officer with the Dallas Police Department two months before the assassination and was allegedly acquainted with Officer Jefferson Davis Tippit, who was murdered in the Oak Cliff, Dallas area approximately 45 minutes after JFK's assassination. Tippit, according to the Warren Commission, was trying to apprehend Lee Harvey Oswald, when Oswald shot him to death. White left the DPD about a year later.

White, who was born on 18 November 1935, died suspiciously from injuries suffered in a fire. On his death bed, White told a local minister (Reverend Jack Shaw, who himself has been linked with the US intelligence community) that several months earlier he had made known his desire to sever his affiliation with US intelligence. He also confessed to have been a professional killer. White went on to say that he owned a 7.65 German Mauser, which he gave to his son before his death. (The rifle found on the sixth floor of the Texas School Book Depository close to Oswald's alleged firing position soon after the assassination was originally identified as a 7.65 German Mauser by several police officers. Those same officers later recanted their identification of the rifle, being told they had made a mistake; the weapon found was then identified as a 6.5 Italian Mannlicher–Carcano. This weapon was later traced to Oswald).

Among Geneva White's possessions after her husband's death was a previously unknown photograph of Lee Harvey Oswald. The photo was one of a series of shots which purport to show the accused assassin in varying poses such as holding weapons and Communist literature. According to Geneva, Roscoe told her to hang onto the photo as it was likely to be of value one day. According to the Warren Commission, these photos were taken by Lee's wife, Marina, in their Neeley Street backyard (in the Oak Cliff area of Dallas). Oswald, after his arrest, told police officers that the series of photographs were indeed fake; that his face had been pasted onto someone else's body and that, in time, he would prove it. Several photographic experts agree that the photos are phoney, citing differences in shadow patterns, the ratio of the size of Oswald's head to his body, and other inconsistencies. Two of the photos were made public, one appearing on the cover of *Life Magazine*, where it did much to convince the public of Oswald's guilt and a third, apparently, belonged exclusively to Roscoe White. Photographic experts, including Robert Groden, who have studied the famous 'backyard' photos of Oswald holding a rifle, have noticed that there appears to be a lump on 'Oswald's' right wrist. Photographic evidence indicates that, while Oswald did not have such a lump on his wrist, Roscoe White did. Was Oswald's head pasted onto Roscoe White's body? According to researcher and author Anthony Summers, in his book 'Conspiracy', the Dallas police must have, at one time, known about the White photograph, as they used the same pose shown in that photograph during their re-enactments for the Warren Commission.

Ricky White learned of his father's involvement in the JFK assassination in 1978 when a family friend – who was allegedly involved with US intelligence – told Ricky to, somewhat dramatically, prepare himself for a mental shock; he told the teenager that his father had killed President John Fitzgerald Kennedy and that this fact was bound to become public sooner or later. Ricky refused to believe the man, considering the tale a fabrication.

Four years later, sometime in 1982, Ricky discovered a military footlocker that had belonged to his father. Inside the footlocker was a handwritten diary and a key to a safety deposit box. In 1988, Ricky contacted the Dallas District Attorney seeking his help in locating the deposit box to match the key. The DA notified the FBI and Ricky was interviewed by them. Following one of these interview sessions the diary was discovered to be missing. Ricky claims that he had no intention of telling the public what he knew regarding his father's diary until the FBI began to persistently question him. In 1990, Ricky searched his grandfather's empty house in Paris, Texas, and there he discovered a steel container. Inside were three cablegram messages alluding to the JFK assassination. These were apparently Roscoe's orders to eliminate a 'National Security threat'. The messages are said to have included Roscoe's codename 'Mandarin' and his military serial number. This is what the cables are said to have contained:

NAVY INT.
Code A MRC
Remarks data
1666106
NRC VDA NAC
(illegible) 63
Remarks Mandarin: Code A

Foreign affairs assignments have been cancelled. The next assignment is to eliminate a National Security threat to world wide peace. Destination will be Houston, Austin or Dallas. Contacts are being arranged now. Orders are subject to change at any time. Reply back if not understood.

C. BOWERS
OSHA
NAVY INT.
CODE A MRC
REMARK data
1666106
Sept. 63
Remarks Mandarin: Code A

Dallas destination chosen. Your place hidden with the department. Contacts are within this letter. Continue on as planned.

C. BOWERS
OSHA
RE-rifle code AAA destroy/on/
NAVY INT.
CODE A mrc
Remark data
1666106
NRC VDC NAC
Dec. 63
Remarks Mandarin: Code G

Stay within department, witnesses have eyes, ears and mouths. You [illegible] do of the mix up. The men will be in to cover up all misleading evidence soon. Stay as planned wait for further orders.

C. BOWERS
RE-rifle Code AAA destroy/on/

Ricky claimed his father's now missing diary contained the following entries:

1) Roscoe shot twice at the President with his Mauser from behind the wooden fence on top of the now infamous grassy knoll, in front of and to the right of JFK. One of those two shots struck JFK in the right temple and killed him instantly. (A computer-enhanced version of a Polaroid photograph taken of the assassination by witness Mary Moorman shows a man firing a rifle from behind that fence. The man, called 'Badge Man' by some researchers, appears wearing the uniform of a Dallas Police Officer).

2) According to the diary, Roscoe White was one of three shooters in Dealey Plaza that day. Each of the shooters had a codename. Roscoe was 'Mandarin', and the other shooters were referred to by their codenames 'Saul' and 'Lebanon'. These two men allegedly shot at the President from two locations behind the President, one from the Texas School Book Depository building and the other from the Dallas County Records Building (diagonally opposite the Book Depository).

3) Roscoe White shot and killed Dallas Police Office J D Tippit in the Oak Cliff section of Dallas approximately 45 minutes after Kennedy was shot. Ricky then claims that Lee Oswald was involved in the assassination plot but did not actually fire any of the shots at either JFK or Tippit. Roscoe White and Oswald were, reportedly, attempting to convince Tippit to give them a ride to Dallas' Redbird Airport, where a getaway plane was waiting for them. Tippit, hearing about the assassination on the radio, refused to take the men to the airport. Roscoe then shot and killed Tippit and he and Oswald fled the scene on foot. According to author Harrison Edward Livingstone, in his book High Treason 2, 'There is a report that an extra police shirt was found in the backseat of Tippit's car, and we surmise that this belonged to Roscoe, who changed clothes there. It was thought that Tippit's car was the one that stopped at Oswald's house and beeped, and then picked him

up down the street.' There are no reports of anyone seeing Tippit's killer (or killers) changing their clothes before, during or after the murder of Tippit.

Roscoe's wife Geneva tells an almost equally absurd story: Geneva claims to have worked for Jack Ruby at his Carousel Club for a short period in September 1963, just two months before the assassination.

In August 1990, Geneva lay on her death bed (she would succumb later to cancer), where she was interviewed by journalist Ron Laytner in the presence of author Harrison Edward Livingstone. During that interview Geneva claimed that, while working at the Carousel Club in Dallas, she had overheard her husband and Jack Ruby plotting to kill the president. When they caught her eavesdropping, Ruby wanted to kill her but White talked him out of it, saying they should just give her electroshock treatments until she forgot what she had heard. This was apparently done and although the effects of the treatments were successful for a while, she was later able to recall the incident. She was, she claims, plagued with mental health problems for the remainder of her life.

Geneva's other claims include the usual things: she once went to a rifle range with Roscoe and Lee Oswald before the assassination and Oswald proved to be a 'real bad shot'. After the assassination, she went to New Orleans and was threatened by mobster Charles Nicoletti. Nicoletti said that her children would be tortured and killed if she ever spoke about 'what she knew'. Geneva and Roscoe knew the Tippits well and she had personal knowledge that the conspirators 'took care' of Tippit's wife and kids after JD's death. During the interview, Geneva offered her opinion as to who was behind JFK's death: 'We at first thought the assassination was more mob [but later realised] it was more CIA.'

Ex-CIA contract employee Robert Morrow, who has confessed to playing a part in Kennedy's death and to having foreknowledge of the assassination, claims that he was told in 1976 that Roscoe White had been placed within the Dallas police department two months before the assassination, and was the man shooting from the grassy knoll.

★

Gary Underhill was born in Brooklyn on 7 August 1915 and graduated from Harvard in 1937. During the Second World War he served with the Military Intelligence Service (6 July 1943 to May 1946). After leaving the Office of Strategic Services (OSS) he worked on specific projects for the Central Intelligence Agency. Underhill was also military affairs editor for *Life* Magazine. He is alleged to have had high-level Pentagon connections.

Following the assassination of President John F Kennedy, Underhill, by now in a highly agitated state, told his friend, Charlene Fitzsimmons, that he was convinced that JFK had been murdered by members of the Central Intelligence Agency. Underhill also said that 'Oswald is a patsy. They set him up. It's too much. The bastards have done something outrageous. They've killed the President! I've been listening and hearing things. I couldn't believe they'd get away with it, but they did!' He also said 'that the Kennedy murder wasn't as cut and dried as it might appear.' According to Fitzsimmons, he also said that, 'he knew the people involved (and that they knew he knew) and he fled Washington for his life.' He indicated that 'A small clique in the CIA were responsible' who 'were conducting a lucrative business in the Far East' in 'gunrunning and other contraband, manipulating political intrigue to serve their ends.' Underhill told his friend 'Kennedy had gotten wind of something going on so he was killed before he could blow the whistle.' The friends at first did not believe this fantastic story and assumed that 'he had gone completely mad,' despite their respect for his credentials and intelligence.

Gary Underhill was found dead in Washington on 8 May 1964 by District of Columbia police, the case being ruled a 'suicide'. Friends wondered if his death was really a suicide since two people who first examined the body indicated that he had been shot behind the left ear. Gary Underhill was right-handed. Friends also began to wonder about the frightened claims he had made about the assassination less than six months earlier. Other friends however accepted the death as a suicide indicating their belief that he had been troubled by personal problems and had been under the care of a psychiatrist.

★

Lee Oswald's mother, Marguerite Oswald frequently expressed the opinion that her son was recruited by an agency of the US Government and sent to Russia in 1959. Marguerite had believed this before her son returned from the Soviet Union.

New Orleans DA Jim Garrison, who in 1967 brought Clay Shaw to trial for the assassination of President Kennedy, stated in the documentary, The Men Who Killed Kennedy, '[Oswald] was employed by the Central Intelligence Agency and was obviously drawn into a scapegoat situation and made to believe ultimately that he was penetrating the assassination. And then when the time came, they took the scapegoat – the man who thought he was working for the United States government – and killed him real quick. And then the machinery, disinformation machinery, started turning and they started making a villain out of a man who genuinely was probably a hero.'

James Botelho, a former roommate of Oswald who would later become a California judge, stated in an interview with lawyer Mark Lane, 'Oswald, it was said, was the only Marine ever to defect from his country to another country, a Communist country, during peacetime, when the Marine Corps and American intelligence decided not to probe the reasons for the 'defection', I knew then what I know now: Oswald was on an assignment in Russia for American intelligence.'

According to Richard Buyer, Oswald never fired a shot at the President. [162] James W Douglass described Oswald as 'a questioning, dissenting CIA operative who had become a security risk' and 'the ideal scapegoat'.[163] According to Josiah Thompson, Oswald was in the Texas School Book Depository during the assassination, but it is 'quite likely' he was not the shooter on the sixth floor.[54]

In a 2013 interview with CBS journalist Charlie Rose, Robert F Kennedy, Jr said that his father, Senator Robert F Kennedy, was 'fairly convinced' that others besides Oswald were involved in the assassination [of his brother]. Robert Kennedy looked destined for the White House before he, too, was assassinated in Los Angeles after winning the 1968 California Primary.

In 1995, former US Army Intelligence officer and National Security Agency executive assistant John M Newman published evidence that both the CIA and FBI deliberately tampered with their files on Lee Harvey Oswald both before and after the assassination. Moreover, he found that both agencies withheld information that might have alerted authorities in Dallas that Oswald posed a potential threat to the President. Subsequently, Newman expressed a belief that CIA chief of counter-intelligence James Angleton was probably the key figure in the assassination. According to Newman, only Angleton 'had the access, the authority, and the diabolically ingenious mind to manage this sophisticated plot.' However, Newman surmised that the cover operation was not under James Angleton, but under Allen Dulles (the former CIA director who had been dismissed by Kennedy after the failed Bay of Pigs invasion).

According to investigative reporter Joseph Trento, among senior government officials, only James Angleton continued to express the belief that Kennedy assassination was not carried out by a lone gunman.

The Warren Commission reported that they had investigated 'dozens of allegations of a conspiratorial contact between Oswald and agents of the Cuban Government' and that they found no evidence that Cuba was involved in the assassination of President

Kennedy. The HSCA also wrote: 'The committee believes, on the basis of the evidence available to it, that the Cuban Government was not involved in the assassination of President Kennedy.'

In the early 1960s, Clare Booth Luce, wife of Time-Life publisher Henry Luce, was one of a number of prominent Americans who sponsored anti-Castro groups. This support included funding exiles in commando speedboat raids against Cuba. In 1975, Clare Luce said that on the night of the assassination, she received a call from a member of a commando group she had sponsored. The man claimed he was calling her from New Orleans.

According to Luce, the caller told her that Oswald had approached his group with an offer to help assassinate Castro. He further claimed that he and his associates eventually found out that Oswald was a communist and supporter of Castro. He said that with this new-found knowledge, his group kept a close watch on Oswald until Oswald suddenly came into money and went to Mexico City and then Dallas. Finally, according to Luce, the caller told her, 'There is a Cuban Communist assassination team at large and Oswald was their hired gun.'

Luce said that she told the caller to give his information to the FBI. Subsequently, Luce would reveal the details of the incident to both the Church Committee and the HSCA. Both committees investigated the incident, but were unable to uncover any evidence to corroborate the allegations.

In May 1967, CIA Director Richard Helms told President Lyndon Johnson that the CIA had tried to assassinate Castro. Helms further stated that the CIA had employed members of the Mafia in this effort, and 'that CIA plots to assassinate Fidel Castro dated back to August of 1960 – to the Eisenhower Administration.' Helms also said that the plots against Castro continued into the Kennedy Administration and that Attorney General Robert Kennedy had known about both the plots and the Mafia's involvement.

On separate occasions, Johnson told two prominent television newsmen that he believed that JFK's assassination had been organized by Castro as retaliation for the CIA's efforts to kill Castro. In October 1968, Johnson told veteran newsman Howard K Smith of ABC that 'Kennedy was trying to get to Castro, but Castro got to him first' In September 1969, in an interview with Walter Cronkite of CBS, Johnson said that in regard to the [JFK] assassination [that] he could not 'honestly say that I've ever been completely relieved of the fact that there might have been international connections' and referenced unnamed 'others.' Finally, in 1971, Johnson told his former speechwriter Leo Janos of *Time* magazine that he 'never believed that Oswald acted alone'.

Fidel Castro has always denied anything to do with the assassination and that, 'It would have been absolute insanity. It would have been a provocation. Needless to say, it would have been to run the risk that our country would have been destroyed by the United States.'

President Lyndon Johnson also implicated the CIA in the assassination. According to a FBI document released in 1977, Johnson's postmaster general, Marvin Watson told the FBI 'that [Johnson] was now convinced there was a plot in connection with the assassination. Watson stated the President felt the CIA had something to do with this plot.'

In 'Allegations of PFC Eugene Dinkin' the Mary Farrell Foundation summarizes and archives documents related to Private First Class Eugene B Dinkin, a cryptographic code operator stationed in Metz, France. Dinkin went AWOL in early November 1963, entered Switzerland using a false ID, and visited the United Nations' press office and declared that officials in the US government were planning to assassinate President Kennedy, adding that 'something' might happen to the Commander in Chief in Texas. Dinkin was arrested nine days before Kennedy was killed, placed in psychiatric care, and released shortly thereafter. His allegations eventually made their way to the Warren Commission, but, according to the Ferrell Foundation account, the Commission 'took no interest in the matter' and indeed omitted any mention of Dinkin from its purportedly encyclopaedic 26 volumes of evidence.'

## CLAY SHAW

Guy Banister had succumbed to a heart attack in 1964, Jack Ruby had died in early 1967 and David Ferrie had just been found dead in his apartment. New Orleans DA Jim Garrison had only one 'principle' subject to investigate: New Orleans businessman Clay LaVerne Shaw.

Shaw was a decorated Second World War veteran who helped start the International Trade Mart in New Orleans which facilitated the sales of both domestic and imported goods. He was known locally for his efforts to preserve buildings in New Orleans' historic French Quarter.

In 1979, former director of the CIA Richard Helms testified under oath that Clay Shaw had been a part-time contact of the Domestic Contact Service of the CIA, where Shaw volunteered information from his travels abroad, mostly to Latin America. This was not, however, unusual as by the mid-1970s, 150,000 Americans (businessmen, journalists, etc.) had provided such information to the DCS.

In 1979, the *House Select Committee on Assassinations* stated in its Final Report that the Committee was 'inclined to believe that Oswald was in Clinton, Louisiana, in late August, early September 1963, and that he was in the company of David Ferrie, if not Clay Shaw, and that witnesses in Clinton, Louisiana established an association of an undetermined nature between Ferrie, Shaw and Oswald less than three months before the assassination'.

A decade before, Garrison was fully aware of the Clinton story, but was unable to prove it. That said, Clay Shaw would prove be the most difficult of the New Orleans group to convict. He was receiving help from CIA Director, Richard Helms. Proof of Helms's concern about Shaw surfaced in 1975 in an interview of a former, high ranking CIA staff officer, Victor Marchetti. Marchetti had published a book in 1974 entitled 'The CIA and the Cult of Intelligence'. The book is impossible to read in its entirety as most of it has been censored by the CIA, who demanded that he omit 399 passages from the manuscript. Eventually only 168 passages were omitted and Marchetti and his publishers (Alfred A Knopf) decided to publish the book anyway, leaving the censored parts out of the book, leaving many blank pages.

Marchetti disclosed in *True* magazine: 'I, was then told, "Well Shaw, a long time ago, had been a contact of the Agency. He was in the export-import business he knew people coming and going from certain areas–the Domestic Contact Service – he used to deal with them and it's been cut off a long time ago" and then I was told, "well of course the Agency doesn't want this to come out now because Garrison will distort it, the public would misconstrue it."'

In the interview, Marchetti added: 'At that time or shortly thereafter this [other] guy Ferrie came up and I was given a similar kind of explanation, that he's been involved in the Bay of Pigs and been a contract agent or contact at the time.'

Despite Garrison's best efforts, his prosecution was flawed. Shaw ultimately received a verdict of not guilty within hours of the judge's instructions to the jury.

Several years later, the events surrounding Shaw's death were, according to Garrison, 'mysterious'. On 14 August 1974, a neighbour saw some men carrying a body on a stretcher in the front door of Shaw's carriage house. The entire body, including the head, was covered with a sheet. The neighbour, finding this unusual, called the coroner's office, which promptly sent its investigators to Shaw's residence. By the time they arrived, the place was empty. After a day of inquiry, the Orleans Parish coroner's investigators learned Shaw had just been buried in Kentwood, in Tangipahoa Parish where he was born.

The New Orleans coroner, Dr Frank Minyard, concerned about the circumstances and the speed of the burial, decided to exhume Shaw's body so that he could assure himself that Shaw had not died a victim of foul play. However, before he could obtain the court order, word of the proposed exhumation reached the media. This caused the local New Orleans papers to publish scathing editorials protesting the callous desecration of Shaw's remains. With the heated publicity, the coroner reconsidered his action. There was no exhumation.

Richard Helms admitted that Shaw had worked as a contract man for Tracy Barnes's Domestic Contact Division (known facetiously as the Domestic Dirty Tricks Operation Division).

In a 1979 trial, Helms was asked if he knew Clay Shaw. He responded, under oath: 'The only recollection I have of Clay Shaw and the Agency is that I believe that at one time as a businessman he was one of the part-time contacts of the Domestic Contact Division (Tracy Barnes's operation), the people that talked to businessmen, professors, and so forth, and who travelled in and out of the country.'

In a subsequent trial, in 1984, this answer was repeated to Helms, and he was asked, 'Do you recall making that statement under oath on 17 May 1979?' He responded, 'If it says here I did make it under oath, I guess I did.'

## TRACY BARNES

After working in Germany (1954-1956) Tracy Barnes was made CIA station chief in London and was there from 1957 to 1959, before he returned to the United States. In 1960 Barnes was with the Directorate for Plans (the CIA's clandestine service and covert action arm) and helped Central Intelligence Agency officer Richard Bissell organize the Bay of Pigs operation. The invasion was a disaster, and within seventy-two hours all the invading troops had been killed, wounded or had surrendered. Bissell had a meeting with John F Kennedy about the operation. Kennedy admitted it was his fault that the operation had been a disaster. Kennedy added: 'In a parliamentary government, I'd have to resign. But in this government I can't, so you and Allen (Dulles) have to go.'

As author Evan Thomas points out in 'The Very Best Men': 'Bissell had been caught in his own web. 'Plausible deniability' was intended to protect the president, but as he had used it, it was a tool to gain and maintain control over an operation [and] without plausible deniability, the Cuba project would have turned over to the Pentagon, and Bissell would have become a supporting actor.'

President John F Kennedy asked his Chairman of The Joint Chiefs of Staff Maxwell Taylor to investigate what went wrong during the Bay of Pigs operation. Taylor in turn asked Lyman Kirkpatrick, the CIA's inspector general, to write a report on the failed project. Kirkpatrick's report was highly critical of both Bissell and Barnes claiming that they had misled the president and that 'plausible deniability was a pathetic illusion.'

In 1962 Barnes was placed in charge of Domestic Operations Division. Former CIA operative Robert Morrow later claimed that Barnes recruited Richard Case Nagell and sent him to New Orleans in the summer of 1963. Barnes also asked Morrow to purchase several weapons: 'I was told specially to get good ones, 7.35mm Mannlicher-Carcanos. A 6.5mm was not an accurate rifle at all, and not to be considered. I remember going to Sunny's Surplus up in Towson, Maryland. They had a whole wall of Mannlichers, Mausers, and other rifles. I picked out four, which I felt were pretty good.' Morrow claimed that the rifles were picked up by David Ferrie in a private plane and taken to New Orleans.

# E H HUNT

Everette Howard Hunt was born in Hamburg, New York on 9 October, 1918 and served in the Office of Strategic Services during the Second World War. After the wars end, he joined the Central Intelligence Agency (CIA) and for a while was stationed in China. While stationed there he met and married his first wife, Dorothy.

In August, 1978, Victor Marchetti published an article about the assassination of John F Kennedy in the Liberty Lobby newspaper, *Spotlight*. In the article Marchetti argued that the *House Special*

*Committee on Assassinations* (HSCA) had obtained a 1966 CIA memo that revealed Hunt, Frank Sturgis and Gerry Patrick Hemming had been involved in the plot to kill Kennedy. Marchetti's article also included a story that Marita Lorenz had provided information on this plot. Later that month Joseph Trento and Jacquie Powers wrote a similar story for the *Sunday News Journal*. (Marita Lorenz was a German woman who had an affair with Fidel Castro in 1959 and in January 1960 was involved in an assassination attempt by the CIA on Castro's life. She later had a child with the Venezuelan former dictator Marcos Pérez Jiménez. In the 1970s she testified before the *House Select Committee on Assassinations* about the John F Kennedy assassination, stating that she was involved with a group of anti-Cuban militants including Lee Harvey Oswald shortly before the assassination. Lorenz gave sworn testimony that Lee Harvey Oswald, American mercenaries Frank Sturgis and Gerry Patrick Hemming, and Cuban exiles including Orlando Bosch, Pedro Diaz Lanz, and the brothers Guillermo and Ignacio Novo Sampol, had met one November midnight in 1963 at the Miami home of Orlando Bosch and had studied Dallas street maps. She also swore that she and Sturgis were at that time in the employ of the CIA and that they received payment from Howard Hunt under the name 'Eduardo'. Lorenz went further and stated that they arrived in Dallas on 21 November 1963, and stayed at a motel, where the group met Howard Hunt. Hunt stayed for about forty-five minutes and at one point handed an envelope of cash to Sturgis. About an hour after Hunt left, Jack Ruby came to the door. Lorenz says that this was the first time she had seen Ruby. By this time, she said, it was early evening. In her testimony, Lorenz identified herself and her fellow passengers as members of Operation Forty, the CIA-directed assassination team formed in 1960 in preparation for the Bay of Pigs invasion. She described her role as that of a 'decoy'. Lorenz's testimony was carefully investigated by the committee and found to be unreliable.

The HSCA did not publish this CIA memo linking its agents

to the assassination of John F Kennedy. Hunt now decided to take legal action against the Liberty Lobby and in December 1981, he was awarded $650,000 in damages. Liberty Lobby appealed to the United States Court of Appeals. It was claimed that Hunt's attorney, Ellis Rubin, had offered a clearly erroneous instruction as to the law of defamation. The three judge panel agreed and the case was retried. This time Mark Lane defended the Liberty Lobby against Hunt's action.

Mark Lane eventually discovered Marchetti's sources: William Corson. It also emerged that Marchetti had also consulted James Jesus Angleton and Alan J Weberman before publishing the article. As a result of obtaining depositions from David Atlee Phillips, Richard Helms, G Gordon Liddy, Stansfield Turner and Marita Lorenz, plus a skilful cross-examination by Lane of Hunt, the jury decided in January, 1995, that Marchetti had not been guilty of libel when he suggested that John F Kennedy had been assassinated by people working for the CIA.

In 2006 it was announced that Hunt had written his memoirs. This included a claim that Lyndon Baines Johnson might have been involved in ordering the assassination of John F Kennedy. 'Having Kennedy liquidated, thus elevating himself to the presidency without having to work for it himself, could have been a very tempting and logical move on Johnson's part. LBJ had the money and the connections to manipulate the scenario in Dallas and is on record as having convinced JFK to make the appearance in the first place. He further tried unsuccessfully to engineer the passengers of each vehicle, trying to get his good buddy, Governor John Connolly, to ride with him instead of in JFK's car – where he [Connolly] would have been out of danger.'

Hunt suggests that senior CIA official William K Harvey could have been involved in the plot to kill Kennedy: 'Harvey was a ruthless man who was not satisfied with his position in the CIA and its government salary' '[Harvey] definitely had dreams of becoming [CIA director] and LBJ could do that for him if he were president. [LBJ] would have used Harvey because he was available and corrupt.'

Edward Howard Hunt died of pneumonia on 23rd January, 2007. His memoir 'American Spy: My Secret History in the CIA, Watergate, and Beyond' was published in May 2007.

After his father's death, Hunt's son, St John Hunt, released a tape where his father claimed that Lyndon Baines Johnson was the instigator of the assassination of John F Kennedy, and that it was organised by Cord Meyer, David Atlee Phillips, Frank Sturgis and David Sanchez Morales.

## DAVID FERRIE

In 1967, Jim Garrison told the world that David Ferrie was 'one of history's most important individuals' declaring he had evidence that Ferrie was not only a pilot for New Orleans underworld boss Carlos Marcello but that he was also involved with a group of extreme right-wing activists – including Guy Banister, Carlos Bringuier, Eladio del Valle and Clay Shaw amongst others – and that this group were planning the execution of JFK. Garrison also claimed that these men were involved in a conspiracy with the Central Intelligence Agency (CIA) to kill the president and that this 'Executive action' was in direct retaliation for Kennedy's attempts to obtain a peace settlement in both Cuba and Vietnam.

On 17 February 1967, *The New Orleans States-Item* broke the news that Garrison was investigating the assassination of Kennedy. The report also revealed that one of the suspects on Garrison's list was David William Ferrie and that Garrison was about to arrest Ferrie and take him into custody for questioning. Ferrie had been the subject of an FBI investigation just after Kennedy was murdered, but was not mentioned in the Warren Report. As stated above, it was alleged that Ferrie's library card had been found among Lee Oswald's possessions at the time of his arrest.

Five days after the news broke regarding Garrison's enquiry, Ferrie's body was found in his New Orleans apartment. Although two suicide notes were found, the coroner did not immediately classify the death as a suicide, noting there were indications Ferrie may have suffered a brain haemorrhage. It is known that Ferrie suffered from hypertension. A New Orleans physician confirmed to Garrison that if someone suffering from hypertension took a whole bottle of this specific drug [proloid], it would cause death very quickly. Garrison later wrote: 'I phoned immediately but was told that no blood samples or spinal fluid from Ferrie's autopsy had been retained. I was left with an empty bottle and a number of unanswered questions.'

Garrison immediately announced that Ferrie had been a part of the Kennedy conspiracy in this statement – 'The apparent suicide of David Ferrie ends the life of a man who in my judgment was one of history's most important individuals. Evidence developed by our office had long since confirmed that he was involved in events culminating in the assassination of President Kennedy. We have not mentioned his name publicly up to this point. The unique nature of this case now leaves me no other course of action.' Garrison added that he was making preparations to arrest Ferrie when they heard of his death. 'Apparently, we waited too long.'

Another Garrison suspect, Eladio del Valle, was found dead in a Miami parking lot twelve hours after Ferrie's was discovered in his room. Garrison's office had been looking for Del Valle for three days. Police reported that de Valle had been tortured, shot in the heart at point-blank range, and his skull split open with an axe. His murder has never been solved. Close friend Diego Gonzales Tendera later claimed de Valle was murdered because of his involvement in the assassination of President John F Kennedy. A senior member of the Cuban Secret Service, Fabian Escalante, agreed:

'In 1962 Eladio Del Valle tried to infiltrate Cuba with a commando group of twenty-two men. In the middle of 1962. Of course, we knew this. I tell you about this, because one of our agents, who was one of the people helping to bring this group to Cuba, was a man of very little education. They talked English on many occasions on this little island with Eladio Del Valle told this person, on many occasions, that Kennedy must be killed to solve the Cuban problem. After that we had another piece of information on Eladio Del Valle. This was offered to us by Tony Cuesta. He told us that Eladio Del Valle was one of the people involved in the assassination plot against Kennedy.'

Some researchers, including Jim Garrison, believe Ferrie was murdered – two suicide notes, both typed, would suggest that something was not quite right regarding the death of David William Ferrie. However, researcher Gus Russo, author of the excellent book 'Live By the Sword: The Secret War Against Castro and the Death of JFK' disagrees: 'David Ferrie has long been portrayed on paper and in film as an American grotesque: a raving hater of President Kennedy, who threatened to kill the President. He was said to be angry at JFK for failing to help the Cuban exiles restore liberty to their land. It seems certain he made a celebrated statement after the Bay of Pigs fiasco on which much of the portrait has been based. That incident occurred in July 1961, when Ferrie was addressing the New Orleans chapter of the Order of World Wars. Ferrie became so critical of Kennedy's handling of the Bay of Pigs invasion that he was asked to discontinue his remarks. But that was almost certainly taken out of context and misinterpreted.'

British author and presenter Anthony Summers has also pointed out: 'David Ferrie, [an] aide in Carlos Marcello's apparatus, and anti-Castro activist, attracted brief official attention less than forty-eight hours after the assassination. Just hours before Ruby killed Oswald, and while Ferrie was still away on his peculiar marathon around Texas, a disaffected member of Banister's staff called New Orleans authorities to say he suspected Ferrie of involvement in the President's murder. This was Jack Martin, a Banister investigator, and he voiced suspicion that Ferrie had been in contact with Oswald. Within hours of the assassination, Martin had been involved in a dispute with Banister – a confrontation that may have occurred when Banister caught Martin trying to examine confidential files.

For whatever reason, Banister injured Martin by hitting him on the head with a revolver butt. It was the day after this, following a visit to the hospital, that Martin raised the alarm over Ferrie. A hue and cry began, but Ferrie was away somewhere in Texas. His associates, questioned in his absence, proved uninformative.'

Finally, in 2007, Edward Haslam published 'Dr Mary's Monkey'. Haslam claims that Alton Ochsner (a surgeon and medical researcher who worked at Tulane University and other New Orleans hospitals before he established his own world-renowned The Ochsner Clinic, now known as Ochsner Foundation Hospital) organised 'one of the 159 covert research centers which the CIA had admitted to setting up.' Haslam believes that Ochsner recruited Mary Sherman, a prominent orthopedic surgeon and expert in cancer research, to run the research operation. The basic project was set up on 23 March 1962, using conventional facilities, which then expanded out of the loop for its final phases. Haslam believes that Sherman was involved in carrying out secret research into developing a vaccine to prevent an epidemic of soft-tissue cancers. This work included using a linear particle accelerator located in the Infectious Disease Laboratory at the Public Health Service Hospital in New Orleans. According to Haslam there was a second-lab working on this project. This was being run by David Ferrie on Louisiana Avenue Parkway. Mary Sherman was murdered on 21 July 1964, the very same day that the Warren Commission was scheduled to hear testimony about Lee Harvey Oswald's activities in Louisiana. Haslam has further claimed that Sherman and Oswald had participated in a secret effort to develop a vaccine against Simian virus 40, which was a contaminant in the polio vaccines that were administered to tens of millions of people in the 1950s and 1960s, and that Sherman was murdered because she knew too much about the assassination of President John F Kennedy.

★

In 1978 Jim and Elsie Wilcott, former husband and wife employees of the CIA station in Tokyo, Japan, went to the *San Francisco Chronicle*. Their story was, if correct, nothing short of a bombshell. 'It was common knowledge in the Tokyo CIA station,' they claimed, 'that Oswald worked for the agency. Right after the president was killed, people in the Tokyo station were talking openly about Oswald having gone to Russia [sic] for the CIA. Everyone was wondering how the agency was going to be able to keep the lid on Oswald. But I guess they did.'

Senator Richard Schweiker, who was a member of the United States Senate Select Committee on Intelligence, stated: 'We do know Oswald had intelligence connections. Everywhere you look with him, there are fingerprints of intelligence." Schweiker also told told author Anthony Summers in 1978, 'I believe that the Warren Commission was set up at the time to feed pabulum to the American public for reasons not yet known, and that one of the biggest cover-ups in the history of our country occurred at that time.'

Richard Sprague, himself interim staff director and chief counsel to the HSCA, said, 'If he had it to do over again, he would begin his investigation of the Kennedy assassination by probing Oswald's ties to the Central Intelligence Agency.'

In 2003, Robert Blakey, staff director and chief counsel for the HSCA, stated [that] 'I no longer believe that we were able to conduct an appropriate investigation of the [Central Intelligence] Agency and its relationship to Oswald.'

# MYSTERIES, MALCONTENTS AND MURDER

Fifty years after this world changing event, the dark shroud of mystery, deception and double talk surrounding the assassination is only a little clearer. That said, Lee Oswald's links to US Intelligence, in an official capacity or otherwise, remain tantalisingly in the shadows; his actions in the Soviet Union and those upon his return to the United States bear the hallmarks of manipulation, subversion and evasion.

Was Oswald simply a lone, malcontent young man eager to put an indelible mark on history in the most heinous way possible or was he secretly infiltrating and trying to prevent a movement intent on changing that same history?

Was Oswald really a hero, a man playing a dangerous role in the hotbed of US/Soviet/Cuban politics in the early 1960s, caught up in such a tangled web of deceit he couldn't get out or was he the villain who murdered a president and a police officer only to be cut down himself?

Oswald was taken from us before he had the chance to face his accusors; taken from the situation in such a convenient way that people now doubt he was a killer at all and that Ruby's act was to silence him forever.

The coincidences stack up: how did he get his rifle into the building? How could no one see him racing down the stairwells of the Book Depository, just seconds after the assassination? How could he be so calm having allegedly murdered Kennedy, run the length of the building, hidden the murder weapon, run down those same stairwells and appear calm and collected when confronted by a police officer in the first floor lunch room?

Did his widow Marina know Robert Webster, another 'disillusioned' young former Marine defector? Why wasn't Oswald arrested and tried upon his return from the Soviet Union? What was he doing handing out pro-Castro leaflets in New Orleans right in the middle of the US intelligence community?

The list of questions is endless.

Either way, hero or villain, Lee Oswald remains an enigma; the JFK assassination and its surrounding cast of characters throws up more questions than answers at every turn. As eye witnesses to the assassination and its surrounding events become fewer, as time inevitably blurs the truth and as the whole tragedy recedes further into history, it is vital those questions are answered. Today.

# Bibliography

Anson, Robert Sam. *"They've Killed The President!"* The Search for the Murderers of John F Kennedy. Bantam Books, Inc., 666 Fifth Avenue, New York, 10019, U.S.A.

Benson, R B: Destiny in Dallas. 1964.

Berkley, Edmund C., Editor. *People and the Pursuit of Truth*. May 1975–September 1978. 815 Washington Street, Newtonville, Mass., 02160, U.S.A.

Blumenthal, Sid and Yazijan, Harvey, Edited by. Government By *Gunplay: Assassination Conspiracy Theories From Dallas to Watergate*. The New American Library, 1301 Avenue of the Americas, New York, N.Y. 10019, U.S.A.

Brewer, Milton E. *The Garrison Case, A Study in the Abuse of Power*. Clarkson N. Potter, Inc. New York.

Brown, Madeleine Duncan. *Texas in the Morning: The Love Story of Madeleine Brown and President Lyndon Baines Johnson*. The Conservatory Press, Baltimore, MD. 1997.

Buchanan, Thomas C. *Who Killed Kennedy?* Putnam, New York, N.Y.

Byrd, David Harold. *I'm an Endangered Species: The Autobiography of a Free Enterpriser*. 1978.

Cockburn, Alex. *Echoes of Dallas: The JFK Assassination Fifteen Years Later. Magill Monthly*, 14 Merrion Row, Dublin 2.

Cover Magazine. Kelley, Kitty. *The Dark Side of Camelot*. 1988.

Curry, Jesse. *JFK Assassination File*. American Poster and Printing

Company, Inc. 1969.

Cutler, Robert B. *The Flight of C.E. 399 - Evidence of Conspiracy*. Box 1465, Manchester, MA 01944.
- *Seventy Six Seconds in Dealey Plaza*. Ibid.
- *Mr Chairman : Evidence of Conspiracy*. Ibid.
- *The Day of the Umbrella Man*. Ibid.

Eddowes, Michael. *November 22: How They Killed Kennedy*. Neville Spearman Ltd., London.
- The Oswald File. Clarkson N. Potter, New York, N.Y.

Estes, Billie Sol. *Billie Sol Estes: A Texas Legend*. BS Productions, Granbury Texas, 76048. 2005.

Evica, George Michael. *And We Are All Mortal: New Evidence and Analysis in the Assassination of John F. Kennedy*. University of Hartford, 200 Bloomfield Avenue West Hartford, Conn., 06117, U.S.A.

Epstein, Edward, J. *Inquest: The Warren Commission and the Establishment of Truth*. Bantam Books, Inc., 625 Madison Avenue, New York, N.Y. 10022.
- *Legend: The Secret World of Lee Harvey Oswald*. McGraw Hill, New York.

Fleming, Glenn B.
- *Patsy*. Unpublished manuscript, 1976.
- *The Oswald Papers : Rumours and Research*. Unpublished manuscript, 1985.
- *Roger Dean Craig: A Man in History*. Privately Published 1999.

Flint, Larry. *JFK Murder Solved*. L.A. Free Press, Special Report no. 1, Press West, Inc., 5850 Hollywood Blvd., Los Angeles, CA.
- *Garrison Charges that Pentagon Planned JFK Killing*. December 22 1972. Ibid.

Ford, Gerald R., with Stiles John R., *Portrait of the Assassin*. Simon & Schuster, New York, N.Y.

Fox, Sylvan. *The Unanswered Questions about President Kennedy's Assassination.* Award Books, New York, U.S.A.

Garrison, Jim. *A Heritage of Stone.* Berkley Publishing Corporation, 200 Madison avenue, New York N.Y. 10016.

Gibson, Donald. *The Kennedy Assassination Cover-Up.* Nova Science Publishers, Inc. Huntington, NY. 1999.

Glassner, Barry. *Revisiting the Great American Tragedies: From Kennedy to Kent State. In Touch Magazine,* November 1974.

Goldberg, Jeff. *Waiting For Justice.* Inquiry Magazine, 1979.
    - and Yazijian, Harvey. T*he Death of 'Crazy Billy' Sullivan. New Times Magazine* Special Report, 24th July, 1978.
        Groden, Robert J. *The Killing of a President.*Bloomsbury, 1993.
    -    *The Search for Lee Harvey Oswald.*Bloomsbury, 1995.

Gunn, Nerin E. *Red Roses from Texas.* 1964.

Hale, Hazel. *Oswald.* (Unpublished Manuscript) 1978.

Haslem, Edward T. *Dr. Mary's Monkey.* Trine Day. 2007.

Hepburn, James (pseudonym). *Farewell America.* Frontiers Publishing Company, Vaduz, Liechtenstein. 1968.

Irwin, Harry. JFK Assassination Forum. (Newsletter). Harry Irwin, 32 Ravensdene Crescent, Ravenhill, Belfast BT6 0DB, Northern Ireland. 1975-1981.

Jenkins, David. *116 for 1. Time Out,* Time Out Limited, 374 Grays Inn Road, London WC1X 8BB. 1973.

Joesten, Joachim. *How Kennedy Was Killed.* Peter Dawney Ltd, in association with Tandem Books. 1968.

Jones, Penn jnr. *Forgive My Grief* Volumes 1, 2, 3 and 4. P.O. Box 1140, Midlothian, Texas, U.S.A. 1965-67.

Joesten, Joachim. *Oswald, Assassin or Fall Guy?* Marzani & Munsell Publishers Inc., New York, N.Y.

- *Oswald, The Truth*. Peter Dawney, London. 1967.
- *Marina Oswald*. Ibid.

Kantor, Seth. *Who Was Jack Ruby?* Everest House, New York, N.Y., U.S..A. 1978.

Kelley, Kit. *People Weekly,* February 29th, 1988. Time & Life Building, Rockefeller Center, New York, N.Y. 10020.

Kirkwood, James. *American Grotesque: An Account of the Clay Shaw - Jim Garrison Affair in New Orleans*. Simon and Schuster, New York, U.S.A. 1969.

Kruger, Henrik. *The Great Heroin Coup: Drugs, Intelligence & International Fascism*. South End Press, Box 68 Astor Station, Boston, MA 02123.

Lane, Mark. *Rush To Judgment*. Holt, Rinehart & Wilson, New York. 1966.
- *A Citizen's Dissent*. Fawcett World Library, 67 West 44th Street, New York, N.Y., 10036, U.S.A. 1968.

*Las Vegas Magazine*: Kennedy in Vegas: The Women, the Mob, How his Indiscretions May Have Got Him Killed. Summer, 1997.

*Life*, July 10th, 1964. Time Inc., 540 N. Michigan Av., Chicago, Illinois 60611, U.S.A.
- John F Kennedy Memorial Edition. 1963.
- *The Warren Report: How the Commission Pieced Together the Evidence*. October, 1964.
- *Why Kennedy Went to Dallas*. November, 1967.
- November 24th, 1967. Ibid.

Latzen, Morris S. *The Kennedy Assassination : The Full Story*. Confidential Detective Yearbook 1964, Sterling House, Inc., 260 Park Avenue South, New York, N.Y., 10010.

Lime, Vic and Ramsey, Robin. *Cover-ups & Conspiracies : A Unique Investigation Into the Dark Side of the Kennedy Legend*. Revelations

Magazine, P.O. Box 150, London E5 0LU.

Lutz, Tom. *Tracking Down Kennedy's Killers. Newsreal,* July 1977. Newsreal Series, P.O. Box 147, Morton Grove, Ill. 60053.
    - Newsreal, October 1977. Ibid.

MacFarlane, Ian. *Proof of Conspiracy in the Assassination of President Kennedy.* Book Distributors, Australia. 1975.

Manchester, William. *The Death of a President: November 20-25, 1963.* Harper & Row, New York, N.Y. 1968.

McDonald, Hugh and Moore, Robin. *L.B.J. and the J.F.K. Conspiracy.* Condor Publishing Company Inc., 29 East Main Street, Westport, Connecticut 06880.

MacMillan, Priscilla Johnson. *Marina and Lee.* Harper & Row. 1977.

Meagher, Silvia. *Accessories After The Fact: The Warren Commission, The Authorities and The Report.* Vintage Books, U.S.A.

Moldea, Dan E. *The Hoffa Wars, Teamsters, Rebels, Politicians and the Mob.* Paddington Press, U.S.A. 1978.
    - *Who Killed Jimmy Hoffa and Why. Playboy,* November 1978.

Morrow, Robert D. Betrayal, *A Reconstruction of Certain Clandestine Events from the Bay of Pigs to the Assassination of John F. Kennedy.* Warner Books Inc., 75 Rockefeller Plaza, New York, N.Y. 10019.

*Newsweek* Magazine: Thomas, Evan. *The Real Cover-Up.* November 1993.

Noyes, Peter. *Legacy of Doubt.* Pinnacle Books, New York, N.Y.

Norden, Eric. Jim Garrison. *A Candid Conversation with the Embattled District Attorney of New Orleans.* Playboy, October 1967. HMH Publishing, Michigan Avenue, Chicago, Ill, U.S.A.
    - *High Noon in Dallas.* Lords, The Gentleman's Companion, (Summer 1969) Lords Magazine Ltd., 2 Bramber Road, London W14.

Oglesby, Carl. *The Yankee and Cowboy War: Conspiracies from Dallas to Watergate and Beyond.* Berkley Publishing Corporation, 200 Madison Avenue, New York, N.Y. U.S.A.

O'Toole, George. *The Assassination Tapes: An Electronic Probe into the Murder of John F Kennedy and the Dallas Cover-up.* Penthouse Press, New York, N.Y.

President John F Kennedy Assassination Records Collection Act; National Archives and Records Administration, Adelphi Road College Park, MD 20740.

Prouty, Fletcher L. *An Introduction to the Assassination Business.* Gallery. Gallery, September 1975. Montcalm Publishing Corporation, 99 Park Avenue, New York, N.Y. 10016.
- *The Guns of Dallas*, Gallery, October 1975. Ibid.
- *The Guns of Dallas Update*. Gallery, May 1976. Ibid.

Popkin, Richard H. *The Second Oswald.* Avon Library–New York Review Books, New York, U.S.A.

Ramsey, Robin. *The Jemstone File.* International times, 97A Talbot Road, London W11.

Roberts, Craig. *Kill Zone: A Sniper Looks at Dealey Plaza.* 1994.

Roffman, Howard. *Presumed Guilty.* Associated University Presses, Inc. Cranbury, New Jersey 08512, U.S.A. 1976.

Russell, Dick. *The Man Who Knew Too Much.* Carroll & Graf. 1992.

Russo, Gus G. *Live By the Sword: The Secret War Against Castro and the Death of JFK.* Bancroft Press. 1998.

Russo, Gus G. *Brothers in Arms: The Kennedys, the Castros, and the Politics of Murder.* Bloomsbury USA. 2008.

Sahl, Mort. *Heartland.* Harcourt Brace and Jovanovich. New York and London. 1977.

Sauvage, Leo. *The Oswald Affair: An Examination of the Contradictions* and Omissions of the Warren Report. World Publishing Co., Cleveland.

Scally, Christopher. *"So near ... and yet so far"* The *House Select Committee on Assassinations'* Investigations into the Murder of President John F. Kennedy. Privately published, Essex. 1981.

Schotz, Martin E. *History Will Not Absolve Us: Orwellian control, Public Denial, and the Murder of President Kennedy.* Kurtz, Ulmer & DeLucia Book Publishers, Brookline, Massachusetts. 1996.

Scott, Peter Dale, with Hoch, Paul and Stetler, Russell. *The Assassinations: Dallas and Beyond - A Guide to Cover-ups and Investigations.* Pelican Books, 625 Madison Avenue, New York, N.Y.

Shaw, J. Gary, and Harris, Larry R. *Cover-up; The Governmental Conspiracy to Conceal the Facts about the Public Execution of John Kennedy.* Cleburne, Texas. (Available from the Author). 1975.

Sloan, Bill. *The Other Assassin.* Tudor Publishing, Inc., 276 Fifth Avenue, New York, N.Y. 10001.

Sneed, Larry A. Three Forks Press, PO Box 823461, Dallas, Texas. 1998.

Sprague, Richard E. *The Assassination of John F. Kennedy: The Application of Computers to the Photographic Evidence. Computers and Automation,* May 1970.

   - *The Taking of America 1-2-3.* (Privately Published) 1976.

Stafford, Jean. *A Mother In History: Mrs. Marguerite Oswald.* Farrar, Strauss and Giroux, New York. 1965.

Stark, Andrew. *The CIA's Secret Weapons Systems.* Gallery, June 1978. Montcalm Publishing Corporation, 99 Park Avenue, New York, N.Y. 10016.

Summers, Anthony. *Conspiracy: Who Killed President Kennedy?* Fontana Paperbacks, U.K. 1978.

   - *The Kennedy Cover-up. The Listener,* 9th March, 1978. Published by the BBC.

Staff Writer. *Where is it now? Sunday Express Magazine*, 6th November 1983. Express Newspapers p.l.c., Fleet Street, London EC4P 4JT.

William Shawcross. *The Day of the Conspirator. Sunday Times Magazine,* July 27th, 1975, Times Newspapers Ltd., P.O. Box 7, New Printing House Square, Gray's Inn Road, London WC1X 8EZ.

Thompson, Josiah. *Six Seconds in Dallas: A Microstudy of the Kennedy Assassination.* Bernard Geiss, New York, N.Y.

Truby, David J. *Mystery of the Umbrella Man.* The Globe, 29th July, 1980.

Turner, William W. *The Garrison Commission on the Assassination of President Kennedy. Ramparts,* January 1968. 301 Broadway, San Francisco, California 94133, U.S.A.

United States Government Printing Office, Washington D. C. *The President's Commission on the Assassination of President Kennedy:* REPORT and 26 Volume's of Evidence.

Various. *The JFK Assassination. Gallery,* Special Report, July 1979. Montcalm Publishing Corporation, 99 Park Avenue, New York, N.Y. 10016.

Various. *The Death of Marilyn Monroe. Scandal (Part 2).* Orbis Publishing Ltd., Griffin House, 161 Hammersmith Road, London W6 8SD.

Weisberg, Harold. *Post Mortem.* Harold Weisberg, Route 12, Old Receiver Road, Frederick, MD, 21701, U.S.A.
   - *Whitewash 1 : The Report on the Warren Report.* Ibid.
   - *Whitewash 2: The FBI - Secret Service Cover-up.* Ibid.
   - *Photographic Whitewash : Suppressed Kennedy Assassination Pictures.* Ibid.

- *Whitewash 4 : JFK Assassination Transcript.* Ibid.
- *Oswald In New Orleans - Case for Conspiracy with the CIA.* Canyon Books, New York, N.Y.

Wilber, Charles G (Ph.d). *Medicolegal Investigation of the President John F Kennedy Murder.* Charles C Thomas, Springfield, Illinois. 1978.

Zirbel, Craig I. *The Texas Connection.* Warner Books, New York, NY 10020.

# Index